Edwin A. Sherm

The Engineer Corps of Hell

Rome's Sappers and Miners

Edwin A. Sherm

The Engineer Corps of Hell
Rome's Sappers and Miners

ISBN/EAN: 9783744785754

Printed in Europe, USA, Canada, Australia, Japan

Cover: Foto ©ninafisch / pixelio.de

More available books at **www.hansebooks.com**

THE
ENGINEER CORPS OF HELL;

OR,

Rome's Sappers and Miners.

CONTAINING THE TACTICS OF THE "MILITIA OF THE POPE," OR THE SECRET MANUAL OF THE JESUITS, AND OTHER MATTER INTENSELY INTERESTING, ESPECIALLY TO THE FREEMASON AND LOVERS OF CIVIL AND RELIGIOUS LIBERTY, WHITHERSOEVER DISPERSED THROUGHOUT THE GLOBE.

COMPILED AND TRANSLATED BY

EDWIN A. SHERMAN, 32°,

Past Grand Registrar of the Grand Consistory of the 32d Degree of the Ancient and Accepted Scottish Rite of Freemasonry of the State of California, and Secretary of the Masonic Veteran Association of the Pacific Coast, etc.

Sold by Private Subscription only, and under Stipulated Conditions.

COPYRIGHT SECURED.

To the

REV. CHARLES CHINIQUY,

of St. Anns, Kankakee County, State of Illinois, the Martin Luther of America, the Client and Friend of Abraham Lincoln, "the Martyr President of the United States," this work is most respectfully and affectionately dedicated by

THE COMPILER.

PART FIRST.

CONTENTS.

The SECRET MONITOR OF THE JESUITS, embracing a brief history of this Society of Thugs, with their secret instructions and code, with an introduction by Charles Sauvestre, the whole translated from the Spanish. Copy now in the hands of the translator, Edwin A. Sherman, the compiler of this work.

PART SECOND.

CONTENTS.

Why Abraham Lincoln, the Martyr President, was assassinated; the initial point of the conspiracy against him by the Jesuits in Illinois in 1856; the Papal conspiracy against him and the Union while he was President, and the tragic fate of the victim of their foul plot, which was consummated on the 14th of April, 1865.

PART THIRD.

The Papal Syllabus of Errors, by Pope Pius IX.; extracts from Den's and Kenricks' Theology; Bishop Dupanloup's tirade against Freemasonry, and other miscellaneous matters of interest to Freemasons and other fraternal associations.

PREFACE.

BY THE TRANSLATOR.

In presenting to our readers this translation from the Spanish of the "MONITA SECRETA" (SECRET MONITOR) of the Jesuits, it is but due that a clear and truthful statement of how the work came into our hands should be given.

In the month of August of 1870, the Secretariat of all the bodies of the Ancient and Accepted Scottish Rite of Freemasonry in the City of San Francisco, California, had been placed in our hands, and we then occupied an office, which had been assigned to us, in the Masonic Temple of this city. Scarcely had we then entered upon our duties, when one morning in the month of September, 1870, a rap was heard at our door, and, on opening it, a stranger, feeble in body, with a pallid face bearing the evidence of great suffering and of sickness, inquired if that was the office of the Secretary of the Scottish Rite of Freemasonry, which we answered in the affirmative and invited him in and gave him a seat.

He then took from his pocket a package of papers, covered with leather and oil-silk, which he carefully unwrapped and presented for our inspection. Being in Spanish and Latin, we found upon examination that they were his patents or certificates of the various degrees of the Scottish Rite of Freemasonry, duly signed and attested by the officers, and bearing the seal of the Supreme Council of the Thirty-third Degree of Peru. Upon further examination, we found the stranger to be a "Brother of the Light," and, with other letters and credentials which he bore, that he was a gentleman of refinement and culture, and a member of and explorer for various scientific societies in Europe, but more especially for the Archæological Society of France, with its principal seat at Paris, and with its members and correspondents scattered throughout Europe and America. He was a Frenchman, and, if we mistake not, a Huguenot. He spoke English, but rather brokenly, yet correctly in grammar and diction. He inquired where our Scottish Rite bodies met, and desired to see the hall where our brethren of that Rite assembled. We conducted him up the stairs, which he slowly ascended to the ante-room of the Chapter Hall, where, pausing a few moments, we then entered the main hall, and with uncovered head he reverently approached the altar, knelt and embraced it, and bowed his head in silent prayer. We were peculiarly struck with his manner and attitude, and looked on in silence, wondering what he would do next. He then raised his head, and, reaching behind, took out a handkerchief from his pocket in the skirt of his coat and spread it out upon the altar. He then reached his hand to the back of his neck inside of his collar and slowly pulled up and out a soiled Masonic Rose Croix apron and spread it out upon the handkerchief upon the altar, and then clasping his hands together and raising his eyes towards heaven, offered a prayer in French of gratitude and thanksgiving. These strange proceedings, at such a time and to which Americans are not accustomed, greatly intensified our curiosity, and the first thought that passed through our mind was, Is he a crank? While waiting for him to finish his devotions, we observed that the apron was badly stained and had several holes in it, and there was something about it which held our attention fixed upon it. At last he arose, and we asked of him the meaning of all this, which was strange to us, never having witnessed anything of this sort before, we having then been a Mason nearly seventeen years. We were aware of the difference in the rituals of foreign jurisdictions, and the customs of our foreign brethren, especially those of the Latin races, and could make an allowance for their exuberance and intensity of feeling in their affection and ardor for Freemasonry. He replied: "If you will return to your room down-stairs, where it is warmer than it is in this hall, I will explain to you all." We then returned to the office, and he, looking to see if the door was bolted and secure, asked us to assist him in removing his coat and vest, and we did so. Then pulling up his outer and under shirts, he showed us his back, and what a sight was there presented to us! There were several bullet wounds and those made by stabs with a knife or poinard, but nearly healed, two or three of which were still slightly suppurating. We said to him, "You need a surgeon." "Oh, no," he answered, "I am pretty near well now." We then assisted him to adjust his clothing, which having done, we then asked of him to explain to us the history and meaning of all this, which he did in the following manner, which is given as correctly as possible and as our recollection serves us. He said: "I am a member of various scientific societies in Europe, one of which is the Archæological Society of France, whose seat is in Paris, and of which country I am a native. This society has many corresponding members in other countries, and is engaged in making archæological and antiquarian researches in various parts of the globe. As one of its scientific explorers, I was assigned to Spanish America, especially to the countries of Chili, Peru, Bolivia, Ecuador, New Granada and Venezuela. After having laid out my plan of exploration, I directed my principal attention to the western slope of the Andean Range in South America, and to that portion in northeastern Chili, Bolivia and southeastern Peru, as that presented the most interesting unexplored territory for my research and examination. Every facility had been accorded to me by the principal government officials of those countries; the people of Chili being the most liberal and enlightened, while those of Peru and Bolivia were the most superstitious and priest-ridden of any under the sun. I was greatly indebted to my Masonic brethren at Callao and Lima for kind and fraternal courtesies and hospitalities extended to me, and after bidding them *adieu*, I entered upon my tour of exploration and started for my destination to examine the ruins of ancient Temples of the Sun and of towns and cities long since perished, which were once populated by the subjects of the Incas, and destroyed by the ravages of war with other nations, the invasion by the Spaniards under Pizarro, and the terrible *temblors* or earthquakes which had helped in the general destruction which had been wrought at the hands of the invaders, both of their native continent and from across the Atlantic from the Sierra Moreña of Old Spain — a people now remotely and sparsely settled, excepting in the few cities and towns, but nearly the whole sunk in ignorance, and both soul and body fettered and bound to a licentious and merciless priesthood, where every cathedral and church was a citadel and fortification, and every monastery a barracks garrisoned with lustful and armed monks, with innumerable nunneries as harems for the gratification of their passions and lustful desires. Morals were at a low ebb, and a *compagñon de noche* was furnished with the general bill of fare to the guest of the hostelry, to be accepted or not, according to the taste or wish of the sojourning traveller.

"Having determined the point of my destination and commenced my explorations, the nearest habitation to the locality of the ruins which I had selected to examine was nearly six miles, and, at times when being excessively fatigued with my labor, I found that it would be necessary to camp upon the spot, and then afterwards where I was domiciled I could write up my reports from the sketches I had made and the notes taken down. The house which I occupied while so engaged was built of massive *adobe* walls (or unburnt brick), nearly four feet thick, one story in height, and the windows without glass were barred with iron grating and shutters inside. It had originally been constructed during the Spanish occupation of the country, and evidently been built as an outpost fortification for military purposes, against the inroads of the mountain tribes of Indians, with whom a constant predatory warfare had been maintained, some of whom, no doubt, were the descendants of the original occupants of the country, the ruins of whose labors I had undertaken to explore.

"The room which had been assigned to me by the family who occupied this house was about thirty feet square, with bare walls, and a seat of the same material (*adobe*) extending nearly around the room, whitewashed, and with patches of the furniture knocked off in many places. The *cama* or bed consisted of an *adobe* bedstead laid up in masonry to about the same height and shape as an ordinary blacksmith's forge, but somewhat larger and covered with a very large bullock's hide. Owing to the frequent changes of the bed linen and to remove the many lively occupants of this downy couch, repeated sweepings of the bedstead had made an incline plane inwards, with a narrow gutter next the wall. In that country, as it used to be in California, every traveller is expected to carry his blankets, take up his bed and walk when necessary. Some cheap pictures of the Virgin and saints and a crucifix adorned the walls, and with a chair and table of rude manufacture, nailed and screwed together with thongs of rawhide, my furnished apartments were complete. During my absence at the ruins, my room was not unfrequently occupied by other travelling gentry, passing through the country.

"It was on my return upon one occasion that I learned that a distinguished '*Obispo Padre de Jesus*,' or Jesuit Bishop Father, had also stopped one night and had occupied my room and bed, and had left there only two days previous to my return. Having thrown my poncho and cloak upon the bed, I made my ablutions, satisfied my hunger, and went to work transcribing from my notes and arranging my sketches in order. While so engaged, I had occasion to rise and go to my bed to get some things out of the pocket in my cloak, and in doing so I disarranged the rawhide mattress, and my attention was directed to a small package in the gutter of the bedstead next the wall, which had been covered up. I unrolled it, and to my great astonishment I found that I had made a great discovery of the 'Secret Manual of Instructions, together with the ceremonies of induction of members of the Society of the Jesuits,' printed in Latin, and bearing the seal and signature and attestation of the General and Secretary of the Order at Rome, embracing also the co-lateral branch of the Society of San Fedistas, or Fathers of the Holy Faith. Accompanying the same were manuscript additions and amendments made to the general work. Carefully concealing the fact of my discovery, I immediately set to work and in stenographic hand copied the entire work from the Latin into French, and, knowing that it would be exceedingly dangerous to be found with the original in my possession, if not positively fatal, I wrapped the whole up with the same care with which I had undone it, replaced it in the corner of the gutter of my bedstead and pushed the rawhide mattress over it in the same manner as I had found it.

"I started the next morning, after having completed my copying, to renew my explorations and to peruse the copy I had made. In a week I again returned to the house where I had been staying, when I was informed by the family that the *Obispo* with his servant had returned in great trepidation and anxiety, asking if they or any one had found a small parcel done up, describing its outward appearance, for he had lost it and would be ruined if it was not to be found. He had ridden on muleback over one hundred and fifty leagues and had searched for it in vain. On entering my apartment, which he had also occupied, and on approaching the bedstead and lifting the rawhide, he had discovered the lost parcel and was greatly overjoyed on again getting possession of it. He rigidly questioned them concerning the *extrangero* who rented the apartments, but gaining no information that would throw any additional light on the subject, went away satisfied with what he had recovered.

"Having when in Paris heard of such a work that had been printed and used by Eugene Sue in his great work of the 'Wandering Jew,' which precipitated the Revolution of 1848 and made France a republic, I sent for a copy of that work, if it could possibly be obtained, which I was fortunate in being able to do through an officer of the Grand Orient of France. On comparing the two, I found that they were identically alike, with the exception only of late additions and emendations, which, with some other matters, were in manuscript form as already stated. I therefore adopted the copy sent me with the introduction by Charles Sauvestre and other addenda, and at my leisure translated the whole printed matter into Spanish, sent the manuscript to my friends in the city of Boston, in the United States, and had it printed in Spanish for the benefit of my Masonic brethren in Spanish America, but the imprint, the better to conceal the source and protect my friends, was made to appear as having been printed at a certain number and street in Paris. I succeeded in getting quite a large number of copies smuggled through the custom-house at Callao, Peru, and distributed some of them among my Masonic brethren in that country. But, alas! unfortunately for myself and the fraternity, the Jesuits were to be found even among them, and, being duly warned by true brethren, it became necessary, in order to save my life, to flee from the country, and I made my arrangements to leave accordingly. But being detained longer than I expected, I had to take another route to reach another seaport than the one originally contemplated, and in doing so had to run the gauntlet, as it were, and was shot and stabbed in the back, as you see by the wounds nearly healed. Fortunately none proved to be fatal. I succeeded in reaching the seacoast, and through kind brethren was put on board of an English steamer bound for Panama, from whose surgeon and officers I received every courtesy and attention, and on arriving at Panama, I took the Pacific Mail Company's steamer, receiving the same tender treatment, and arrived here only a few days ago, nearly well, and here I am just as you see me. Through it all I have carried one copy of this work safely, and here it is. If I could get it translated into English and have it printed, it would be a most valuable weapon in the hands of the Masonic fraternity."

At that time we were the Associate Editor of the *Masonic Mirror*, published by A. W. Bishop & Co., afterwards Bishop & Sherman. We offered to make the translation, and did a small portion of it at that time and sent copies of the oath of the *San Fedistas* and Colloquy to our subscribers, and we went with him to Messrs. H. H. Bancroft & Co., Roman & Co., and other publishers of San Francisco at that time, to see if they would print the work, but all of them declined, either out of indifference, fear or policy, and the publication of it at that time had to be abandoned. This gentleman then went with me to Dr. Washington Ayer, with whom the book was left. It had been lost, and for a period of about twelve years could not be found, when, as good fortune would have it, the book was again recovered in the fall of 1882, and, as translated, it is here given to our readers. The original owner is supposed to now be in Mexico or Central America, pursuing his scientific researches there. His name is withheld for prudential reasons and for safety. He is a gentleman of high character, and was warmly and favorably indorsed by Señor Don José Raymundo Morales, 33°, Active Member of the Supreme Council of the Ancient and Accepted Scottish Rite of Freemasonry of Peru at the time of his visit to the Grand Consistory of the State of California, at its organization in San Francisco, October 12th, 1870, at which time we were chosen as the Grand Registrar of that Grand Body.

The difficulty in adhering to the original text, being a translation from the Spanish into English, and the Spanish itself being a translation from the Latin and the French at the same time, we have endeavored to give the same true to the spirit and literally as possible; and though there are some paragraphs and sentences somewhat awkward in expression, dubious in their meaning and hard to be understood, yet the reader will be ready, when he comes to them, to understand the full force of the language of the Jesuit Talleyrand, "that words are only intended to conceal ideas."

Asking the indulgence of our readers for the imperfections contained in this our first edition, which when exhausted will be supplied by another, and thanking our Masonic and other brethren, who have encouraged us in bringing forth this work, that we may see the devil as he is, we remain,

Fraternally yours,

EDWIN A. SHERMAN,

Translator and Compiler.

SAN FRANCISCO, CAL., August 24, 1883.

INTRODUCTION.

By CHARLES SAUVESTRE.

[TRANSLATION BY EDWIN A. SHERMAN.]

THE COMPANY OF JESUS,

OR THE

SOCIETY OF THE JESUITS.

Imagine an association whose members having destroyed all ties of family and of country, to be singled out from among men, and whose forces are to be concentrated at last to one united and formidable end, its plan devised and it establishes its dominion by all possible means over all the nations of the earth.

Imagine this immense conspiration having in place substituted its rules and its policy, yet, to the same principles of religion, that, little by little, they have arrived to dominate over the princes of the church, to maintain a royal slavitude, although not confessed, and of such a manner, that those who officially have the titles and assume the responsibility, are nothing but the docile instruments *of a force hidden and silent.* SUCH ARE THE JESUITS. Always expelled, forever returning, and little by little clandestinely and in the darkness throwing out its vigorous roots. Its wealth may be confiscated, its losses cannot be detained for they are covered. Practicing at a time the caption of inheritances and the commerce of great adventures. Confessors, negotiators, brokers, lenders, peddlers of pious gewgaws, inventors of new devotions to make merchandise. At times mixing in politics, agitating states and making princes to tremble upon their thrones, *for they are terrible in their hate.* WO UNTO HIM WHEN THEY TURN UPON HIM AS HIS ENEMY ! By very especial grace from heaven, any who may raise obstacles against them, although they may be found at the summit of the most lofty grandeur, *yet will they be stricken down as with a thunderbolt.*

Henry IV, "the one king of whom the people have treasured his memory," found three assassins successively, and died under the knife of a fanatic, at the same time he was about to attack the favorite government of the Jesuits—Austria. Clement XIV, *a Pope!* supreme above the Order of the Jesuits, dies of colic pains by poison. At this moment the Jesuits have established themselves anew amongst us (in France), in spite of the edicts and the laws. As of old, they have returned to open their colleges and to persist in moulding the youth to their own spirit.

Its society grows and increases in riches and influence by all sorts of means; and no one can attack them, for everywhere we find men prompt to serve them, to obtain from them some advantage of position or pride. This book which we present is the SECRET MANUAL of this most celebrated company. Many times have we desired to make ourselves believe that it is an apocryphal work, and so absolve the entire Order, whose code has been made known to us. The whole of this evil matter is deniable when it is said that *"these are good Fathers."* But in all conscience, can one place confidence in the words of men, when they teach that *"lying is lawful to those who can make it useful."*

"We can swear that we have not done a thing, although in effect we may have done it, understanding by this *that we did not do it on such a day or before being* born; understanding over any other similar circumstance, that we have some way by it, which can discover the words by which one can save himself; *and this is very convenient in critical circumstances* and *just when it is necessary or useful* for the health, for honor or well being." [*Opera Moralia*, R. P. Sanchez, page 2, Book III, Chap. 6, number 13.]

We well know that the Jesuits are immutable in their doctrines as in all their modes of being *sint aut sunt aut non sint*. But to give some weight to the negation, it will be found necessary to show that the conduct of the Jesuits, nothing is had in common with the precepts contained in the book of the Monita Secreta (Secret Monitor); well then, it is most evident that the contrary exists in truth, and that their works are in perfect conformity with it.

It is a great thing to be noted, that the influence of this Society has been extended over the secular clergy; we have seen its methods developed among them at the same time as its spirit. The proofs are so very numerous and public that we have the right to insist upon this point, and the reader who desires to be convinced can recur to the collection of the periodicals of these last times. It is sufficient to read the "Secret Instructions" to understand the Jesuit spirit that dictated them. Let us give a glance among the chapters—

"System that must be employed with Widows and the manner to dispose of their Properties." "Methods by which the Sons of Rich Widows are to be made to embrace the Religious State or that of Devotion." "The Method by which we must charge the Confessors and Preachers to the Great of the Earth." "Mode of making Profession of Despising of Riches." Read them all, omitting nothing, and say afterward if these precepts are a dead letter. Having ceased *to care for the widow*, to capture the inheritances, to rob the children from their families, of intriguing near the great, *of influencing in the politics of the nations*, of working to the last with but one object, that is not the triumph of religion, but the engrandisement of the "Company of Jesus" and the establishment of its dominion in the earth.

Well, then, if the conduct of the Jesuits is the faithful execution of the "Secret Instructions" it is the whole indispensable point of admitting the reality of this book. For why, or are, the Jesuits those which are modeled upon it, or has the book been copied on them ? In both cases, we cannot say that *it is an invention or a calumny*. That which is incontestable is, that the "SECRET INSTRUCTIONS" have been printed for the first time in Paris in 1661; and that of those there are existing manuscript copies of anterior date.

We read in the edition of 1824, which we have before our sight, "In the religious wars of which Germany was the theatre, many Jesuit colleges were assaulted and robbed by the Reformers. We encounter in their archives exemplary manuscripts of the 'SECRET MONITOR;' and we also find at one time in Paris two editions, one under the rubric of Praga and the other under that of Padua. This last is printed on parchment and in accordance with the '*Constitutions of the Company of Jesus.*' The three editions, although made from different manuscripts, are perfect in conforming with each other."

In all the epochs in which the Jesuits have menaced the State, a zealous hand has always thrust anew this book which has always been preserved from those that would destroy it, safely passed the trial, though the "Company" have ever sought to purchase it in secret, and cause all evidences of it to disappear entirely from view. The present edition of the "SECRET MONITOR" has been collected from the manuscript of FATHER BROTHIER and from the French editions of 1718, 1819, 1824 and 1845—this last made in Blois by Mr. Ducoux, afterwards member of the Constituent Assembly and Prefect of Police in 1848, which has served us in the edition of last June. In this is included an excellent notice, *but it has been made to disappear as has the most of all other books against the Jesuits.*

We have given in the following a brief historic sketch of the Order. Here we see that the Jesuits have been successively expelled from all parts, but that also they have returned to all parts, and entered furtively without being disturbed; in France, solemnly condemned for their acts and doctrines.

Not for this has it been left open with less audacity in the lap of the country from which they have been thrice expelled. The Ministers of State pass away, governments fall, revolutions tear up the countries, the laws are renewed, the Jesuits are always permanent and weigh down the whole. *They, only, never change.* This immutability, which is the sign of its strength, is also that of its condemnation. For that the movement is the law of its existence; all who live are subject to change—this same is the essence of progress. The formidable "Company of Jesus" *is a society of dead men! perinde ac cadaver* is also a work of death that is realized.

Founded in an epoch in which European society was lifted up at last from the long and bloody night of the Middle Ages, it imposed the mission of repelling the current which bore humanity along to the light and to science. To the torch of reason, it opposed the dogma of passive obedience and *to be as a corpse;* to the pure brilliant lights of the conscience, the corruptions of doubt and of casuistry.

The worship of the saints replaces that of God; puerile practices are substituted for those that are moral; religion has given way to the grossest superstitions; and, as the human spirit cannot be detained in its road, the separation has to be made between faith and the reason; atheism is disseminated everywhere; Jesuitism aims to kill all religious sentiment; truth, which should be in its place, is given to hypocrisy!

Established and directed with the proposition of universal domination, this Society presents in the means of its organization such power of invasion that we cannot think of it without being oppressed by a species of fear. Well, can it be that the aim of its first founders was only to assist in the unity of its beliefs? Perhaps to-day many of its members are of good faith, and mounting artifice upon artifice, hypocrisy upon hypocrisy, with the best of intentions imaginable. It is not the first example presented of hallucination. But not for this is to be left to be less pernicious its action in the world; it is all contrary.

It is true the statutes of the "COMPANY OF JESUS" forbid to

its members *all personal ambition;* but in this nothing is lost to the devil. The *good fathers* do not labor with less earnestness for the exaltation and enrichment of the Company, whose power and splendor is reflected upon each member. The pride of the body with all the passions of the spirit of sect replaces the interest of person. In one word, each one is left to be one particular entity—that is, *a Jesuit.*

For them the disinterested individual absolves the most reprehensible actions at the time they are inspired with the pride of perfection. "It is always," says the profound wisdom of Pascal, "that if an angel desired to be converted, he would return an imbecile." The excessive humility is that which is more assimilated to arrogance. It is, then, by this mode that the Jesuits have come to be believed to be superior to the most of the members of the clergy, whatever may be their dignity or how high they may be found. It is also by this method that they have imposed upon themselves the task of dominating the whole Catholic world.

For themselves, they are nothing, not having pompous titles, no sumptuous ornaments, no croziers, no mitres, no capes of the prebendiaries, but pertain to that one Order everywhere governing and directing. Of command, others have the appearance; but these possess the reality. *In whatever place of the Catholic world a Jesuit is insulted or resisted, no matter how insignificant he may be, he is sure to be avenged*—AND THIS WE KNOW.

NOTE BY THE TRANSLATOR.—See in Part Second the assassination of Abraham Lincoln and its causes, in the trial of Rev. C. Chiniquy.

PREFACE

OF THE

FOURTH FRENCH EDITION.

The three first editions of this book were exhausted in so short a time that we could not carry out our intention of important changes; but we now present new proofs and augment our citations, answering with them to our adversaries.

The events of Switzerland stamping out the Jesuits as agitators of civil war; their black robes spattered with blood—but, as on other occasions, the blood was not distinguished, because it was confounded with that of the Protestants and inhabitants of the New World. And we offer the testimony of the riches of the Jesuits, of their duplicity and of their bad faith. This complete book is to-day the condemnation of the Jesuits by themselves, being the one answer conceded by us to the Jesuit journals which so cowardly attacked us.

A thousand laurels to the Jesuits! Awakening Europe out of its lethargy and running unitedly to the conquest of democratic ideas, for the reaction of tyranny always produces liberty.

In 1833, the Jesuits made exclamation to the Pope. "*It would be an absurdity to concede to the people the liberty of conscience.*"

The CARDINAL ALBANI having framed his plan of action that decimated Italy and dictated this impious oath: "*I swear to erect the throne and the altar upon the bones of the infamous Liberals, and to exterminate them one by one, without being moved by the clamors of children, old men and women!*"

In 1843, we take the events of Helvetia and note that the Jesuits were the prime movers of the civil war; the Holy Father having *counseled* them to abandon Switzerland, but did not satisfy the exit of the *reverend fathers, and they persisted in another struggle.* Shall it be that the blood shall be poured upon their heads, drop by drop! Shall they not receive the maledictions of men and fall beneath the anathema of God!

THE JESUITS,

FROM 1541 UNTIL OUR OWN DAYS.

In vain we question the step; in vain we ask ourselves if the odium against the Jesuits has not been unjust, to see them constantly hated for three centuries, with the curses of peoples and the sentences even of popes and of kings. Who can answer to human infallibility? Infamous persecutions cannot pursue entire peoples. Have not the Hebrews been a thousand times condemned? And at the end of eighteen centuries man has avoided the injury and maledictions. Where was the season of justice? Where that of equality? Who can assure me that the Jesuits, as in other times the Templars, have not been victims? The truth is, popes and sovereigns excluded their doctrines; but was it not a Pope who condemned Galileo? Was it not another who sentenced Bossuet and Fenelon? Certainly posterity annulled many unjust sentences, but in turn maintained and sanctioned all the decisions which struck down the Jesuits, petitioning yet against the Order of the Jesuits the sentence pronounced against them by Pope Clement XIV., *who was poisoned by them!*

We hurriedly trace the history of the Jesuits, descending beyond all comprehension of our tasks, to the sepulchre in which Loyola interred the doctrines, "*the bounden duty of making of man and of intelligence a corpse.*"

A Spanish chieftain, called Ignatius Loyola, was the founder and lawgiver of the Jesuits. This man was a fanatic, insensible, and given an iron and omnipotent will, created a sect in the midst of Catholicism, frightened them with the clamorous apostacy of Luther; covering his haughty ideas with the habit of the monk and the cape of the mendicant, ridiculous in the extreme but terrible in his results. Spain having inaugurated a tribunal (the Inquisition) with the intent of killing the body, under the pretext of saving the soul. Ignatius Loyola assassinated the soul, despising the body—in this manner, in the two extremities of the world, in Spain and the Indies, and accounted the two societies which destroyed the body, "the *inquisitors* and *stranglers*, by other name—*thugs*, and the Company of Jesus placed its tents between them both."

Jesus created the life and the thought; Ignatius Loyola created death—the death of the soul and of intelligence, of love and charity, of all that is grand, noble and generous. Loyola was the creator and the one light-giver of the Society of the Jesuits, an ardent and passionate man, rancorous and persevering, oppressive towards his disciples, in his institutions, poesy and enthusiasm, in genius and human passions. In the Order of the Jesuits there must be only one man—*the General*—his inferiors being nothing more than passive instruments; then Loyola in the bed of death prescribed blind obedience—*obedientia sœca*. His institutions which we present from thence, form a monument, are few and minute; the attention given by readers that they must spring from casuists, deceivers and perverse, and also that they must betray the timorous and honorable. This code has only one base—*mutual vigilance and despising of the human race.*

"The Superior," says Michelet, "is always surrounded by counsellors, professors, novices and graduates, and his brethren who can and must be denouncers; taking shameful precautions, although against other members who have given the greatest proof of their adhesion; prescribing friendship in the seminaries and being prohibited to walk two by two, and it is necessary to be alone or three together, but not less, for it is well known that the Jesuits never establish any intimacy before a third, *for the third is a spy;* for when there are three, which is indispensable, *there cannot be found a traitor.*"

In the celebrated *Constitutions* it is prescribed "to have the sight much lower than that of those to whom they speak and dissimulate the wrinkles which form in the nose and the forehead." The *Constitutions* instruct the confessors in sophistries, and these serve them to direct them before the eyes of the penitents. In the power of Loyola in converting into a corpse, the faculty of free will—*perinde ac cadaver*. "His successors (1) organized the grand scholastic moral or casuistry, that for all whom we may meet either a *distinguished individual* or a *nobody* (*nisi*). THIS ART OF DECEIVING WITH THE MORAL WAS THE PRINCIPAL CONSISTENCY OF HIS INSTITUTION; THE OMNIPOTENT ATTRACTION OF A CONFESSIONARY SEDUCED THE MULTITUDE; THE SERMON WAS SEVERE AND INDULGENT IN DIRECTION, concluding at last with such foreign merchandise introduced among the feeble consciences of the great of the world and the political direction of society.

The birth of the "Company of Jesus" was at an appropriate time, of the great revolution of Luther, valiantly fighting the Reform of the Sixteenth Century, serving the Pope with these auxiliaries who did not see whom they were that were as succor sent from heaven.

The Jesuits augmented their numbers very soon at the side of *the tiara* to whom they gave power in his day, and in 1547, Bobadilla of Germany was expelled for his seditious doctrines. Meanwhile the accomplices of Charles IX and Cathererine de Medicis took counsel of the Jesuits and were assembled in their den on the bloody night of St. Bartholomew, August 24th, 1572, when Gaspard de Coligny was assassinated with 30,000 other Huguenots, and over 70,000 in the provinces were butchered, being at the time when Francis Borgia was the General of the Order. In 1568 they intended to establish a seminary in Paris, but the University, great and powerful then, was opposed to the progress of the Sons of Loyola, whose chief in France was ODON PIGENAT, a furious colleague, to whom Arnaud gave the appellation of "*the fanatic priest of Cybele*," and the historian gave the title of "*The Tiger*."

In 1570, Elizabeth expelled the Jesuits from England, being at the same time that they were banished from Portugal and Amberes in 1578. During the reign of Henry III., they

---

(1) MICHELET of the Jesuits. See Pascal "The Provincials."

stirred up a rebellion and famished the country by becoming monopolists, the infallible method of sharpening the poniards of Jacob Clement and Chatel. In 1593, the Jesuit Varade armed the hand of the assassin Barriere against Henry IV.; in 1594, Jean Chatel, with the intent of assassinating Henry IV., had for his accomplice the Father Guinaud, who was hung for the crime on the 7th of June, 1595. Pope Clement VII. charged the Jesuits with the dissensions of the church; in 1598 they were expelled from Holland for attempting to assassinate Maurice of Nassau, as they had by order of Pope Gregory XIII assassinated William the Silent, Prince of Orange, on the 10th of July, 1584. An edict of Henry IV expelled them from France, but, dragging along until the planting of the French monarchy they were tacitly permitted to enter. The Conqueror of the League, the king who dreamed of a universal monarchy, the threatening aspect of these men *whom* it is said *had secret treaties and correspondence everywhere and ability to cause others to treat with them by their agreeable manners (Qui ditil ont des intelligences et correspondances partout et grande dextiente a disposea les esprit ainsi qu'il leur plait).*

• In 1604 Cardinal Borromeo was dispatched from the Seminary of Breda; being hung in London in 1605, the Jesuits Garnet and Oldecorn as authors of the "Gunpowder Plot;" and in 1606 they were driven from Venice.

Ravaillac assassinated Henry IV. in the year 1610, and the Jesuit Mariana, in his work "*De Rege*," made the apology of the regicide.

Following so notorious a Society, its tracks are imperishable—a trench filled with the corpses of kings. In 1618 they were expelled from Bohemia; in 1619, from Moravia; and in 1621, from Poland. Inflamed in 1641 with the great contest of *Jansenism*, in 1843, they were thrust out of Malta; and in Seville, where they commenced merchandising and were broken up in 1646, after having been the adversaries of all the illustrious men of their epoch, after having been routed by Arnaud and De Thou, who fell under the lash of Pascal;

the provincial decrees of justice and forced out of the Royal
Ports by repeated blows, the eloquent voice of Bossuet breaking forth in invectives against them, and by the declaration
of 1682 all the French clergy treated them with indignation
and contempt. But following their subterranean ways, they
returned to their elevation again, ruling Louis XIV., by Maintenon and the Father Lachaise, who was very influential over
the mind of the widow of Scareon, who, dying, ceded his
power to the Father Letellier. The Edict of Nantes, which
sheltered the Protestants, was shamefully revoked; the Jesuits profaned the cemetery of Porte Royal; the *Bull Unigenitus*, provoked by them, produced 80,000 letters — orders
against the *Jansenists;* Jouvenez, historian of the Jesuits,
placed the assassins of our kings in the number of martyrs,
(1) and in 1723 Peter the Great drove them out of his territory. The Jesuits were reduced to poverty, and in 1753 the
bankruptcy of the Father Lavallete made known to Europe
their common riches and bad faith. In 1757, Louis XV. perished at the hands of Damiens, a new regicide, a native of
Arras, and educated by the Jesuits in a city where they exercised full power; his confessors were Jesuits and designers
against France as accomplices with a similar purpose.

In 1758, the King of Portugal was assassinated in consequence of a mutual oath by the Father Malagrida, Matus and
Alexander; the Parliament proceeded judicially against them
and they were expelled. In 1762, the Parliament of Paris
suppressed them.

On the 9th of September, 1767, they were expelled from
Peru by the Viceroy Amaty Junient, after one hundred and
ninety-nine years establishment in that country, by order of
the government of Spain, dated in Prado on the 5th of April,
1767.

On the 21st of July, 1773, they were abolished forever by
Clement XIV., after having carefully studied their history
and doctrines for the space of four years. The church was

---

(1) His book was condemned to be burned, weighted down with
many of the works of Father Letellier.—(N. del T.)

united for their degradation and destruction—the whole world repelled and cursed them; is it to be believed that they succumbed to all this? No! Their enemies are those who have ceased to exist; they have preached regicide for so long a time, nothing to them is the cost of so monstrous a crime —this crime which no human law can foresee—this crime that must stain the world for that, which but none will disown, committed upon the person of Pope Clement XIV., the Vicar of Jesus Christ and successor of St. Peter (so-called), *died poisoned!*

Scarcely had the stranger put his foot on the soil of France when the Jesuits appeared by their same footsteps, (1) although at that time wearing a mask, and called then "THE FATHERS OF THE FAITH!" (2)

Presenting themselves among the people under the guise of missionaries, but in a short time they threw off the mask, preaching the counter-revolution and *ultramontanism*. Mont Rouge and Saint Archeuil were quartered Generals of the Order of "THE FATHERS OF THE FAITH," humbled during the reign of Louis XVII., who were nicknamed "*Sectaries of Voltaire*," manifesting to their death, dominated the throne of Charles X. and precipitated his fall. Obliged to renounce the light of day, *the holy fathers* returned to their subterranean mine. Denying their own existence, they annulled all that was possible, but did not desist from turning anew to power; annihilated by the Revolution of 1830, re-establishing themselves little by little, and hoping for victory, for they counted with more arms than Briareus to the side of calumny, hypocrisy and falsehood.

II.

Two learned Professors gave the signal of contest against the Jesuits; thanks be given to them for the prompt notes of

---

(1) The Bull that re-established the Jesuits had the significant date of August 6th, 1814.

(2) The San Fedistas, see their oath and words of recognition at the end of this work.

alarm, that the snares of Jesuitism, of new dextrous covering which had covered the world. "Who are the Jesuits?" exclaimed everybody; "let us fight them now!" The Jesuits are a monstrous body, illegal, and also anti-canonical. This body is fictitious in France, and does not dwell here but by its cunning, being in continuous rebellion against the laws for which they have been banished and proscribed. For everywhere the clandestine place is, it is a post of observation. At its own time it is *ecclesiastical and secular*, regular and secular, of all classes and of all religions; *then even in Protestantism it has its affiliates*. The famous General Ricci manifested that its true name was the "WHAT IS IT?"

The Order of the Jesuits had devoted themselves to poverty, but accumulated continually. Appointed confessors and physicians to the soul, they were its perverters; they valued its moral influence to augment its riches with gifts and cunning advantages—approaching the pillows of the dying to speak of holy things, and terrorizing with the infernal (1) to at last obtain a testamentary will that dispossessed the widow and orphans, claiming the title of "Protector of Kings," they gave the example to the regicide; they were armed with the most audacious privileges, ultramontanes, against laws, kings, magistrates and priests like themselves. Passive instruments of the Pope or of the General, they were independent of all ecclesiastical authority; they depended on no other than Rome; devoted buffoons and able directors; they knew how to move, terrorize and subjugate the ignorant, but were weak and indulgent towards the powerful of the earth; converting their crimes into virtues, *and always having a distinguished person at their service*.

"*Il est avec le ciel accommodements*"—"There are composures in heaven"—they exclaimed, and pretended that the gospel was the same with morality. In their object to be-

---

(1) He also succeeded with the President—Don Miguel San Roman—to apostatize from his Masonic doctrines was the Reverend Pedro Gual, in extremis he destroyed his apostization.

come rich, they were either hypocrites or incautious, but either one or another they were the most humble of agents.

In its code there was only one unpardonable crime; not being that of the parricide, the assassin, the sacrilegious, robber, incestor or violator. That of *scandal, only!* Corrupter of the faith and dogma, of the ecclesiastical customs and discipline; bold to present in the pulpit its casuistries with the assured guarantees of being the true doctrine.

Manufacturers in Asia and America of idolatrous rites, we have seen in its dark missions its pretended symbol with the savages, and in the same moment of singing victory at the arrival of Protestantism; and all the courage, all the self-denial of its missionaries was but to open a road to the Calvinists or the English. One only country where they remained was Paraguay, where one of them was proclaimed king; Paraguay, which offered the image of nothing and the tomb.

Let us write with the eloquence of Quinet: "How tranquilly to my country have I invited an alliance, that such a price to pay to them the most, and none can notice that we are guarded, for others having the experience with preference, that the most infamous people of Europe, those of the least credit and authority are of the habitation of the Society of Loyola, * * * and that we shall not be worn out until suspended by that *poisoned* sleep which for two centuries has prevailed in Spain and South America."[1]

How many have been taken by Jesuitism? how many others have perished? There is no rest beneath its shade, for the shade of the manzanillo is death.[2] We have said that the

---

(1) Jesuits. Now they have domineered over Ecuador, where they rule despotically, by the dictator Garcia Moreno, who has submerged the soil of his country in blood, in floods and seas of the blood of the Liberals conforming to the oath of Cardinal Albani, which we publish at the end of this book ; and how rapidly grew the power of Peru un der the shadow of the Coronel Don Jose Balta, its actual President.

(2.) Manzanillo : tree of the Antilles, whose fruit is poisonous and whose shade is noxious.

Jesuits are the destroyers of dogmas, and the citations we make in this book prove it; we read the "*hundred easy devotions,*" a book created for the *superstitious* without religion; for the men who desire to have one foot in paradise and the other in hell; for they at one instant cannot reform within and consecrate themselves to prayer; but that they who desire to be saved without any labor and without abandoning a life of orgies and of pleasure. Who are these who create proselytes, and for all find excuses, making religion a victim of their doctrines, guilty indulgencies and alliances carnal or political, so notorious and deplorable, saying to the rich libertine "*Apply to me and I will save you at little cost*"; and to the Virgin, saluting her in this manner: to those who rise up "*Good Morning, Mary! and Good Night! to those who retire, or without lifting a scapulary or a sacred heart.*" All this is said without our perceiving how ridiculous are our beliefs and how ultra is Christianity!

Who are they? The agents of espionage, intrigue, and accusations; *the prime movers of the leagues, civil wars and dragonnades*[1] *schisms, murderers; that is what they are! Incarnate enemies of legitimate liberty, partners of despotism; that is what they are! Disturbers of the peace of all states and of all families, seducers and conspirators; instructors of the assassins of kings; authors of slavery and the stolidity of peoples; vassals and oppressors in the name of God to popes, kings, peoples and to the most holy and illustrious men;* THAT IS YOUR HISTORY! In vain we seek for a crime that they have not committed or excused. Where are your works? Perhaps you can cite the noble efforts of some missionaries. You caused the Stuarts to perish and the Bourbons must disappear forever. This is your future, your destiny.[2]

For a long time they humbled themselves before making

---

(1) Persecution that was made in France during the siege of Louis XIV. of the Protestants for which they employed dragoons.—(N. del T.)

(2) This treatise, written in France, in 1845 foretold the last of Doña Isabel de Bourbon, Queen of Spain.—(N. del T.)

their appearance in public, and now they have invaded the soil of our country. We are the tyrants of forty thousand priests, your friends say with pride. France possesses to-day 960 Jesuits.[1]

Are we not threatened by the presence of the Jesuits? Who has not advised us of their existence? Anti-revolutionary tendencies, ultramontane systems, an evil that is undefinable, and over all the division that is so powerful of the paternal household; tyrants of 40,000 priests the Jesuits have disposed of 40,000 pulpits, being its moral and proxy of the souls of women, and whom they possess, has said Michelet, reckoning debit with the remainder. Proxies also of the mothers to obtain their children, for which they demand in high voice the *liberty of their teaching*, with the object of *monopolizing to their own profit*, the actual generation they repel, for they are confident of forming the heart of the coming posterity; illusory confidence; for on giving the cry of liberty, all the world has divined that slavery was the primordial object of its efforts and denying arbitrary liberty because arbitrariness or actual liberty was not desired.[2]

But if the Jesuits are to be the directors of learning, must we despair of the future generation which issues from their hands? No; because the Jesuits educated Voltaire and Diderot their greatest enemies; and further the disciples of the Jesuits with their writings precipitated the Revolution of 1789. The education by the Jesuits created philosophers, casuists, and certainly is it shown atheists, over all!

Who can predict with certainty, what shall be the results of the education by the Jesuits? The habits are relaxed in the extreme; egotism and rivalry dry up the hearts; what will the world be if the perverse *doctrines* have access to modern society?

---

(1) We have at the time of the date of this little work to-day in France many more Jesuits —(N. del T.)

(2) Long live the Revolution of September which brought to us the liberty of teaching.—[N. del T.]

"Death kills only the body! but they kill the soul. What care? To the deadly murderers living on are to be left our children; here will be lost our children in the future. Jesuitism is the soul of policy and of impeachment; the most ugly habits of the tattling scholar, surrendering all society for the college convent; what a deformed spectacle! A whole people living as an establishment of Jesuits, is to say, that they have arrived at the lowest occupation of denunciation; treason in the same home; then the wife is a spy upon her husband, the brothers spy upon one another, but without any bustle, we perceive only a sad murmur, a confused noise of people who confess strange sins, which torment them mutually and at which they blush in silence."[2]

The Jesuits destroy the moral and never reach to purify their habits, carrying forward religious quarrels to centuries without any object of lesson. The Pombal may be reborn and a new Clement VI. perhaps may not delay to avenge the universe.

To re-establish the Jesuits solidly, it will be necessary to destroy man; the Jesuits are impossible in the meanwhile when we can consult our soul and our reason; in the meanwhile we notice the palpitation of our heart.

III.

The actual position of the French clergy to-day is the object of many grave fears. When the immortal declaration of 1682, the clergy having expelled the Jesuits, they measured an abyss between them and the others. Who is blind to this abyss? The French clergy remember the eloquent words of Bossuet: "*The Shepherd will unite with the Wolf to guard the flock.*"

A similar alliance is more than a scandal, it is a sacrilege.

---

(1) Michelet of the Jesuits.—(N. del T.)

(2) See for example the actual state of Ecuador, the whole of which country is converted into a college of Jesuits and Peru following behind.—(N. del T.)

The French clergy we do not doubt very promptly detest the Jesuits; they observe with honor its moral and its history; expelling the sellers of the temple and marching at the head of progress, prove that the Gospel is not the precursor of the sepulchre. Christianity must not be only the religion of the dead; the Gospel is the charter of man and the proclamation of his liberty. Minister of God, explain until the last, the Gospel of Christ. Eighteen centuries have we hoped. The people, Christ anew has been nailed to the cross; and for a long time have we seen the blood flow from his wounds; the generous blood which has flowed for our redemption, running yet all the days; but the proclamation of the gospel will cicatrize the bloody gashes.

The French Revolution has commenced the work of equality and liberty. The apostles of Christ must explain to all the law of God!] The tablets of Mt. Sinai was the code of the Hebrews; but we are not ambitious for any other laws than those of the Gospel. But the soul of the Gospel that is in the sepulchre and the Church is the door which covers its entrance; and we trust that only the stone may be broken and be scattered in every part. The moral of Christ is eighteen centuries old and has lost nothing of its eloquence or force. Already is the time that the people see in the Gospel something else than a theory of what is beyond the tomb. Rest is the only thing that can be given to the ashes of the dead; *but to the living must be given liberty!*

The French clergy will know very soon where are their true friends. But the priests of false Gods may incense to emperors and preach inequality and slavery; but the priests of Christ will find the footsteps of their Master in the paths of love and liberty.

And now, young men, be careful that ye do not have to repent of living sepulchres when the catastrophe shall be inevitable. Great things are for you to do. Persist wherever is the combat of the soul, the danger of life and the reward. Do not be lost, or then yourselves will become the sepulchre of the catacombs: "as I, know ye, that God is not the God of the dead, he is the God of the living."

NOTE BY THE TRANSLATOR.—If such are the opinions of a liberal Catholic so beautifully, ardently and eloquently expressed, what ought not Protestants, Hebrews and liberals to do in America and around the globe, to throw off the yoke of Rome entirely wherever it is attempted to be fastened to fetter the people. Repudiate the whole thing entirely, Jesuits, Dominicans, Franciscans, Augustinians, Carthusians, Paulist Fathers, Fathers of the Holy Faith, Pope, Cardinals, Archbishops, Bishops, Priests, Curates, Convents, Monasteries filled with lazy, licentious Friars, and clean out the whole business of this caravansary of prostitution and lust, under the name of the Roman Catholic religion.

SUDDEN DEATHS OF SOME OF THE POPES OPPOSED TO THE JESUITS.

I.

Sextus V was stricken down by premature death (*immature morte precepti*) at the time of attaining the subjection of the Jesuits to his established law.

II.

The same fate attended Clement VIII, but his death did not immediately happen; it was predicted with certainty by the Father Bellarmin until the very moment of going to condemn the doctrine of *Moline* favored by the Jesuits.

III.

Innocent XIV died immediately when he meditated upon the measures for abolishing the Society.

IV.

Clement XIV died immediately after having dissolved the Jesuits.

It is to be noted that these different corpses and many others of bishops and cardinals who were as little disposed toward the Jesuits and always died by them, and have contributed evidence for us to regard them with sinister suspicions.

The Jesuit PEDRO JANIGE having written against the Society a work called "*The Jesuit upon the Scaffold*," was surprised by the *Holy Fathers*, who compelled him to sign a retraction. Their action was continued until the removal of FATHER JANIGE, in consequence of a crime that they took care to exempt. MELCHOIR INCHOFFER, a Jesuit suspected to be the author of the "*Monarchy of Solipsos*," was violently carried away clandestinely from Rome, whither he had returned to petition the Pope. The FATHER SCOTTI, the true author of the "*Solipsos*," escaped with difficulty the poniard and the poison.

HISTORIC DOCUMENTS AGAINST THE SOCIETY OF THE JESUITS.

THE AUTHORS ARE

Pope Clement VIII, Francisco de Borgia, third General of the Jesuits, Geromo Lazuna, San Carlos, The Blessed Palafoz, Cardinal Turon, Parliament of Paris, Id., Charles III, The last moments of Clement XIV, Palafoz to Innocent X, Monclas, Bull of Benedict IV, The Father Lachaise, Innocent XIII, The Charlotaise, etc.

"The Jesuit is a sword whose hilt is in Rome and its point everywhere," says GENERAL FOY.

HISTORIC TESTIMONIES.

I.

"*Vede il signor, di questa camero io governo non dico Pirigi, mala China, non guia la China, ma tutto il mondo, senzache messuno sappio come si fa.*—(TAMBURINI, the General of the Jesuits.)

"See, sir, from this chamber I govern not only to Paris. but to China; not only to China, but to all the world, without any one to know how I do it."

Effectively, not being the Jesuits, but its *institutes*, subjects of no king, its general is the first in the world. In 1773 the Jesuits were 22,000, to-day (1846) they number 46,000, and who does not fail to ask, "*Where are the Jesuits?* (God and the Devil can only answer correctly.—*Translator.*) OCCULIHABENT SED NON VIDEUNT.

II.

Opinion of Pope Clement VIII.
(1592.)

"The CURIOSITY drawn to the Jesuits is gathered from everywhere; over all, *in the confessionals*, to *know* from the penitent, whatever passes in her house, *between her children, servants, or other persons who are domiciled with them, or to whom they come, and every incident which may happen*. If they confess a Prince *they have the power to govern all his States*, desiring to govern for him, and making him to believe that nothing will go well without their care and industry."

It is not a philosopher who looks out for the Jesuits, it is the Chief of the Church; let us see the judgments by its third General, Francisco Borgia.

III.

"The time will arrive very soon, in which the 'Company of Jesus' will become very solicitous in the human sciences, *but without a single application to virtue*, the ambition will be to dominate, the overbearing and pride penetrating its soul, to rule alone and no one can refrain them. The spirit of our brethren is trampled upon by an unlimited passion for temporal goods, an eagerness to accumulate with the utmost ardor of the worldly."

Here is a prediction that does not pertain to Voltaire nor to Michelet but to Gerome Lanuza, Bishop of Albarracin.

IV.

"Robbing the alms given to the poor, to the beggars and

the sick, drawing to them the rabble. * * * *Contracting familiarities with women and teaching them to wrong their husbands and to give them their goods to hide.*"

V.

"A long time have we seen the Society of the Jesuits in imminent danger of a sudden decadence, for many bad heads and evil maxims predominate among them."
(Letters of San Carlos of the 15th of April, 1759, to M. Speciaup.)

VI.

"We have no religious order more prejudicial to the universal Church, or who have made themselves more revolting to Christian provinces, etc."
(Bishop Palafoz to Pope Innocent X. Letter II, Chapter III, Pages 115, 116.)

VII.

We read in the sentence given by the parliament of France of 1662:
"The institute of the Jesuits is inadmissible, for its nature in its whole estate is contrary to natural right, opposed to all authority, spiritual and temporal, and on the road to introduce under the cloak of a religious institution, a body politic, whose essence consists in a continual activity, to reach by whatever way their desire, direct or indirect, secret or public, until first an absolute independence, and successively the usurpation of all authority."

VIII.

The sentence of 1762 contained the following paragraph relating to the moral of the Jesuits:
"The moral practice of the Society of the Jesuits is perverse, destructive of all religious principle and of *probity*; injurious to the Christian morality; pernicious to civil society; seditious and contrary to the rights and nature of the royal power, and to the sacred persons of the sovereigns, and to

the obedience of the subjects; they are adapted to excite the greater revolts in the States, *and to re-form and sustain the most profound corruption in the hearts of men.*"

IX.

In reply to a brief of Pope Clement XIII., Charles III. being King of Spain, he expressed the following, relating to the Jesuits: "I can assure YOUR HOLINESS, that I have the proofs, the most efficacious, of the necessity of expelling the whole Company, and not any one in particular. I repeat to YOUR HOLINESS with a new assurance, and for your consolation I pray God that he will inspire what I believe."

X.

When Clement XIV. had signed *the extinction of the Jesuits* he was found seated in his office, and said in the presence of a person distinguished for his merit and his class, "I have made this suppression, and I do not repent it; but I was not determined until I had examined to the end, and fully reflected, and having believed it useful and necessary for the Church, making it anew if I had not already done so; MA QUESTA SO-PRESSIONE MI DARA LA MORTE "—" although this suppression shall occasion my death."

XI.

No one knew how to interpret a pasquinade at the entrance of the palace of the Holy Father, which contained these five letters: I. S. S. S. V. Clement XIV. explained them in this manner, "*In Settembre Sara Sede Vacante.*" In September the Holy See will be vacant.

Clement XIV. died with a devouring heat in the throat, stomach and intestines, ceasing to exist after terrible colics. At the time of his death, his body was clean, became black and decomposed in great pieces.

Twice had the life of the Holy Father been attempted by poison—in the month of April, and at last in June, 1774.

" *The Jesuits had devoted themselves to poverty!!! We have found the Jesuits in power and perhaps with all the riches of*

South America; not ceasing to augment their wealth by the industry of its traffic which has been extended until they have opened not only markets of cattle, meat and fish, but the stores for the smallest of trade!"

(Second letter of Bishop Palafoz to Innocent X.)

XII.

"Political corrupters of all governments; flatterers of the great and of their passions; prime movers of despotism ; to smother the reason and power of authority; enemies of kings who oppose them and their crooked desires; calumniators of the many who love with sincerity the prince and the state; placing a sceptre of iron in the hands of kings and a dagger in those of their subjects; counseling tyranny and preaching tyrannicide; binding to its interests the most cruel intolerance with the most scandalous indifference and respect to religion and morality; permitting all classes of crimes, and not pardoning disputes over words in subjects little intelligible; serving idolatry which they regard, and persecuting Catholicism which refuses its confidence. A theological quarrel is in Europe a business of state, as much as the superstitious and worship of Confucius which they permit in Asia."

(M. DE MONCLAIR—*Manual of the Jesuits*, note 61.)

XIV.

Benedict XIV., by a Bull of December, 1741, prohibited the Jesuits. "They dare, before us, to enslave the Indians of Paraguay, to sell them, or buy them, etc., * * * separating mothers from their children, and to despoil them of their goods and property." (Page 27.)

XV.

A few days before his death, FATHER LACHAISE said to LOUIS XIV, "Sir, I counsel you to elect a confessor in our company well disposed to your majesty, for at this time they are very much scattered, numerous and composed of characters very diverse and impassioned for the glory of the body. *No one can answer for a misfortune, and* ONE EVIL BLOW MAY

VERY SOON BE GIVEN." The king took care to throw down the proposition, and it was referred to Marechal, his chief physician, the which in his first terror he revealed to Blouin, first chamberlain, and to Bolduc, the first apothecary, his particular friends, and from whom we have this and many other anecdotes.

(*Memoirs of Duclos*, vol. i, page 134.)

XVI.

Pope Innocent XIII. reproached the Jesuits for having been, in Pekin, the prime movers and solicitors of the incarceration of the missionaries, declaring that for that unheard of scandal, re-presenting the paper of the constables for their imprisonment and jailers for keepers, over all for the respect to Pedini, Appiani and Guingues, Italian and French missionaries.

(Vol V of the *Anecdotes upon China*, page 260.)

XVII.

"Is it honorable to form a duty of espionage between religious people, and accustom them to assimulate and lie to tender hearts, and for as much with propensity or inclination to all?" "The corruption of the soul and the degradation of the spirit, to tear away from men all sentiments of honor, and all the causes of emulation; this is to debase humanity under the pretext of perfecting them." *And that use cannot make* of similar instruments *a superior ambitious man* and *a criminal* continually occupied in observing and consequently for sale. Imposing the yoke of belief, that they are sold for *their good*; this is the culmination of fanaticism."

(LA CHALOTAIS, *Manual of the Constitutions of the Jesuits*, page 171, edition in 12.)

XVIII.

"It is for this that the Society of the Jesuits has the power to hide the sun, and make men blind and deaf to its caprice."

(MONTLARC, *Manual* page 60.)

XIX.

"The General is *the true Pope of the Company of Jesus*, and the plan of this institute is to destroy all authority, and all government, having concentrated all in its society."

"This ambitious Company is a nation, a power apart germinating in the loins of all others, changing their substance and surmounting their ruins."

(RIQUET, member of the Parliament of Toulouse.)

[Verily, a tape-worm.—*Translator.*]

XX.

"What other religion possesses secret constitutions, privileges which they do not declare, and regulations which are forever hidden? * * * The Church does not limit that which illumines the reason of man, and by the contrary it abhors totally the darkness, * * * and for this will come, as much as any desire, the privileges, the instructions, statutes and regulations of the conduct of the most religious. Religious men there are in the abodes of the Jesuits, and religious professors *who ignore the constitutions and privileges*, proper rules of the company; but they are the more obliged to submit to them, and made to follow them; for whose motives the superiors conduct them by secret regulations known only to themselves."

(D. PALAFOZ, Bishop of Osmu to Innocent X.)

To conclude such numerous citations we abandon the pen with pleasure; being effectively pained of having to transcribe such maxims, although they may be trampled upon and scoffed at. For the general public who believe that we are deceived and a compiler of dreams better than the thoughts of an individual of a religious society, are the ideas of a bandit. We cannot believe that there are men so miserable, who excuse the *parricide*, the robber, the assassin, and all the vicious, adulating despotism and pointing the daggers against kings.

"A vertigo has for three centuries made the "*Company of*

Jesus; if these abominable doctrines have not been sufficient to horrify the world, without having been thrust forth from the Confessional, who can foretell what we shall be to-day, and who knows if the power not pertaining to the Order that the Nineteenth Century may not have the glory of destroying it forever?"

(GEORGE DARNEVELL.)

CONFESSIONS OF THE JESUITS.

I.

"If we are accused of pride and of intention that all shall pass through our hands, and depend on us; when they do not have that upon which to found similar accusations, we must conduct ourselves in such a manner that the world cannot vituperate us."

(Epistle of MUCIO WITELLESCHI, General of the Jesuits.)

II.

MARIANA concluded that the Society of Jesus was *gangrened*. He believed that it was lost by its crimes, if God did not shortly establish it upon a more solid foundation.

III.

GEROMO FIORAVENTI said; "*I confess it with pain that much contained in the book of MARIANA is very true, and that the Society of Jesus has peremptory necessity of total reform.*"

POWER OF THE POPES AND OF THE JESUITS.

I.

"The Pope must admonish kings and punish them with death."

(P. SANTABEL, *del Papa* 1626, Chap. XXX, page 296.)

II.

"*A man proscribed by the Pope must be put to death every-*

where; for the Pope has one jurisdiction, indirect to the least, over the globe, even to the *temporal.*[1]

(MUSENBAUM.)

III.

"It is a strange thing to see men who have made a profession of religion, (the Jesuits) and to whom no evil or good has been done by any one, *to daily attempt against my existence!*"

(Memoirs of Sully VI. Letter of Henry IV.)

IV.

"I do not judge it to be convenient to surrender to the Jesuits. Can they perhaps guarantee my life? It is well if they are eager for it; then it may be attempted more than once against it; *I have the proof by experience* and can show some cicatrices of its wounds. There is no necessity of more invitations, nor excitements to reach to the extremes, *consenting in his pardon but greatly to my grief and for necessity.*"

(HENRY IV.)

V.

"Whatever man of the people, not to have other remedy, we can kill him who tyranically usurps power; for he is a public enemy."

(EMMANUEL SA, Jesuit.)

VI.

"Evidently," exclaims Andrew Delrio, "it is lawful for any man to assassinate a tyrant, if having become powerful at the summit of power and not having other means by which we can cease the tyrrany."

---

(1) After reading the maxim, who will defend the temporal power when it is so that the Company of Jesus have sanctified the manner in which they do it?

SECRET INSTRUCTIONS

OF THE

COMPANY OF JESUS.

PREFACE.

These particular instructions must be guarded and kept with careful attention by the superiors, communicated with prudent caution to a few of the professors; in the meantime there does not exist any other thing so good for the Society; but we are charged with the most profound silence, and to make a false show, should they be written by any one though founded in the experience we have had. As there are various professors who are in these secrets, the Society has fixed the rule, that those who know these reserved instructions that they cannot pass in any one religious Order, whether it be of the Carthusians, to cause them to retire from that in which they live, and the inviolable silence with which they are to be guarded, all of which has been confirmed by the Holy See. Much care must be taken that they do not get out; for these counsels in the hands of strange persons to the Society, because they will give a sinister interpretation invidious to our situation.

If (unless God does not permit) we reach success, we must openly deny that the Society shelters such thoughts, and to take care that it is so affirmed by those of the Company, that they are ignorant by not having been communicated, which they can protest with truth, that they know nothing of such instructions; and that there does not exist other than the general printed or manuscripts, which they can present, to cause any doubt to vanish. The superiors must with prudence and discretion, inquire if any of the Company have shown these instructions to strangers; for neither for himself, or for another, they must be copied by no one, without permission of the General or of the Provincial; and when it is feared that anyone has given notice of these instructions, we shall not be able to guard so rigorous a secret; and we must assert to the contrary, all that is said in them, it will be so given to be understood, that they only show to all, to be proved, and afterwards they will be dismissed.

CHAPTER I.

THE MANNER OF PROCEDURE WITH WHICH THE SOCIETY MUST BE CONDUCTED WHEN CONSIDERING THE COMMENCING OF SOME FOUNDATION.

1. To capture the will of the inhabitants of a country, it is very important to manifest the intent of the Society, in the manner prescribed in the regulations in which it is said, that the Company must labor with such ardor and force for the salvation of their neighbor as for themselves. For the better inducement of this idea, the most opportunely that we practice the most humble offices, visiting the poor, the afflicted, and the imprisoned. It is very convenient to confess with much promptness, and to hear the confessions, showing indifference, without teasing the penitents; for this, the most notable inhabitants will admire our fathers and esteem them; for the great charity they have for all, and the novelty of the subject.

2. To have in mind that it is necessary to ask with religious modesty, the means for exercising the duties of the Society, and that it is needful to procure and acquire benevo-

lence, principally of the secular ecclesiastics, and of persons of authority, that may be conceived necessary.

3. When called to go to the most distant places, where alms are to be received, they are to be accepted, no matter how small they may be, after having marked out the necessities of ourselves. Notwithstanding, it will be very convenient at the moment to give those alms to the poor, for the edification of those who do not have an exact understanding of the Company; and, *"but we must in advance be more liberal with ourselves."*

4. All must labor as if we were inspired by the same spirit; and each one must study to acquire the same styles, with the object of uniformity among so great a number of persons, edifying the whole; those who do the contrary must be expelled as pernicious.

5. In a beginning it is not convenient to purchase property; but in case they can be found, some good sites may be bought, saying that they are to belong to other persons, using the names of some faithful friends, who will guard the secret. The better to make our poverty apparent, the property nearest our colleges must belong to colleges the most distant, that we can prevent the princes and magistrates from ever knowing that the income of the Society has a fixed point.

6. We must not ourselves go out to reside to form colleges, except to the rich cities; for in this we must imitate Christ, who remained in Jerusalem; and as he alone, passed by the less considerable populations.

7. We must obtain and acquire of the widows all the money that we can, presenting ourselves at repeated times to their sight our extreme necessity.

8. The Superior over each province is the one to whom we must account with certainty, the income of the same; *but the amount to the treasurer at Rome, it is, and must always be, an impenetrable mystery.*

9. It is for us to preach and say in all parts and in all conversations, that *we have come to teach the young and aid the people*; and this without interest in any single species and without exception of persons, and that *we are not so onerous to the people as other religious orders.*

CHAPTER II.

THE MANNER WITH WHICH THE FATHERS OF THE SOCIETY MUST CONDUCT THEMSELVES TO ACQUIRE AND PRESERVE THE FAMILIARITY OF PRINCES, MAGNATES AND POWERFUL AND RICH PERSONS.

1. It is necessary to do all that is possible to gain completely the attentions and affections of princes and persons of the most consideration; for that, who, being on the outside, but in advance, all of them will be constituted our defenders.

2. As we have learned by experience that princes and potentates are generally inclined to the favor of the ecclesiastics, when these disseminate their odious actions, and when they give an interpretation that they favor, as is to be noted among the married, contract with their relations or allies; or in other similar things; assembling much with them, to animate those who may be found in this case, saying to them that we confide in the assurance of the exemptions, that by intervention of us fathers, which the Pope will concede, if he is made to see the causes, and will present other examples of similar things, exhibiting at the same time the sentiments that we favor, *under the pretext of the common good and* THE GREATER GLORY OF GOD *that is the object of the Society.*

3. If at this same assembly the prince treats of doing something, that will not be agreeable to all the great men, for which we are to stir up and investigate, meanwhile,

counselling others to conform with the prince, without ever descending to treat of particularities, for fear there may not be a successful issue of the matter, for which the Company will be imputed blame; and for this, if this action shall be disapproved, there will be advertences presented to the contrary that may be absolutely prohibited and put in jeopardy, the authority of some of the fathers, of whom it can be said with certainty, that they have not had notice of the secret instructions; for that, it can be affirmed with an oath, that the calumny to the Society, is not true in respect to that which is imputed to it.

4. To gain the good will of Princes, it will be very convenient to insinuate with skill; and for third persons, that we fathers, are a means to discharge honorable and favorable duties in the courts of other kings and princes, and more than any one else in that of the Pope. By this means we can recommend ourselves and the Society; for the same, no one must be charged with this commission but the most zealous persons and well versed in our institute.

5. Aiming especially to bring over the will of the favorites of princes and of their servants, by means of presents and pious offices, that they may give faithful notice to us fathers of the character and inclinations of the princes and great men. Of this manner the Society can gain with facility as much to one as to others.

6. The experience we have had, has made us acquainted with the many advantages that have been taken by the Society of its intervention in the marriages of the House of Austria, and of those which have been effected in other kingdoms, France, Poland, and in various duchies. Forasmuch assembling, proposing with prudence, selecting choice persons who may be friends and families of the relatives, and of the friends of the Society.

7. It will be easy to gain the princesses, making use of their valets; by that, coming to feed and nourish with rela-

tions of friendship, by being located at the entrace in all parts, and thus become acquainted with the most intimate secrets of the familiars.

8. In regard to the direction of the consciences of great men, we confessors must follow the writers who concede the greater liberty of conscience. The contrary of this is to appear too religious; for that they will decide to leave others and submit entirely to our direction and counsels.

9. It is necessary to make reference to all the merits of the Society; to the princes and prelates, and to as many as can lend much aid to the Society, after having shown the transcendency of its great privileges.

10. Also, it will be useful to demonstrate, with prudence and skill, such ample power which the Society has, to absolve, even in the reserved cases, compared with that of other pastors and priests; also, that of dispensing with the fasts, and of the rights which they must ask and pay, in the impediments of marriage, by which means many persons will recur to us, whom it will be our duty to make agreeable.

11. It is not the less useful to invite them to our sermons, assemblies, harangues, declamations, etc., composing odes in their honor, dedicating literary works or conclusions; and if we can for the future, give dinners and greetings of divers modes.

12. It will be very convenient to take to our care the reconciliation of the great, in the quarrels and enmities that divide them; then by this method we can enter, little by little, into the acquaintance of their most intimate friends and secrets; and we can serve ourselves to that party which will be most in favor of that which we present.

13. If there should be some one at the service of a monarch or prince, and he were an enemy of our Society, it is necessary to procure well for ourselves better than for others, making him a friend, employing promises, favors, and ad-

vances, which shall be in proportion to the same monarch or prince.

14. No one shall recommend to a prince any one, nor make advances to any who have gone out from us, being outside of our Company, and in particular to those who voluntarily verified, for yet when they dissimulate they will always maintain an inextinguishable hatred to the Society.

In fine, each one must procure and search for methods to increase the affection and favor of princes, of the powerful, and of the magistrates of each population, that whenever occasion is offered to support, we can do much with efficacy and good faith, in benefiting ourselves, though contrary to their relations, allies and friends.

CHAPTER III.

HOW THE SOCIETY MUST BE CONDUCTED WITH THE GREAT AUTHORITIES IN THE STATE, AND IN CASE THEY ARE NOT RICH WE MUST LEND OUR SERVICES TO OTHERS.

1. The care consigned to us, that we must do all that is possible, for to conquer the great; but it is also necessary to gain their favor to combat our enemies.

2. It is very conducive to value their authority, prudence and counsels, and induce them to despise wealth, at the same time that we procure gain and employ those that can redeem the Society; tacitly valuing their names, for acquisition of temporal goods if they inspire sufficient confidence.

3. It is also necessary to employ the ascendant of the powerful, to temper the malevolence of the persons of a lower sphere and of the rabble against our Society.

4. It is necessary to utilize, whenever we can, the bishops, prelates and other superior ecclesiastics, according to the diversity of reason, and the inclination we manifest.

5. In some points it will be sufficient to obtain of the prelates and curates, that which it is possible to do, that their subjects respect the society; and that obstructing the exercise of its functions among those who have the greatest power, as in Germany, Poland, etc. It will be necessary to exhibit the most distinguished attentions for that, mediating its authority and that of the princes, monasteries, parishes, priorates, patronates, the foundations of churches and the pious places, can come to our power. Because we can with more facility where the Catholics will be found mixed with heretics. It is necessary to make such prelates see the utility and merit that we have in all this, and that never will they have so much valuation from the priests, friars, and for the future from the faithful. If making these changes, it is necessary to publicly praise their zeal, although written, and to perpetuate the memory of their actions.

6. For this it is necessary to labor, to the end, that the prelates will place in the hands of us fathers, as confessors and counsellors: and if they aspire to more elevated positions in the Court of Rome, we must unite in their favor and aid their pretensions with all our forces, and by means of our influence.

7. We must be watchful that when the bishops are instituting principal colleges and parochial churches, that the faculties are taken from the Society, and placed in both vicarious establishments, with the charge of cures, and that the Superior of the Society to be, that all the government of these churches shall pertain to us, and that, the parishioners shall be our subjects, of the method that all can be placed in them.

8. Where there are those of the academies who have been driven out from us, and are contrary; where the Catholics or the heretics obstruct our installation, we will compound with the prelates, and make ourselves the owners of the first cathedrals; for thus shall we make them to know the necessities of the Society.

9. Over all, we must be very certain to procure the protection and affection of the prelates of the Church, for the cases of beatification or canonization of ourselves; in whose subjects convened further, to obtain letters from the powerful and of the princes, that the decisions may be promptly attained in the Catholic Court.

10. If it shall be accounted that the prelates or magnates should send commissioned representatives, we must put forth all ardor, that no other priests, who are in dispute with us, shall be sent; for the reason, that they shall not communicate their animadversion, discrediting us in the cities and provinces we inhabit; and that if they pass by other provinces and cities, where there are colleges, they will be received with affection and kindness, and be so splendidly treated as a religious modesty will permit.

CHAPTER IV.

OF THAT WHICH WE MUST CHARGE THE PREACHERS AND CONFESSORS OF THE GREAT OF THE EARTH.

1. Those of us who may be directed to the princes and illustrious men, of the manner in which we must appear before them, with inclination unitedly *"to the greater glory of God,"* obtaining—with its austerity of conscience, that the same princes are persuaded of it; for this direction we must not travel in a principle to the exterior or political government, but gradually and imperceptibly.

2. Forasmuch there will be opportunity and conducive notices at repeated times, that the distribution of honors and dignities in the Republic is an act of justice; and that in a great manner it will be offending God, if the princes do not examine themselves and cease carrying their passions, protesting to the same with frequency and severity, that we do not desire to mix in the administration of the State; but when it shall become necessary to so express ourselves thus, to

have your weight to fill the mission that is recommended. Directly that the sovereigns are well convinced of this, it will be very convenient to give an idea of the virtues that may be found to adorn those that are selected for the dignities and principal public changes; procuring then and recommending the true friends of the Company; notwithstanding, we must not make it openly for ourselves, but by means of our friends who have intimacy with the prince that it is not for us to talk him into the disposition of making them.

3. For this watchfulness our friends must instruct the confessors and preachers of the Society near the persons capable of discharging any duty, *that over all, they must be generous to the Company;* they must also keep their names, that they may insinuate with skill, and upon opportune occasions to princes, well for themselves or by means of others.

4. The preachers and confessors will always present themselves so that they must comport with the princes, lovable and affectionate, without ever shocking them in sermons, nor in particular conversations, presenting that which rejects all fear, and exhorting them in particular to faith, hope and justice.

5. Never receive gifts made to any one in particular, but that for the contrary; but picture the distress in which the Society or college may be found, as all are alike; having to be satisfied with assigning each one a room in the house, modestly furnished; and noticing that your garb is not over nice; and assist with promptness to the aid and counsel of the most miserable persons of the palace; but that you do not say it of them, but only those who have agreed to serve the powerful.

6. Whenever the death occurs of any one employed in the palace, we must take care of speaking with anticipation, that they fail in the nomination of a successor, in their affection for the Society; but giving no appearance to cause suspicion that it was the intent of usurping the government of the prince; for which, it must not be from us that it is said; take

a part direct; but assembling of faithful or influential friends who may be found in position of rousing the hate of one and another until they become inflamed.

CHAPTER V.

OF THE MODE OF CONDUCTING THE SOCIETY WITH RESPECT TO OTHER ECCLESIASTICS WHO HAVE THE SAME DUTIES AS OURSELVES IN THE CHURCH.

1. It is necessary to help with valor these persons, and manifest in their due time to the princes and lords that are always ours, and being constituted in power, that *our Society* contains essentially the perfection of all the other orders, with the exception of singing and manifesting an exterior of austerity in the mode of life and in dress; and that if in some points they excel the communities of the Society, this shines with greater splendor in the Church of God.

2. We must inquire into and note the defects of the other fathers, and when we find them, we must divulge among our faithful friends, as condoling over them; we must show that such fathers do not discharge with certainty, that we do ourselves the functions, that some and others recommend.

3. It is necessary that the fathers of our Society oppose with all their power the other fathers who intend to found houses of education to instruct the youths among the populations where ours are found teaching with acceptation and approval; and it will be very convenient to indicate our projects to princes and magistrates, that such people will excite disturbances and commotions if they are not prohibited from teaching; and that in the last result, the damage will fall upon the educated, by being instructed by a bad method, without any necessity; posting them that the Company is sufficient to teach the youth. In case that the fathers bear letters of the Pontificate, or recommendations from the Cardinals, we must work in opposition to them, making the

princes and great men to point out to the Pope the merits of the Society and its intelligence for the pacific instruction of the youths, to which end, we must have and obtain certifications of the authorities upon our good conduct and sufficiency.

4. Having notwithstanding to form duties, our fathers in displaying singular proofs of our virtue and erudition, making them to exercise the alumnos (graduates) in their studies in methods of functions, scholars of diversion, capable of drawing applause, making for supposition, these representations in the presence of the great magistrates and concurrence of other classes.

CHAPTER VI.

OF THE MODE OF ATTRACTING RICH WIDOWS.

1. We must elect effective fathers already advanced in years, of lively complexion and conversation, agreeable to visit these ladies, and whence they can promptly note in them appreciation or affection for our Society; making offerings of good works and the merits of the same; that, if they accept them, and succeed in having them frequent our temples, we must assign to them a confessor, who will be able of guiding them in the ways that are proper, in the state of widowhood, making the enumeration and praises of satisfaction that should accompany such a state; making them believe and yet with certainty that they who serve as such, is a merit for eternal life, being efficacious to relieve them from the pains of purgatory.

2. The same confessor will propose to them to make and adorn a little chapel or oratory in their own house, to confirm their religious exercises, because by this method we can shorten the communication, more easily hindering those who visit others; although if they have a particular chaplain, and will content to go to him to celebrate the mass, making op-

portune advertencies to her who confesses, to the effect and treating her as being left to be overpowered by said Chaplain.

3. We must endeavor skillfully but gently to cause them to change respectively to the Order and to the method of the House, and to conform as the circumstances of the person will permit, to whom they are directed, their propensities, their piety, and yet to the place and situation of the edifice.

4. We must not omit to have removed, little by little, the servants of the house that are not of the same mind with ourselves, proposing that they shall be replaced by those persons who are dependent on us, or who desire to be of the Company; for by this method we can be placed in the channel of communication of whatever passes in the family.

5. The constant watch of the confessor will have to be, that the widow shall be disposed to depend on him totally, representing that her advances in grace are necessarily bound to this submission.

6. We are to induce her to the frequency of the sacraments, and especially that of penitency, making her to give account of her deeper thoughts and intentions; inviting her to listen to her confessor, when he is to preach particular promising orations; recommending equally the recitation each day of the litanies and the examination of conscience.

7. It will be very necessary in the case of a general confession, to enter extensively into all of her inclinations; for that it will be to determine her, although she may be found in the hands of others.

8. Insist upon the advantages of widowhood, and the inconvenience of marriage; in particular that of a repeated one, and the dangers to which she will be exposed, relatively to her particular businesses into which we are desirous of penetrating.

9. We must cause her to talk of men whom she dislikes, and to see if she takes notice of anyone who is agreeable,

and represent to her that he is a man of bad life; procuring by these means disgust of one and another, and repugnant to unite with anyone.

10. When the confessor has become convinced that she has decided to follow the life of widowhood, he must then proceed to counsel her to dedicate herself to a spiritual life, but not to a monastic one, whose lack of accommodations will show how they live; in a word, we must proceed to speak of the spiritual life of Pauline and of Eustace, &c. The confessor will conduct her at last, that having devoted the widow to chastity, to not less than for two or three years, she will then be made to renounce a second nuptial forever.

In this case she will be found to have discarded all sorts of relations with men, and even the diversions between her relatives and acquaintances, we must protest that she must unite more closely to God. With regard to the ecclesiastics who visit her, or to whom she goes out to visit, when we cannot keep her separate and apart from all others, we must labor that those with whom she treats shall be recommended by ourselves or by those who are devoted to us.

11. In this state, we must inspire her to give alms, under the direction, as she will suppose, of her spiritual father; then it is of great importance that they shall be employed with utility; more, being careful that there shall be discretion in counsel, causing her to see that inconsiderate alms are the frequent causes of many sins, or serve to foment at last, that they are not the fruit, nor the merit which produced them.

CHAPTER VII.

SYSTEM WHICH MUST BE EMPLOYED WITH WIDOWS AND METHODS OF DISPOSING OF THEIR PROPERTY.

1. It will be necessary to inspire her to continue to persevere in her devotion and the exercise of good works and of disposition, in not permitting a week to pass, to give away

some part of her overplus, in honor of Jesus Christ, of the Holy Virgin and of the Saint she has chosen for her patron; giving this to the poor of the Company or for the ornamenting of its churches, until she has absolutely disposed of the first fruits of her property as in other times did the Egyptians. (Hebrews.)

2. When the widows, the more generally to practice their alms, must be given to know with perseverance, their liberality in favor of the Company; and they are to be assured that they are participants in all the merits of the same, and of the particular indulgencies of the Provincial; and if they are persons of much consideration, of the General of the Order.

3. The widows who having made vows of chastity, it will be necessary for them to renew them twice per annum, conforming to the custom that we have established; but permitting them notwithstanding, that day some honest freedom from restraint by our fathers.

4. They must be frequently visited, treating them agreeably; referring them to spiritual and diverting histories, conformable to the character and inclination of each one.

5. But that they may not abate, we must not use too much rigor with them in the confessional; that it may not be, that they by having empowered others of their benevolence, that we do not lose confidence of recovering their adhesion, having to proceed in all cases with great skill and caution, being aware of the inconstancy natural to woman.

6. It is necessary to have them do away with the habit of frequenting other churches, in particular those of convents; for which it is necessary to often remind them, that in our Order there are possessed many indulgencies that are to be obtained only partially by all the other religious corporations.

7. To those who may be found in the case of the garb of mourning, they will be counselled to dress a little more agreeable, that they may at the same time, unite the aspect of

mourning with that of adornment, to draw them away from the idea of being found directed by a man who has become a stranger to the world. Also with such, that they may not be very much endangered, or particularly exposed to volubility, we can concede to them, as if they maintained their consequence and liberality, for and with the Society, that which drives sensuality away from them, being with moderation and without scandal.

8. We must manage that in the houses of the widows there shall be honorable young ladies, of rich and noble families; that little by little they become accustomed to our direction and mode of life; and that they are given a director elected and established by the confessor of the family, to be permanently and always subject to all the reprehensions and habits of the Company; and if any do not wish to submit to all, they must be sent to the houses of their fathers, or to those from which they were brought, accusing them directly of extravagance and of glaring and stained character.

9. The care of the health of the widows, and to proportion some amusement, it is not the least important that we should care for their salvation; and so, if they complain of some indisposition, we must prohibit the fast, the hair cloth girdle, and the discipline, without permitting them to go to church; further continue the direction, cautiously and secretly with such, that they may be examined in their houses; if they are given admission into the garden, and edifice of the college, with secresy; and if they consent to converse and secretly entertain with those that they prefer.

10. To the end that we may obtain, that the widows employ their utmost in obsequiousness to the Society, it is the duty to represent to them the perfection of the life of the holy, who have renounced the world, estranged themselves from their relations, and despising their fortunes, consecrating themselves to the service of the Supreme Being with entire resignation and content. It will be necessary to produce the same effect, that those who turn away to the Con-

stitutions of the Society, and their relative examination to the abandonment of all things. We must cite examples of the widows who have reached holiness in a very short time; giving hopes of their being canonized, if their perseverance does not decay; and promising for their cases our influence with the Holy Father.

11. We must impress in their souls the persuasion that, if they desire to enjoy complete tranquility of conscience it will be necessary for them to follow without repugnance, without murmuring, nor tiring, the direction of the confessor, so in the spiritual, as in the eternal, that she may be found destined to the same God, by their guidance.

12. Also we must direct with opportunity, that the Lord does not desire that they should give alms, nor yet to fathers of an exemplary life, known and approved, without consulting beforehand with their confessor, and regulating the dictation of the same.

13. The confessors must take the greatest care, that the widows and their daughters of the confessional, do not go to see other fathers under any pretext, nor with them. For this, we must praise our Society as the Order most illustrious of them all; of greater utility in the Church, and of greater authority with the Pope and with the princes; perfection in itself; then dismiss the dream of them, and menace them, that we can, and that we are no correspondents to them, we can say, that we do not consent to froth and do as among other monks who count in their convents many ignorant, stupid loungers who are indolent in regard to the other life, and intriguers in that to disorder, &c.

14. The confessors must propose and persuade the widows to assign ordinary pensions and other annual quotas to the colleges and houses of profession for their sustenance with especialty to the professed house at Rome; and not forgetting to remind them of the restoration of the ornaments of the temples and replenishing of the wax, the wine, and other necessaries for the celebration of the mass.

15. If they do not make relinquishment of their property to the Company, it will be made manifest to them, on apparent occasion in particular, when they are found to be sick, or in danger of death; that there are many colleges to be founded; and that they may be excited with sweetness and disinterestedness, to make some disbursements as merit for God, and in that they can found his eternal glory.

16. In the same manner, we must proceed with regard to princes and other well doers, making them to see that such foundations will be made to perpetuate their memory in this world, and gain eternal happiness, and if some malevolent persons adduce the example of Jesus Christ, saying, that then he had no place to recline his head, the Company bearing his name should be poor in imitation of himself, we must make it known and imprint it in the imagination of those, and of all the world, that the Church has varied, and that in this day we have become a State; and we must show authority and grand measures against its enemies that are very powerful, or like that little stone prognosticated by the prophet, that, divided, came to be a great mountain. Inculcate constantly to the widows who dedicate their alms and ornaments to the temples, that the greater perfection is in disposing of the affection and earthly things, ceding their possession to Jesus Christ and his companions.

15. Being very little, that which we must promise to the widows, who dedicate and educate their children for the world, we must apply some remedy to it.

CHAPTER VIII.

METHODS BY WHICH THE CHILDREN OF RICH WIDOWS MAY BE CAUSED TO EMBRACE THE RELIGIOUS STATE, OR OF DEVOTION.

1. To secure our object, we must create the custom, that the mothers treat them severely, and show to them, that we are in love with them. Coming to induce the mothers to do

away with their tastes, from the most tender age, and regarding, restraining, &c., &c., the children especially; prohibiting decorations and adornments when they enter upon competent age; that they are inspired in the vocation for the cloister, promising them an endowment of consideration, if they embrace a similar state; representing to them the insipidity that is brought with matrimony, and the disgust that has been experienced in it; signifying to them the weight they would sit under, for not having maintained in the celibate. Lastly, coming to direct in the conclusions arrived at by the daughters of the widows, so fastidious of living with their mothers, that their feet will be directed to enter into a convent.

2. We must make ourselves intimate with the sons of the widows, and if for them an object or the Company, and cause them to penetrate the intent in our colleges, making them to see things that can call their attention by whatever mode, such as gardens, vineyards, country houses, and the farm houses where the masters go to recreate; talk to them of the voyages the Jesuits have made to different countries, of their treating with princes, and of much that can capture the young; cause them to note the cleanliness of the refectory, the commodiousness of the lodges, the agreeable conversation we have among ourselves, the suavity of our rule, and that we have all for the object of *the greater glory of God;* show to them the preëminence of our Order over all the others, taking care that the conversations we have shall be diverting to pass to that of piety.

3. At proposing to them the religious state, have care of doing so, as if by revelation; and in general, insinuating directly with sagacity, the advantage and sweetness of our institute above all others; and in conversation cause them to understand the great sin that will be committed against the vocation of the Most High; in fine, induce them to make some spiritual exercises that they may be enlightened to the choice of this state.

4. We must do all that is possible that the masters and professors of the youth indicated shall be of the Company, to the end, of being always vigilant over these, and counsel them; but if they cannot be reduced, we must cause them to be deprived of some things, causing that their mothers shall manifest their censure and authority of the house, that they may be tired of that sort of life; and if, finally, we cannot obtain their will to enter the Society, we must labor; because we can remand them to other colleges of ours that are at a distance, that they may study, procuring impediment, that their mothers show endearment and affection, at the same time, continuing for our part, in drawing them to us by suavity of methods.

CHAPTER IX.

UPON THE AUGMENTING OF REVENUE IN THE COLLEGES.

1. We must do all that is possible, because we do not know if bound with the last vow of him, who is the claimant of an inheritance, meanwhile we do not know if it is confirmed, to not be had in the Company a younger brother, or of some other reason of much entity. Before all, that which we must procure, are the augmentations of the Society with rules to the ends agreed upon by the superiors, which must be conformable; for that the Church returns to its primitive splendor *for the greater glory of God;* of fate that all the clergy shall be found animated by a united spirit. To this end, we must publish by all methods, that the society is composed in part of professors so poor, that are wanting of the most indispensable, to not be for the beneficence of the faithful; and that another part is of fathers also poor, although living upon the product of some household property; but not to be grievous to the public, in the midst of their studies, their ministry, as are other ordinary mendicants. The spiritual directors of princes, great men, accommodating widows, and of whom we have abundant hope, that they will be disposed at last to make gifts to the Company in exchange for spiritual and

eternal things, that will be proportioned, the lands and temporalities which they possess; for the same, carrying always the idea, that we are not to lose the occasion of receiving always as much as may be offered. If promises and the fulfillment of them is retarded, they are to be remembered with precaution, dissimulating as much as we can the coveting of riches. When some confessor of personages or other people, will not be apt, or wants subtility, that in these subjects is indispensable, he will be retired with opportunity, although others may be placed anticipatedly; and if it be entirely necessary to the penitents, it will be made necessary to take out the destitute to distant colleges, representing that the Society has need for them there; because it being known that some young widows, having unexpectedly failed, the Company not having the legacy of very precious movables, having been careless by not accepting in due time. But to receive these things, we could not attend at the time, and only at the good will of the penitent.

2. To attract the prelates, canonicals and other rich ecclesiastics, it is necessary to employ certain arts, and in place procuring them to practice in our houses spiritual exercises, and gradually and energetically of the affection that we profess to divine things; so that they will be affectioned towards the Society and that they will soon offer pledges of their adhesion.

3. The confessors must not forget to ask with the greatest caution and on adequate occasions of those who confess, what are their names, families, relatives, friends, and properties, informing their successors who follow them, the state, intention in which they will be found, and the resolution which they have taken; that which they have not yet determined obtaining, having to form a plan for the future to the Company. When it is founded, whence directly there are hopes of utility; for it will not be convenient to ask all at once; they will be counseled to make their confession each week, to disembarrass the conscience much before, or to the title of penitence. They will be caused to inform the con-

fessor with repetition, of that which at one time they have not given sufficient light; and if they have been successful by this means, she will come, being a woman, to make confession with frequency, and visit our church; and being a man, he will be invited to our houses and we are to make him familiar with ourselves.

4. That which is said in regard to widows, must have equal application to the merchants and neighbors of all classes, as being rich and married, but without children, of that plan by which the Society can arrive to be their heirs, if we put in play the measures that we may indicate; but over all, it will be well to have present, as said, near the rich devotees that treat with us, and of whom the vulgar can murmur, when more, if they are of a class not very elevated.

5. Procuring for the rectors of the colleges entrance for all the ways of the houses, parks, groves, forests, lawns, arable lands, vineyards, olive orchards, hunting grounds, and whatever species of inheritances which they meet with in the end of their rectory; if their owners pertain to the nobility, to the clergy, or are negotiators, particulars, or religious communities, inquiring the revenues of each one, their loads and what they pay for them. All these dates or notices they are to seek for with great skill and to a fixed point, energetically yet from the confessional, then of the relations of friendship, or of the accidental conversations; and the confessor meets with a penitent of possibles, he will be placed in knowledge of the rector, obtaining by all methods the one conserved.

6. The essential point to build upon, is the following: that we must so manage, that in the ends we gain the will and affections of our penitents, and other persons with whom we treat, accommodating ourselves to their inclinations if they are conducive. The Provincials will take care to direct some of us to points, in which reside the nobility and the powerful; and if the Provincials do not act with opportunity, the rectors must notice with anticipation, the crops (the field of operations) that are there, which we go to examine.

7. When we receive the sons of strong houses in the Company, they must show whether they will be easy to acquire the contracts and titles of possession; and if so they were to enter of themselves, of which they may be caused to cede some of their property to the college, or the usufruct (profit) or for rent, or in other form, or if they can come for a time into the Society, the gain of which may be very much of an object, to give a special understanding to the great and powerful, the narrowness in which we live, and the debts that are pressing us.

8. When the widows, or our married devoted women, do not have more than daughters, we must persuade them to the same life of devotion, or to that of the cloister; but that except the endowment that they may give, they can enter their property in the Society gently; but when they have husbands, those that would object to the Company, they will be catechized; and others who desire to enter as religiouses in other Orders, with the promise of some reduced amount. When there may be an only son, he must be attracted at all cost, inculcating the vocation as made by Jesus Christ; causing him to be entirely disembarrassed frem the fear of its fathers, and persuading him to make a sacrifice very acceptable to the Almighty, that he must withdraw to His authority, abandon the paternal house and enter in the Company; the which, if he so succeeds, after having given part to the General, he will be sent to a distant novitiate; but if they have daughters, they will primarily dispose the daughters for a religious life; and they will be caused to enter into some monastery, and afterwards be received as daughters in the Company, with the succession of its properties.

9. The Superiors will place in the channel of the circumstances, the confessors of these widows and married people, that they on all future occasions may act for the benefit of the Society; and when by means of one, they cannot take out part he will be replaced with another; and if it is made necessary, he will be sent to great distances, of a manner that he cannot follow understandingly with these families.

10. If we can succeed in convincing the widows and devoted persons, who aspire with fervor to a perfect life, and that the better means to obtain it is by ceding all their properties to the Society, supporting by their revenues, that they will be religiously administered until their death, conforming to the degree of necessity in which they may be found, and the just reason that may be employed for their persuasion is, that by this mode, they can be exclusively dedicated to God; without attentions and molestations, which would perplex them, and that it is the only road to reach the highest degree of perfection.

11. The Superiors craving the confidence of the rich, who are attached to the Company, delivering receipts of its proper hand writing whose payment afterwards will differ; not forgetting to often visit those who loan, to exhort them above all in their infirmities of consideration, as to whom will devolve the papers of the debt; because it is not so to be found mention of the Company in their testament; and by this course we must acquire properties, without giving cause for us to be hated by the heirs.

12. We must also in a grand manner ask for a loan, with payment of annual interest, and employ the same capital in other speculation to produce greater revenues to the Society; for at such a time, succeeding to move them with compassion to that which they will lend to us, we will not lose the interest in the testament of donation, when they see that they found colleges and churches.

13. The Company can report the utilities of commerce, and value the name of the merchant of credit, whose friendship we may possess,

14. Among the peoples where our fathers reside, we must have physicians faithful to the Society, whom we can especially recommend to the sick, and to paint under an aspect very superior to that of other religious orders, and secure direction that we shall be called to assist the powerful, particularly in the hour of death.

3*

15. That the confessors shall visit with assiduity the sick, particularly those who are in danger, and to honestly eliminate the other fathers, which the superiors will procure, when the confessor sees that he is obliged to remove the other from the suffering, to replace and maintain the sick in his good intentions. Meanwhile we must inculcate as much as we can with prudence, the fear of hell, &c., &c., or when, the lesser ones of purgatory; demonstrating that as water will put out fire, so will the same alms blot out the sin; and that we cannot employ the alms better, than in the maintaining and subsidizing of the persons, who, by their vocation, have made profession of caring for the salvation of their neighbor; that in this manner the sick can be made to participate in their merits, and find satisfaction for their own sins; placing before them that charity covereth a multitude of sins; and that also, we can describe that charity, is as a nuptial vestment, without which, no one can be admitted to the heavenly table. In fine it will be necessary to move them to the citations of the scriptures, and of the holy fathers, that according to the capacity of the sick, we can judge what is most efficacious to move them.

16. We must teach the women, that they must complain of the vices of their husbands, and the disturbances which they occasion, that they can rob them in secret of some amounts of money, to offer to God, in expiation of the sins of their husbands, and to obtain their pardon.

CHAPTER X.

OF THE PARTICULAR RIGOR OF DISCIPLINE IN THE SOCIETY.

1. If there shall be anyone dismissed under any protest, as an enemy of the Society, whatever may be his condition, or age; all those who have been moved to become the devotees of our churches; or of visiting ourselves; or who having been made to take the alms on the way to other churches; or

who having been found to give to other fathers; or who having dissuaded any rich man, and well intentioned towards our Society, of giving anything; or in the time in which he can dispose of his properties, having shown great affection for his relations with this Society; because it is a great proof of a mortified disposition; and we conclude that the professions are entirely mortified; or also, that he having scattered all the alms of the penitents, or of the friends of the Society, in favor of his poor relations. Furthermore, that he may not complain afterwards of the cause of his expulsion, it will not be necessary to thrust him from us directly; but we can prohibit him from hearing confessions, which will mortify him, and vex him by imposing upon him most vile offices, obliging him each day to do things that are the most repugnant; he will be removed from the highest studies and honorable employments; he will be reprimanded in the chapters by public censures; he will be excluded from the recreations and prohibited from all conversation with strangers; he will be deprived of his vestments and the uses of other things when they are not indispensable, until he begins to murmur and becomes impatient; then he can be expelled as a shameful person, to give a bad example to others; and if it is necessary to give account to his relatives, or to the prelates of the Church, of the reason for which he has been thrust out, it will be sufficient to say that he does not possess the spirit of the Society.

2. Furthermore, having also expelled all those who may have scrupled to acquire properties for the Society, we must direct, that they are too much addicted to their own judgment. If we desire to give reason of their conduct to the Provincials, it is necessary not to give them a hearing; but call for the rule, that they are obligated to a blind obedience.

3. It will be necessary to note, whence the beginning and whence their youth, those who have great affection for the Society; and those which we recognize their affection until the furthest orders, or until their relatives, or until the poor

shall be necessarily disposed, little by little, as carefully said, to go out; then they are useless.

CHAPTER XI.

HOW WE MUST CONDUCT OURSELVES UNITEDLY AGAINST THOSE WHO HAVE BEEN EXPELLED FROM THE SOCIETY.

1. As those whom we have expelled, when knowing little or something of the secrets, the most times are noxious to the Company; for the same, it shall be necessary to obviate their efforts by the following method, before thrusting them out; it will be necessary to obligate them to promise, by writing, and under oath, that they will never by writing or speaking, do anything which may be prejudicial to the Company; and it will be good that the Superiors guard a point of their evil inclinations, of their defects and of their vices; that they are the same, having to manifest in the discharge of their duties, following the custom of the Society, for that, if it should be necessary, this point can serve near the great, and the prelates to hinder their advancement.

2. Constant notice must be given to all the colleges of their having been expelled; and we must exaggerate the general motives of their expulsion; as the little mortification of their spirit; their disobedience; their little love for spiritual exercises; their self love, &c., &c. Afterwards, we must admonish them, that they must not have any correspondence with them; and they must speak of them as strangers; that the language of all shall be uniform, and that it may be told everywhere, that the Society never expels any one without very grave causes, and that as the sea casts up dead bodies, &c., &c. We must insinuate with caution, similar reasons to these, causing them to be abhorred by the people, that for their expulsion it may appear plausible.

In the domestic exhortations, it will be necessary to persuade people that they have been turned out as unquiet persons; that they continue to beg each moment to enter anew into the Society; and it will be good to exaggerate the misfortunes of those who have perished miserably, after having separated from the Society.

4. It will also be opportune to send forth the accusations, that they have gone out from the Society, which we can formulate by means of grave persons, who will everywhere repeat that the Society never expels any one but for grave causes; and that they never part with their healthy members; the which they can confirm by their zeal, and show in general for the salvation of the souls of them that do not pertain to them; and how much greater will it not be for the salvation of their own.

5. Afterwards, the Society must prepare and attract by all classes of benefits, the magnates, or prelates, with whom those who have been expelled begin to enjoy some authority and credit. It will be necessary to show that the common good of an Order so celebrated as useful in the Church, must be of more consideration, than that of a particular one who has been cast out. If all this affliction preserves some affection for those expelled, it will be good to indicate the reasons which have caused their expulsion; and yet exaggerate the causes the more that they were not very true; with such they can draw their conclusions as to the probable consequences.

6. Of all modes, it will be necessary that they particularly have abandoned the Society by their own free will; not being promoted to a single employment or dignity in the Church; that they would not submit themselves and much that pertains to the Society; and that all the world should withdraw from them that desire to depend on them.

7. Procuring soon, that they are removed from the exercise of the functions celebrated in the Church, such as the sermons, confessions, publication of books, &c., &c., so that they do not win the love and applause of the people. For this, we must come to inquire diligently upon their life and their habits; upon their occupations, &c., &c., penetrate into their intentions, for the which, we must have particular cor-

respondence with some of the family in whose house they live, of those who have been expelled. In surprising something reprehensible in them or worthy of censure, which is to be divulged by people of medium quality; giving in following the steps conducive to reach the hearing of the great, and the prelates, who favor then, that they may be caused to fear that the infamy will relapse upon themselves.. If they do nothing that merits reprehension, and conduct themselves well, we must curtail them by subtle propositions and captious phrases, their virtues and meritorious actions, causing that the idea that has been formed of them, and the faith that is had in them, may little by little be made to disappear; this is of great interest for the Society, that those whom we repel, and more principally those who by their own will abandon us, shall be sunk in obscurity and oblivion.

8 We must divulge without ceasing the disgraces and sinister accidents that they bring upon them, notwithstanding the faithful, who entreat for them in their prayers, that they may not believe that we work from impulses of passion. In our houses we must exaggerate, by every method these calamities, that they may serve to hinder others.

CHAPTER XII.

WHO MAY COME THAT THEY MAY BE SUSTAINED AND PRESERVED IN THE SOCIETY.

1. The first place in the Company pertains to the good operators; that is to say, those who cannot procure less for the temporal than for the spiritual good of the Society; such as the confessors of princes, of the powerful, of the widows, of the rich pious women, the preachers and the professors who know all these secrets.

2. Those who have already failed in strength or advanced in years; conforming to the use they have made of their talents in and for the temporal good of the Society; of the man-

uer which has attended them in days that are passed; and further, are yet convenient instruments to give part to the Superiors of the ordinary defects which are to be noted in ourselves, for they are always in the house.

3. We must never expel but in case of extreme necessity, for fear of the Society acquiring a bad reputation.

4. Furthermore, it will be necessary to favor those who excel by their talent, their nobleness and their fortune; particularly if they have powerful friends attached to the Society; and if they themselves have for it a sincere appreciation, as we have already said before. They must be sent to Rome, or to the universities of greater reputation to study there; or in case of having studied in some province, it will be very convenient that the professors attend to them with special care and affection. Meanwhile, they not having conveyed their property to the Society, we must not refuse them anything; for after confirming the cession, they will be disappointed as the others, notwithstanding guarding some consideration for the past.

5. Having also especial consideration on the part of the Superiors, for those that have brought to the Society, a young notable, placed so that they are given to know the affection made to it; but if they have not professed, it is necessary to take care of not having too much indulgence with them, for fear that they may return at another time, to carry away those whom they have brought to the Society.

CHAPTER XIII.

OF THE YOUTH WHO MAY BE ELECTED TO BE ADMITTED INTO THE SOCIETY, AND OF THE MODE OF RETAINING THEM.

1. It is necessary that much prudence shall be exercised, respecting the election of the Youth; having to be sprightly, noble, well liked, or at the least excellent in some of these qualities.

2. To attract them with greater facility to our institute, it is necessary in the meanwhile, to study that the rectors and professors of colleges shall exhibit an especial affection; and outside the time of the classes, to make them comprehend how great is God, and that some one should consecrate to his service all that he possesses: and particularly if he is in the Society of his Son.

3. Whenever the opportunity may arrive, conducive in the college and in the garden, and yet at times to the country houses, that in the company of ourselves, during the recreations, that we may familiarize with them, little by little, being careful, notwithstanding, that the familiarity does not engender disgust.

4. We cannot consent that we shall punish them, nor oblige them to assemble at their tasks among those who are the most educated.

5. We must congratulate them with gifts and privileges conforming to their age and encouraging above all others with moral discourses.

6. We must inculcate them, that it is for one divine disposition, that they are favorites among so many who frequent the same college.

7. On other occasions, especially in the exhortatious, we must aim to terrify them with menaces of the eternal condemnation, if they refuse the divine vocation.

8. Meanwhile frequently expressing the anxiety to enter the Society, we must always defer their admission, that they may remain constant; but if for these, they are undecided, then we must encourage them incessantly by other methods.

9. If we admonish effectively, that none of their friends, nor yet the fathers, nor the mothers discover their vocation before being admitted; because then, if then, they come to the temptation of withdrawing; so many as the Society desires to give full liberty of doing that which may be the most

convenient; and in case of succeeding to conquer the temptation, we must never lose occasions to make them recover spirit; remembering that which we have said, always that this will succeed during the time of the novitiate, or after having made their simple vows.

10. With respect to the sons of the great, nobles, and senators, as it is supremely difficult to attract them, meanwhile living with their fathers, who are having them educated to the end, that they may succeed in their destinies, we must persuade, vigorously, of the better influence of friends that are persons of the same Society; that they are ordered to other provinces, or to distant universities in which there are our teachers; careful to remit to the respective professors the necessary instructions, appropriate to their quality and condition, that they may gain their friendship for the Society with greater facility and certainty.

11. When having arrived at a more advanced age, they will be induced to practice some spiritual exercises, that they may have so good an exit in Germany and Poland.

12. We must console them in their sadness and afflictions, according to the quality and dispositions of each one, making use of private reprimands and exhortations appropriate to the bad use of riches; inculcating upon them that they should depreciate the felicity of a vocation, menacing them with the pains of hell for the things they do.

13. It will be necessary to make patent to the fathers and the mothers, that they may condescend more easily to the desire of their sons of entering the Society, the excellence of its institute in comparison with those of other orders; the sanctity and the science of our fathers; its reputation in all the world; the honor and distinctions of the different great and small. We must make enumeration of the princes and the magnates, that, with great content, have lived until their death, and yet living in the Society. We must show how agreeable it is to God, that the youth consecrate themselves to Him, particularly in the Society of his Son: and what

thing is there so sublime as that of a man carrying the yoke of the Lord from his youth. That if they oppose any objections because of their extreme youth, then we must present the facility of our institute, the which not having anything to molest, with the exception of the three vows, and that which is most notable, that we do not have any obligatory rule, nor yet under penalty of venial sin.

CHAPTER XIV.

UPON RESERVED CASES AND MOTIVES THAT NECESSITATE EXPULSION FROM THE SOCIETY.

1. To most of the cases expressed in the Constitutions, and of which only the Superior or the ordinary confessor, with permission of this, can absolve them, where there is sodomy, unnatural crime, fornication, adultery, of the unchaste touch of a man, or of a woman; also if under the pretext of zeal, or whatever motive, they have done some grave thing against the Society; against its honors and its gains; these will be just causes for reason of the expulsion of the guilty.

2. If anyone confesses in the confessional of having committed some similar act, he will not be promised absolution, until he has promised to reveal to the Superior, outside of the confessional, the same or by his confessor. The Superior will operate the better for it, in the general interests of the Society; further, if there is founded hope of the careful hiding of the crime, it will be necessary to impose upon the guilty a convenient punishment; if otherwise he can be expelled much before. With all the care that is possible, the confessor will give the penitent to understand that he runs the danger of being expelled.

3. If any one of our confessors, having heard a strange person say, that he had committed a shameful thing with one of the Society, he will not absolve such a person, without his

having said, outside of his confession, the name of the one with whom he has sinned; and if he so says, he will be made to swear that he will not divulge the same, without the consent of the Society.

4. If two of ourselves have sinned carnally, he who first avows it will be retained in the Society; and the other will be expelled; but he who remains permanent, will be after such mortification and bad treatment, of sorrow, and by his impatience, and if we have occasion for his expulsion, it will be necessary for the future of it that it be done directly.

5. The Company being a noble corporation and preëminent in the Church, it can dismiss those that will not be apt for the execution of our obj ct, although giving satisfaction in the beginning; and the opportunity does not delay in presenting itself; if it procures continuous maltreatment; and if he is obliged to do contrary to his inclination; if they are gathered under the orders of gloomy Superiors; if he is separated from his studies and from the honorable functions, &c., &c., until he gets to murmuring.

6. In no manner must we retain in the Company, those that openly reveal against their Superiors, or that will complain publicly, or reservedly, of their companions, or particularly if they make them to strangers; nor to those who are among oureelves, or among persons who are on the outside, censure the conduct of the Society in regard to the acquisition or administration of temporal properties, or whatever acts of the same; for example, of crushing or oppressing many of those whom we do not wish well, or that they the same having been expelled, &c., &c. Nor yet those, that in conversation, who tolerate, or defend the Venetians, the French or others, that have driven the Company away from their territories, or that have occasioned great prejudices.

7. Before the expulsion of any *we must vex and harrass them in the extreme;* depriving them of the functions that they have been accustomed to discharge, dedicating them to others. Although they may do well, it will be necessary to

censure them, and with this pretext, apply them to another thing. Imposing by a trifling fault that they have committed the most severe penalties, that they blush in public, until they have lost all patience; and at last will be expelled as pernicious to all, for which a future opportunity will present itself when they will think less.

8. When some one of the Company has a certain hope of obtaining a bishopric, or whatever other ecclesiastical dignity, to most of the ordinary vows of the Society he will be obliged to take another; and that is, that he will always preserve good sentiments towards the Society; that he will always speak favorably of it; that he will not have a confessor that will not be to its bosom; that he will do nothing of entity without having heard the justice of the same. Because in consequence of not having observed this, the Cardinal Tolet the Society had obtained of the Holy See, that no swinish descendants of Jews or Mahometans were admitted, that he did not desire to take such vows; and that for celebrity that is out, he was expelled as a firm enemy of the Society.

CHAPTER XV.

HOW THE COMPANY MUST BE CONDUCTED WITH THE MONKS AND NUNS.

1. The confessors and preachers must guard well against offending the nuns and occasioning temptations contrary to their vocation; but on the contrary, having conciliated the love of the Lady Superiors, that we obtain to hear, when less, their extraordinary confessions, and that it is predicted that we may hope soon to receive some gratitude from them; because the abbesses, principally the rich and noble, can be of much utility to the Society, by themselves, and by their relatives and friends; of the manner with which we treat with them and influence of the principal monasteries, the Society will little by little arrive to obtain the knowledge of all the corporation and increase its friendship.

2. It will be necessary, notwithstanding, to prohibit our nuns from frequenting the monasteries of women, for fear that their mode of life may be more agreeable, and that the Society will see itself frustrated in the hopes of possessing all their properties. We must induce them to take the vow of chastity and obedience, at the hands of their confessors; and to show them that this mode of life will conform with the uses of the Primitive Church, placed as a light to shine in the house, and that it cannot be hidden under a measure, without the edification of their neighbor, and without fruit for the souls; furthermore, that in imitation of the widows of the Gospel, doing well by giving themselves to Jesus Christ and to his Company. If they were to know how evil it can possibly be, of the life of the cloisters; but these instructions must be given under the seal of inviolable secresy, that they do not come to the ears of the monks.

CHAPTER XVI.

HOW WE MUST MAKE PROFESSION OF DESPISING RICHES.

1. With the end of preventing the seculars from directing attention to our itching for riches, it will be useful to repel at times alms of little amount, by which we can allow them to do services for our Society; though we must accept the smallest amounts from people attached to us, for fear that we may be accused of avarice, if we only receive those that are most numerous.

2. We must refuse sepulture to persons of the lowest class in our churches, though they may have been very attached to our Society; for we do not believe that we must seek riches by the number of interments, and we must hold firmly the gains that we have made with the dead.

3. In regard to the widows and other persons who have left their properties to the Society, we must labor with resolution and greater vigor than with the others; things being

equal, and not to be made apparent, that we favor some more than others, in consideration of their temporal properties. The same must be observed with those that pertain to the Company, after that they have made cession of their property; and if it be necessary to expel them from the Society, it must be done with all discretion, to the end that they leave to the Company a part for the less of that which they have given, or that which they have bequeathed at the time of their death.

CHAPTER XVII.

METHODS TO EXALT THE COMPANY.

1. Treating principally all, though in things of little consequence, we must have the same opinion, or at least exterior dignity; for by this manner we may augment and strengthen the Society more and more; to overthrow the barrier we have overcome in the business of the world.

2. Thus strengthening all, it will shine by its wisdom and good example, that we shall excel all the other fathers, and particularly the pastors, &c., &c., until the people desire us to all. Publicly divulging that the pastors do not need to possess so much knowledge; with such they can discharge well their duties, stating that they can assist them with the counsels of the Society; that for this motive they can dedicate themselves to all classes of studies.

3. We must inculcate this doctrine with kings and princes, THAT THE CATHOLIC FAITH CANNOT SUBSIST IN THE PRESENT STATE, WITHOUT POLITICS; but that in this, it is necessary to proceed with much certainty. Of this mode, *we must share the affection of the great, and* BE ADMITTED TO THE MOST SECRET COUNSELS.

4. We must entertain their good will, by writing from all parts interesting facts and notices.

5. It will be no little advantage that will result, by secretly

and prudently fomenting dissensions between the great, ruining or augmenting their power. But if we perceive some appearance of reconciliation between them, then we of the Society will treat and act as pacificators; that it shall not be that any others shall anticipate to obtain it.

6. As much to the magnates as to the people, we must persuade them by all possible means, that the Society has not been, but by especial Divine Providence, conforming to the prophecies of the Abbot Joachim, for to return and raise up the Church, humbled by the heretics.

7. Having acquired the favor of the great and of the bishops, it will be an entire necessity, of empowering the curates and prebendaries to more exactly reform the clergy, that in other times lived under certain rule with the bishops, and tending to perfection; also it will be necessary to inspire the abbeys and prelacies; the which it will not be difficult to obtain; calling attention to the indolence and stupidity of the monks as if they were cattle; because it will be very advantageous for the Church, if all the bishoprics were occupied by members of the Society; and yet, as if it was the same apostolic chair, particularly if the Pope should return as temporal prince of all the properties; for as much as it is very necessary to extend little by little, with much secrecy and skill, the temporalities of the Society; and not having any doubt that the world will enter the golden age, to enjoy a perfect universal peace, for following the divine benediction that will descend upon the Church.

8. But if we do not hope that we can obtain this, supposing that it is necessary that scandals shall come in the world, WE MUST BE CAREFUL TO CHANGE OUR POLITICS, CONFORMING TO THE TIMES, AND EXCITE THE PRINCES, FRIENDS OF OURS TO MUTUALLY MAKE TERRIBLE WARS THAT EVERYWHERE THE MEDIATION OF THE SOCIETY WILL BE IMPLORED; *that we may be employed in the public reconciliation, for it will be the cause of the*

common good; and we shall be recompensed by the PRINCIPAL ECCLESIASTICAL DIGNITIES; *and the* BETTER BENEFICIARIES.

9. *In fine, that the* SOCIETY *afterwards can yet count upon the favor and authority of princes* PROCURING THAT THOSE WHO DO NOT LOVE US SHALL FEAR US.

CODE OF THE JESUITS.

OF REGICIDE.

(The good doctrines as much as the pernicious, will overcome on all occasions, the circumstances that will originate; and will be left imprinted in the Society.

The doctrine of Regicide that has been preached, during some centuries, corrupt the people, and after having sharpened the daggers against Henry III, Henry IV, Louis XV, against Louis XVI, sharpening also the revolutionary axe in 1703. The "SOCIETY OF JESUS" was the first united Christian society to bear and diffuse the odious principles of rebellion and of the regicide; to prove the certainty of our words, we cite textually, the principal Jesuits that have written upon the regicide. From 1541, the Jesuits maintained that they were calumniated by their enemies, but they themselves shall supply us with weapons, and be condemned for their acts and their words.

I.

PETER BANIERE, a soldier of Orleans, and notorious for his project of attempting the assassination of Henry IV, refused to reveal the names of his accomplices; but having been condemned to be broken on the wheel, on the 26th of August, 1595, declared in his testament, *that he was assisted and protected by the* FATHER VARADE, *rector of the Jesuits in Paris.*

II.

Read in the *Opusculos Theologicus* of MARTIN BECAN, a famous Jesuit, page 130, upon the regicide:

"That every subject can assassinate his prince when he has assumed the power of the throne as a usurper," adding "that his assertion is so just, as that in all the nations, it will be observed, that they will be honored in the extreme, those who immolate similar tyrants. It is necessary yet, however, that he shall be a usurper; because, having a probable right, his death will not be lawful. It is permitted to a nation, continuing, to depose a legitimate prince always, when Le conducts himself as a tyrant."

It will not rebound to us, the odiousness of these maxims, that they thus for themselves will make infamous.

III.

On the 27th of October, 1595, JEAN CHATEL resolved to assassinate Henry IV, when he struck him a blow with a dagger on his lips; declaring that in his adolescence he had contracted an infamous habit, that he could not control; that he was impulsed by the compunctions of remorse which agitated him, *and having heard sustained in the College of the Jesuits, that they were permitted to assassinate heretical monarchs*, having expiated his crime, he himself was assassinated at *Bearnes*. The Jesuits inscribed his name in their martyrology equal to Jacob Clement.

IV.

We read in the *Moral Decisions of* PAUL COMITOLO, an Italian Jesuit, Book IV, Page 158:

"That it is lawful to kill an unjust aggressor, though he may be a general, prince, or king; that innocence is as always useful as injustice; and that a prince that will maltreat citizens is a ferocious beast, cruel and pernicious, that it is necessary to annihilate."

V.

In 1594, JAMES COMMOLET, a French Jesuit, chose for a text of a sermon passages in the Third Chapter of the *Book of Judges* where they refer to Ehud assassinating Eglon, the king of the Moabites; and under this dictated, designating

Henry IV, crying: "*it is necessary for an Ehud, whether he be a monk, soldier or pastor.*" This Jesuit treated of Henry IV, of Nero, of Eglon of Moab, of Holofernes and of Herod; and maintained that the crown should be transmitted by right of election, to a foreign family, anathamatizing in full sermon to his hearers, "for permitting on the throne *a false convert.*"

VI.

DAMIENS, a servant of the Jesuits, intended to assassinate Louis XV. Burnt by the hand of the executioner in the midst of the courtyard. The Moral Theology of Busenbaum.

VII.

"THE GUNPOWDER PLOT," that broke out in England in 1605 was hatched by the Jesuits. The Jesuit GERARD who administered to the oath-bound conspirators, and the FATHER GARNET exclaimed in a public prayer: "*Oh God! destroy this perfidious nation; extirpate from the earth those who live in it, to the end that we may joyfully render to Jesus Christ the praises that are due unto him.*" The English Parliament having returned promptly to the day of its solemn session, but discovered the conspiracy in time and took prisoners the guilty. On the 3d of May, 1606; while upon the scaffold and oppressed by remorse, said to the spectators, "*there would have been a horrible affair.*" In 1603 GARNET was asked if it was lawful, if causing so many heretics to perish, it involved in their ruin some that were not heretics; he ardently responded without wavering, "*that if it is beneficial to the Catholic faction built in this, and having a greater number of the guilty than of the innocent, we can make it legal to destroy them all.*" The conspirators Catesby, Greenwell, Tesmond, Garnet and Oldcorn, Jesuits, were employed a year in opening a mine under the House of Parliament, to blow up the Chambers of the Commons and the Lords, at the proper time with the Queen and her ministers. Garnet made a complete confession, which is preserved in the authorized archives, with the signature of that regicide. We read in a book of the Jesuits, "In the

'Gunpowder Conspiracy' *perished the holy martyr, Henry Garnet,*' with whom heresy invented signal calumny to dishonor him; but it was in vain; then his enemies recognized a manifestation of his innocence; because a drop of his blood that fell on a sword, represented the thousand wonders of his heavenly countenance." (*Garnet was hung!*)

VIII.

EMMANUEL SA said, "The tyrant is illegitimate; and any man whatever of the people has the right to kill him; *uniquisque de populo potest occidere.*" ADAM TANNER, a German Jesuit, said, "To all men it is permitted to kill a tyrant, whatever may be his rank or substance; *tiranus quad substantium:* glorious is his extermination; *exterminare gloriosum est.*

IX.

"The Pope can kill by a single word; *(potest verbo corporalem vitam ausene*); for having received the right of making pasture for the sheep, has he not received the right of cuting the throats of wolves? (*Potestatum lupos interficiendi ?*)"

ALF. SA, Portugese Jesuit.

X.

The Jesuit, JEAN GUIGNARE, who was hanged as the accomplice of James Clement, has said, "it is a meritorious action with God to kill a heretic king."

We find further in their writings the following phrases: "Neither Henry III nor Henry IV, nor the Elector of Saxony, nor the Queen Elizabeth, are true kings. That Clement has done a heroic action in killing Henry III; if it were possible to make war with the Bernese and bring them to the point; and if it was impossible, then to assassinate, (*se le asesinara.*)"

XI.

In 1594, the English Jesuits HOLT, WILLIAMS and YORK, young Jesuits to assassinate the Queen of England, and to aid them in the execution of this crime, Holt had given them the mystic bread. The crime could not take place, and the Jesuit was hung with Henry Garnet.

XII.

GABRIEL MALAGRIDA, a Portugese Jesuit, conspired against the life of Joseph I, king of Portugal, during the ministry of Pombal, and to this end, the conspirators were assured that the assassin of the king *would not be guilty of venial sin;* in attention to said king, *"He is not good for the Jesuits."*

Delivered to the Inquisition (in charge of the Dominicans) in company of the Fathers Mathos and Alexander they were hanged and burned.

XIII.

"Ultimately in France there was executed a signal and magnificent exploit for *the instruction* of impious princes, Clement assassinating the king, and conquered an immense number (*ingins sibi nomen fecit*) who perished. Clement, eternal honor of France, (*æternum Gallica decus*), following the opinion of the greater number, was a youth of sensitive character and of delicate physique, but of a superior strength that was given to his arm and to his resolution."

(MARIANA, Jesuit, *De Rege*, Lib. 1, Chapter IV,)

XIV.

"It is a salutary thought to inspire princes, and persuade them that if they oppress their people, making them insupportable by the excess of their vices and the infamy of their conduct, living with such conditions that they cannot only become so obnoxious, but that they can be gloriously and heroically got rid of, by similar acts." (1)

MARIANA, *De Rege*, Book 1, Chapter VI,)

The book of the *Institution of the King*, from whence we have extracted that which precedes it, was dedicated to Philip

---

(1) What has the Father Mariana written, to live in one epoch, of the dethronement of *Dona Isabella de Bourbon?* Has the same thought that precedes it been taken from his work, *De Rege?*—[N. del T.]

III. This act characterizes the audacity of that infernal Company that has lived until our days, marked upon the daggers and the most odious principles; *corrupting to reign.* Such was its object.

XV.

The Jesuit CARLOS SCRIBANUS has written of Henry IV: "Rome, see this cart driver that governs France, this anthropohagi, this monster that is bathed in blood. * * * Can we not find one that will take up arms against the ferocious beast? * * * Have we not a Pope that will employ an axe in the salvation of France? Calm yourself, young Jesuit, if we fail of the papal axe, we have the dagger of Ravalliac."

XVI.

NICHOLAS SERRANUS, Italian Jesuit, in his *Commentaries upon the Bible*, approves the assassination of the king Eglon, committed by Ehud. He says: "Many wise men think that Ehud had done well, for the reason that he was protected by God; and this reason is not the only one, for there exists another, to-wit; That similar action is of ordinary right against tyrants."

XVII.

"When there is a tyrant by his manner of government, he can be laudably put to death by his vassals and subjects, with daggers or *poison*, notwithstanding the oath, without waiting the sentence or the order of any judge."

XVIII.

"It does not pertain to priests and other ecclesiast'cs to kill kings by means of artifices; nor do the sovereign pontiffs have the right to reprimand by this method, but after having paternally reprimanded thence directly, they can exclude them by censures from the communion of the sacrament; in the following if it be necessary they can absolve their subjects from the oath of fealty, depriving them of their dignity and royal authority; after this, take others who are not ecclesiastics, they will arrive to ways of action (*execucio ad alios pertinet*)."

(BELLARMIN, *De Summa Pontificis Autontate*, Book IV, Page 180.

The canonization of Bellarmin has been asked and *obtained* by the Jesuits.

XIX.

"It is of faith that the Pope has the right of deposing of heretical and rebel kings; not being legitimate king nor prince; a monarch deposed by the Pope, if they refuse obedience to this, after having been deposed, they are converted into notorious tyrants and they may be killed by the first who can reach them."

"If the public cause cannot meet with its defense in the death of the tyrant, it is lawful for the first who arrives to assassinate him."

(SUAZEZ. *Defensis fidei*, Book VI, Chapter IV, Nos. 13 and 14.)

XX.

"Henry IV, who was struck on the lips by Jean Chatel, exclaimed, "Is it necessary that the great Jesuits convince me by my mouth?"

We shall not cite anything further upon this subject, the doctrines of the Jesuits upon Regicide, that horrorize the globe and are those which have for a long time been known and condemned; all the *Histories of Father Loriquet* cannot change a similar opinion. Henry IV pardoned the Jesuits, because he said, " There have been many proposed attempts against my life that have been miserably made and confounded, and I am always in fear of being assassinated; *but these people have delegates and correspondents everywhere, and an amount of cunning to prepare their minds at their pleasure.*"

When we meditate upon the death of Henry IV similar words freeze the blood in the veins, making every movement more terrible, if we reflect that the Jesuits were the poisoners of Pope Clement XIV.

OF PARRICIDE.

"The Christian and Catholic children can accuse their parents of the crime of heresy, although for this they may be set apart to be burned; * * *and not this only, they can refuse them food,* if they pretend that they have removed from the Catholic Faith; but that until then, *they can, without sin and injustice,* if they desire to obligate themselves, *assassinate those who abandon the faith.*"

(STEPHEN FACUNDEZ, Portuguese Jesuit. *Treatises upon the Commandments of the Church,* (*Tratados sobre los Mandamientos de la Iglesia*) 1626, Book I, Chapter 33.

Are these the Apostles of that Christ who died for the redemption of the world and who exclaimed *"Love one another"*?

"Is it lawful for a son to kill his father when he has been proscribed? A great many authors maintain that he can, and if this father becomes obnoxious to the Society, it is my opinion that the same can be done as stated by these authors."

(J. DE DICASTILLE, Spanish Jesuit. *De la Justicia del Derecho,* [Of the Justice of Right] Book II, Page 511.)

OF ASSASSINATION.

Extract from the *Compendis para uso de los Seminarios* (Compendium for the use of Seminaries) by the ABBOT MOULLET, free member of the Society of Jesus, published in the year 1845, in Strasburg. We implore our readers that they will compare the doctrines of the *Compendis* of 1843 with that of the Jesuits of the 17th and 18th centuries contained in this volume.

"Certain it is to be permitted to kill a thief to preserve the goods necessary to life; for that the aggressor does not only attack the goods, but also the life at the same time; but it is doubtful if it is lawful to kill him who attacks the treasury, *not precisely necessary for the life;* in this case if we can not come out victorious in defense, the consequence is proved; being the reason that *Charity does not exist that will permit any single notable loss in your fortune by saving the life of the thief."*

(The Abbot MOULLET, Jesuit.)

I.

"Is it permitted to defend ourselves against him who attacks us, and until we kill him? *Answer.* If you can do so without making a scandal of the assassination, it will not be lawful; that being so that it does not pertain to the right of defending your life only of a private person, against one of the vulgar; an inferior against his superior; a son against his father; a priest or a monk against a layman; and reciprocally, it is clear that there will not be incurred a single irregularity."

(FRANCISES AMICUS, Jesuit, *Curso Theologica*, [Course of Theology] published in 1642.)

II.

"Is it permitted to kill in defense of one's own self, whoever may be the aggressor?

Answer. A son may kill his father; a woman her husband; a servant his master; a layman his priest; a soldier his general; an accused his judge; a scholar his preceptor; a subject his prince."

(*Compendio de los Casos de Consciencia*, Book III, by JOHN AZON, Jesuit.)

Fire! my reverends, with promptness at the travelers! For fortune has the justice, a moral more sure and less docile.

III.

PAUL CAMITOLO, Italian Jesuit, reproduces the doctrines of AMICUS and JOHN AZON.

IV.

"If a priest at the altar is attacked, he can lawfully kill the adversary *e incontinente* [and incontinently] finish the sacrifice of the mass."

(STEPHEN FAGUNDEZ, Com. of the Church.)

4*

V.

"It is permitted to men, although they be priests or monks, to kill for the defense of the life of their neighbor when they cannot defend them by any other mode."
(Idem, idem.)

VI.

"If a judge commits an injustice, and works against the laws, the criminal can defend himself with blows, even though he kills the judge."
(Idem, idem.)

VII.

"Is it lawful for a husband to kill his wife surprised in adultery, and a father have the same right over his daughter for the same cause? *Answer.* That before the sentence has fallen from the judge, it would be a mortal sin for a husband to kill his wife, although she were surprised *in flagrante delictu.* In the second place, that after pronouncing the sentence, the husband may assassinate his wife, without sin; for he is converted into a voluntary executor of justice, and can kill his wife, if it is well to do so."
(VICENTE EILLINCIUS, Italian Jesuit. *Moral Questions*, 1633, tome C, 7.)

VIII.

"If a man kills another, believing that he causes a transcendent evil, that man only sins but lightly; for he does not know the enormity of his election."
(GEORGE OF RHODES, Jesuit. *Theologica Escolastica*, tome 1, Page 322.)

IX.

"Ordinarily, one can kill a man for the value of an escudo, ($2.00.)"
(ESCOBAR.)

X.

"It is lawful for you to kill a man who will rob you of six or seven ducats, if you are seriously impressed to save yourself from the robbery being committed. I have not the hardihood to condemn as a sinner one who intends to kill, rather than to have taken from him anything of the value of an escudo." ($2.00.)

(The Father MOLINA, Book IV, V. 3, disposition 16 of 6.)

TO DESIRE THE DEATH OF YOUR NEIGHBOR.

"A father can desire the death of a husband that maltreats his daughter; for he must love her much more than does his son-in-law."

"It is permitted to a son who desires the death of his father; but it is a cause of inheritance and not of the death itself."

(*Crisis Theologica*, Colonia, 1702, Page 242. JUAN DE CARDENAS, Spanish Jesuit.)

TAMBURINI, (THOMAS,) Italian Casuistic Jesuit, ask the following questions upon homicide:

"Can a son desire the death of his father, for to enjoy the inheritance? Can a mother earnestly desire the death of her daughter; need she be anxiously obliged to feed and endow her? Can a priest covet the death of his bishop, for the hope of succeeding him?" To these questions he answered: "If longed for such only, we can inform you with delight of these events: it is lawful for you to desire and receive them without sin; but you are not to rejoice at this remote evil, but of the good that will result to you."

(*Metodo de la facil confesion*. Page 20.)

The books of the *Casuistic Jesuits* are full of these odious maxims. Pascal discovered them in his *Cartus Provinciales*; but with him as it is with us, has retroceded with an intense adversion against these infamous writings; and we believe we would dishonor our pen if we impose upon ourselves the task of terminating these citations.

OF SUICIDE.

(1843.)

"If a physician orders a prescription, when there is great sickness, the use of food *as a necessary remedy to avoid a certain death*, is one obliged to obey the physician?

Answer. The question is controverted; notwithstanding a *negative* decision, for this may be *more probable*, being also *more common among the doctors.*"

The Abbot Moullet. Compendium for the use of the Seminaries, 1843.)

OF VIOLATION OF CHASTITY, AND OF LUST.

Adultery.

We have translated from some of the Casuistic Jesuits, but it was impossible for us to do so with the book of Bouvier, Archbishop of Rheims. "*The Manual of Confession*" is a book the most immoral of the works of the Marquis De Sade; and notwithstanding published to the truth in Latin, has been printed in France. At the very moment of our writing, while it is being denied as a falsification, they have but scarcely finished the authorization of the work of Bouvier, and already it is at private sale. It is easy to comprehend the motives for abandoning the translation of some texts of this book; we desire to spoil the infamous doctrines and destroy the mask that covers them, but we abhor the scandal; after having read our book, the honorable man will become indignant, and the noble clergymen of France, as in 1682, will thrust far away from them such vile allies.

The assassins of St. Bartholomew, the inquisitors and the Jesuits are monsters produced by malignant imaginations; they are the natural allies of the spirit of darkness and of death; the religion of Christ, entirely to the contrary, is the sublime revelation of the life and of the light.

I.

"He who deflowers a virgin with her own consent, does not incur any other punishment than that of doing penance; because she being the owner of her person, can concede her favors to whom she best pleases; but that her father has the right to prevent that, for that they will assist to avoid that their children offend God."

(FRANCISCO JAVIER FREJELEL, Jesuit. *Cuestiones practicas de las funciones del confesor*, page 284 Augsburg, 1750.)

II.

"He that by force, menace, bribe, or importunity of his entreaties has seduced a virgin without promise of marriage, he shall indemnify her of all the injuries that will result from this act to the young girl and to her father. *If seriously reflecting upon what has been said, we must be careful that the crime is absolutely hidden;* it is the most *probable* that if she were willing, the seducer will not be obliged to make the least reparation."

(The Abbot MOULLET, Jesuit.)

ADULTERY.

"If anyone sustains guilty relations with a married woman, *not because she is married*, but for her beauty, making obstruction of the circumstance of the marriage, these relations, it will be perceived of many authors, *does not constitute adultery; but it is of simple impurity.*"

(1813 *Compendium* of the Abbot MOULLET.)

OF LUST.

I.

STEPHEN BEAUMY, a French Jesuit, says in his work entitled "*De la summa de los pecados*," (Of the amount of the Sins) 1653, page 77: "It is lawful for all classes of persons to enter into the places of prostitution, to convert the lost women, although they may be very likely to sin; although they may have attempted many times; although that person that they have left will drag them down until they sin by the sight and flatteries of these women."

To distinguish the sin of lust. *Rape*, it is said, is when the action with a virgin is against her will and by force; but when the woman accedes amicably and voluntarily it is not *rape*, but *fornication;* and then it is not necessary to endow, and much less to marry with her, because he will not have injured her with whom he has treated."

II.

"If a servant is obliged of necessity to serve a lustful master, this same necessity permits her to execute the most grave things; and they can be proportioned as concubines, leading to the most reprobate places; and if a gentleman desires to scale a window to sleep with a woman, he can sustain her upon his shoulders or follow her with a ladder, *quiat sunt actiones de se indifferentes.*"

(CASTRO PALAS, Portuguese Jesuit. *De las . Virtudes y los vicios,* 1631, page 18.)

III.

In his *"Commentaries upon the Prophet Daniel,"* printed in Paris in the year 1622, CORNEILLE DE LOS PIERLE, Jesuit, expresses himself in the following manner:

"Susanna said to Daniel, '*If I abandon myself to the shameless desires of these old men I am lost.*' In a similar extremity, as fearing the infamy upon the one side and death on the other, Susanna could have said, '*I do not consent to so shameful an action, but will suffer without opening my lips, to the end that I may preserve my life and my honor.*' The young inexperts believe that to be chaste, it is necessary to cry succor, and resist the seducer with all their strength. *But they will not sin without their consent and the co-operation;* and of this manner Susanna could have permitted the old men to have exercised their lust upon her, by not taking any part therein; *certain it is,* that she would not have sinned."

IV.

"*Clericus rem habens cum femina in vase prepostero, non incurrit pœnas bullæ.* Pius V. If he does not make frequent use of the sin."

(Escobar y Mendoza, "*De la Lascivia,*" title I, page 143.)

V.

"*Clericus vitium bestialitatis perpetioras non incurrent*—unless that he is not in the habit of this sin."

(Escobar, id. Id. Book I, page 144.)

VI.

"*Clericus Sodomatice pattens non incurrit in pœnis bullœ.*—If it is not exercised more than two or three times."

(Escobar, id. Id. Book I, page 144.)

VII.

Escobar judges in the first number of his work upon lust, that a priest is not to be despoiled of his habit, nor exposed to excommunication when he has acted by a shameful motive, as to commit fornication, to rob anyone, or for to enter incognito into an orgie.

VIII.

Pascal has made particular burlesque of Escobar, but what particularly characterizes this celebrated Jesuit is, that all the questions have two senses or meanings. Escobar continually uses this duplicity and of the *probabilities*. Escobar asks, " Is a bad disposition such as we see of the woman with the desire of lust, incompatible with the duty of hearing mass? *Answer to this.* It is sufficient to hear mass, although in such dispositions, to satisfy the precepts, always refraining her exterior."

IX.

"A man and a woman who having denuded themselves to

embrace, executing a thing indifferently, and is not a true sin."

(VINCENT FELLUCIOS, Italian Jesuit. *Preguntor Morales*, [Moral Questions] 1633, Book II, Page 316.)

EDIFYING AND CURIOUS HISTORY.

In 1718, JEAN BAPTISTE GERARD, a French Jesuit, was nominated rector of the Royal Seminary at Toulon; there was distinguished in it, at that point, CATHARINE CADIERE, one of the penitents, of eighteen years of age, and endowed with the most rare beauty, whose health became altered by a supernatural change in her. Coming to visit her daily, and with frequency he had surprised Catharine in the most turpid posture, until that one morning he was obliged, in the name of Divine Justice, to cast off his clothing and in that position began to embrace her; promising that he would conduct her to ultimate perfection; but as he feared the consequences of his love, he made her take from time to time a potion that occasioned enormous losses of blood. Subsequently she was conveyed to the Convent of Ollivules, the distance of a league from Toulon, where he could go and see her without witnesses; having been guilty of this despicable snare that commenced to be a scandal, for which the Father Girard had to make a journey by order of the President of Brest, who locked up the young lady of Cadiere in the Convent of the Ursulines; and having asked to confess, revealed to the priest all that had taken place with her former director. The Father Girard was not disturbed by so horrible an accusation; but beforehand, on the contrary, accused Catharine of having been privately detected, and excited the fathers against her; but the subject being transferred to Parliament, an order of imprisonment was issued against the young lady of Cadiere and the Carmelite to which they were directed. But the Jesuit was set at liberty.

The debates upon such an ignominious subject proved that

Girard was guilty of the crimes of sorcery, mysticism, spiritual incest, abortion (of which this horrible transgression has given proof) and bribing of witnesses. On the 11th of September, 1731, the Procurator-General asked that Catharine be condemned to make public retraction in front of the portico of the Church of St. Saviour, and then to be hung immediately thereafter. The act was not passed conforming to these conclusions, Catharine being returned to her mother and father, and the Father Girard was exonerated; recognized by the people, crushed with insults and injuries. Notwithstanding this, she lived to an advanced age and tranquilly passed away.

XI.

"A prostitute can legitimately receive payment, but she must not put the price very high. All young girls or prostitutes have the same right in secret fornication; but a married woman does not have a similar right; for the gains of prostitution are not stipulations in the marriage contract."

(J. GORDON, Scotch Jesuit, *Universal Moral Theology*, Title 2, Book V.)

XII.

"If a priest, although he may be very well instructed in the danger that he will run in penetrating into the room of a woman, and that he unites in amorous bonds, and is surprised in adultery by the husband, whom he may kill in the defense of his life or his members, is not to be considered irregular and may continue in his ecclesiastical functions."(1)

(ENRIQUEZ, Portuguese Jesuit. *Sum of Moral Theology*, Venice, 1600.)

---

(1) The reader who desires to investigate the private life of the individuals of the infernal Company of Jesus, will read and meet with the *"Portrait of the Jesuits,"* a work that was published at the end of the last century. – (N. del T.)

XIII.

"The women do not commit mortal sin when they deck themselves with superfluous adornments or fine clothing that we may see their breasts; it being the custom of the country and not being done with an evil intention."

(SIMON DE LESSAN, Jesuit.)

This is nothing more than the tolerance in disagreeing with the opinion of the hypocrite who said: *Prenez de moi ce mouchoir*, etc. [Take from me this handkerchief, etc.]

XIV.

To be remembered, we will only cite the title of the work of the celebrated SANCHEZ, "THE TREATMENT OF MARRIAGE," which is sown with *lewd discussions*. If we only pertain to these Jesuit charnel places; making some citations, but do not write for the seminaries only; (1) and can fall into whatever hands, we do not desire to be accused of immorality.

XV.

"For how much can a woman sell the pleasures of immorality? *Answer*. It is necessary to estimate in justice; attending to the nobleness of mind, beauty and decorum of the woman. * * An honest woman is of more value than the one who makes her house free to the first recent comer. How shall we distinguish in the treatment of a prostitute or of an honest woman? *Answer*. A prostitute cannot in justice ask one without the same that is received of the other; they must fix a price that must be reduced to a contract between her and him who pays; for the one gives the money and the other puts up her body. But a woman of decorum can exist as she pleases; because in things of this nature she

---

(1) Effectively there are other works introducible, although they are entitled "*Guide de los Confesores*," [The Confessor's Guide] and such is the work of Bouvier, Archbishop of Rheims, a work which we do not see is of sufficient sanctity to translate, but the most easy version will make any woman of lust red hot.— (N. del T.)

does not have a common and established price; the person who sells is the owner of her merchandise. A damsel and an honest woman can sell their honor as dear as they estimate it."

(TAMBURINI, Jesuit, *De la Facil Confesion*, [Of Easy Confession] Book VIII, Chap. 5.)

XVI.

JACOB TIRIN, Jesuit, maintains as Corneille, whom we cited in the first part, that the *Chaste Susannah* might have abandoned her body to the old men, *without*, as has been said of *co-operating and consent;* no one is obliged we say, with the end of preserving her chastity, to declare her dishonor by her cries, and exposing herself to death; *for the reputation and the life are preferable to the purity of the body."*

(1668, *Commentaries upon the Bible*, Page 787.)

XVII.

"We can and must absolve a woman that hides in her house a man with whom she often sins; but freely following her with decorum or having something to detain her."

(FATHER BAUNY, Jesuit.)

OF ROBBERY.

I.

"Is it lawful to kill, rob or fornicate an innocent person? *Answer.* Yes, in virtue of the commandment of the law of God; because God is the arbiter of life and of death; and an obligation to execute in this manner his commandments." "And is it permitted to rob, when we see that we are oppressed by necessity? *Answer.* It is permitted secretly or privately; not having other means succoring your necessities; this is not robbery or rapine, for it conforms to natural right that is common to all in this world."

(PEDES ARAGON, Jesuit. *Compendio de la summa teologica de Santo Tomas de Aquinas*, pages 244, 365.)

II.

"The amount of the robbery to fall into mortal sin, according to the calculation of all men is estimated at the value of sixty pence or three francs. [Read page 226.]"

"To resist is just, under the penalty of mortal sin, to restore that which is robbed, in small portions, *that by the larger shall be the sum total.*"

(ANTONIO PABLO GABRIEL, Jesuit. *Moral Theology.*

III.

"The small thefts made on different days, and of one man only, or of many; for great as the sum may be that is appropriated they never will be mortal sins."

(The Father BAUNY, Jesuit, *Sum of the sins*, Chap. 10, page 143.)

IV.

"If the masters commit any injustice with their servants, respecting their salaries, they can ultimately demand justice against them, or take in justice the value of the compensation."

(J. DE CADENNAS, Jesuit. *Teologica*, page 214.)

V.

"God prohibits robbery, when it is considered as *evil*, and not when it is reputed as good."

(CASNEDI, Jesuit, *Juicios Teologicos*, ['Theological Justice] Book I, page 278.)

VI.

"JAVIER FEGULLI, Italian Jesuit, judges that is lawful for a servant to rob her master for compensation; *but with the condition, that she does not leave herself to be surprised with her hands in the dough.*"

(*Del Confesor*, page 137.)

VII.

Paul Laymann approves the secret compensation, being also the opinion of Father Lepus.

(*Moral Theology*, Book III, page 119.)

VIII.

"If the fathers do not give money to their children, can the children rob them? *Answer.* When a man is subjected to indigency, and the other nothing in riches, inasmuch as he of the riches is obliged to succor him that is indigent, the latter can take in secret, and in a holy amen, the property that is presented, *without sin and without being obliged to make restitution.*"

(Louget, French Jesuit. Question IV, page 2.)

IX.

Juan de Lugo approves the secret compensation and says: "He can rob from all debtors, if he suspects that they do not desire to pay."

(*Treatise of the Incarnation*, Book I, page 408.)

X.

Valeria Regnal admits the secret compensation, but with the obligation that it must be exact.

XI.

"If anyone cannot sell his wine at its just value, it would be a cause of injustice of the judge or malice of the buyers, he can diminish the measure and divide equally with water; drawing off directly the merchandise as pure wine and without alteration."

(F. Tollett, Jesuit. *Of the seven mortal sins*, pages 102 7.)

XII.

"When we see a thief resolved and promptly to rob a poor man, we can dissuade him; designating some rich person *to be robbed in place of the other.*

OF BLASPHEMY.

I.

"If we believe by an insuperable error that the blasphemy of ourselves is commanded by God, it will be blasphemy." (J. Casnedi, Jesuit. *Juy thet.*)

II.

"If the penitent is a renegade from his Creator, and enraged against him, giving vent to his anger by uttering scandalous words, he only sins venially; because his anger deprives him of the means of considering what he says." (Father Bauny, Jesuit. *Sum of the sins*, Chap. 1, page 66.)

III.

"Jesus Christ can say to us, 'Come and surround me, ye blessed, for ye can lie and blaspheme, believing that these were my orders that ye should lie and blaspheme." (J. Carnedi, Jesuit.)

CUNNING LIES.

We have recompiled under this title, maxims that we cannot easily classify. The first place, of right, corresponds to the celebrated Escobar.

JESUITICAL DOCTRINES OF ESCOBAR AND MENDOZA.

"Is gluttony a sin? *Answer.* Yes, and no. It is with respect to its specie; a venial sin, although without necessity; some will stuff themselves to the point of vomiting; excepting that the health does not suffer considerably; and yet, when to that excess of premeditated design of misery, one will never run into mortal sin."

"Can one accept a duel? *Answer.* Yes, and no. It is not lawful when it will make a scandal, but it is permitted

with reserve, to defend your treasure; if to. that, you should see yourself obliged; for a man has the right of guaranteeing his property, although with the death of his enemy."
(*Moral Theology*, Book IV, page 119 and following.)

"He is not drunk who can distinguish a scarecrow from a load of hay."
(BUSENBAUM.)

"IT IS LAWFUL TO HAVE TWO CONFESSORS; ONE FOR MORTAL SINS AND THE OTHER FOR THE VENIAL, TO THE END OF MAINTAINING YOUR GOOD REPUTATION WITH YOUR ORDINARY DIRECTOR; ALWAYS THAT IT SHALL NOT BE THE CAUSE OF REMAINING IN MORTAL SIN."
(ESCOBAR. *Moral Theology*, Book 7, page 135.)

"No one is obliged but to confess the circumstances that attenuate the nature of the sin and not that which aggravates it."
(ESCOBAR.)

"The rapine is not a circumstance that is obliged to be had, to discover when the robbery was committed."
(FAGUNDEZ, Jesuit.)

OF PERJURY.
(1843.)

Question. To what is that man obliged, when he takes an oath in a fictitious manner, and with the intention of gain? *Answer.* He is not obliged to anything *in virtue of the religion*, that not having taken a true vow, but in justice he is obliged to execute that which he has sworn to in a fictitious manner, and with the intent of gain."
Compendium for the use of Seminaries, by the Abbot MOULLET, Strasburg, 1843.)

We have not drained off much of the actual books of the Jesuits, because some are untranslatable because of their brutal immorality, and the others reproduce the doctrines of the 17th and 18th centuries. The extracts from the *Compendium* of the year 1843 prove the veracity of our assertions.

I.

"It is permitted as much in a light matter, as in a grave one, to swear without the intention of fulfilling, if you have good reasons to follow that method."
(CARDENAS, Jesuit. *Crisis Teologica.*)

II.

"You can swear that you have not executed a thing, although effectively it has been executed; understanding by it *that you did not do it before having been born*; and to be understood by any other similar circumstance, that without having some idea by which you can discover the words which cover it; and this is very convenient in circumstances, and just when it is necessary or useful for the health, the honor or the well being."
(SANCHEZ. *Opera Moralis.*)

III.

"But not to lie, you can satisfy, *that what you have done is not that which has been done*; always that you intend to give by your speeches the idea that a man of ability can give."
(SANCHEZ. *Opera Moralis.*)

OF JUSTICE.

I.

"If it is asked, if a judge is obliged to restore that which he has received to administer justice? *Answer.* It must devolve on him who has received the decision, which gave him justice; but if his vote has been given in favor of injustice, then the money that has been gained may be retained."

(J. B. Taberna, Jesuit. *Epitome of Moral Theology*, published in 1736,)

This is more than humanitarian; it is folly. We do not deem it necessary to discuss maxims of such nature.

II.

"When we have received money to commit an evil action, is it necessary to make restitution? *Answer.* We distinguish. If the act is not to be performed which has been paid for, it is necessary to return the quantity; but in fact and in truth it is not necessary."

Molina, Jesuit. *Obras*, Vol. 3, page 138.)

OF USURY.

"Is it permitted to purchase a thing for less than its value of one who is obliged by necessity to sell; for by this means it diminishes the price of things, and makes the merchandise that is offered to be sought for? *Answer.* A thing that is sold of necessity loses not only the third of its value, but the half. It is lawful for a tavern keeper to mix water with wine, and laborers, chaff with wheat, and to sell these goods at a common price; with such that the wine and the wheat will not be worse than that which is sold daily."

(Amadeus Gimenius, Jesuit.)

In the process of Affnaer, it was proved that the Jesuits discounted, bought and sold by deeds, and this with a circulation of five or six millions.

OF INFANTICIDE.

"Can a woman occasion an abortion? *Answer* 1st. If the fœtus is not animated and the pregnancy is not dangerous, she is permitted to do so, directly or indirectly, taking potions that will work in such a manner upon the fœtus that it will be dissolved and evacuated; indirectly caused to flow with blood, or taking remedies that may be favorable and destroy the fœtus.

2d.—If the fœtus is animated, and the mother must die with it, it is lawful, before childbirth, to drink some potion that may indirectly be noxious; that which we can authorize by this comparison; if a ferocious beast pursues a pregnant woman, that she must fly to be saved from death, although it is certain, morally speaking, that it will produce an abortion.

3d.—If a young girl has been seduced, and she repents of her young adultery, she can, before the fœtus is animated for fear of losing her honor which is more precious to her than her own life."

(AIRAULT, Jesuit. *Propositions upon the fifth precept of the Decalogue*, 2, page, 322.)

CALUMNIES.

The Abbot CHAUVELIN, speaking of one article of calumny, s among those details that will excite the indignation of every honorable soul. Following the speech of a magistrate of Parliament, we find that Calumny is the doctrine of the Company of Jesuits.

I.

"Men can, without scruples, attempt some against others, by detraction, calumny and false testimony."

II.

"To cut down the calumnies, we can assassinate the calumniator; but we must hide it, that we avoid the scandal."
(AIRAULT, Jesuit.)

OF LYING AND FALSE SWEARING.

I.

"If you believe in an incontrovertible manner that you are commanded to lie, then lie."

(BASNEDI, Jesuit. *Juicio Teologica*, page 278.)

II.

"If asked about a robbery that has been committed, are we obliged immediately to make compensation; or upon a loan that truly is not due; because being satisfied that in the actuality it is not due, because having conquered the term, or that your poverty will probably excuse you from paying; you can swear that you did not receive any loan; it being understood *that you had paid the amount;* because this is the end that all justice demands for the oath."

CASTROPALAS, Jesuit. "*The virtues and vices,*" 1631, page 18)

III.

"A man surprised in *flagrante delictu,* and who would be obliged to swear that he had contracted matrimony with a dishonored young lady, can swear that he had done so, it being understood, *If I am obliged to in advance of my pleasure.*"

"If anyone desires to swear, without being obliged to comply with his vow, he can destroy the word, and then he does not commit but a venial lie, that is easily pardoned."

(SANCHEZ.)

IV.

"If a woman conceals the value of her dowry, after the goods of her husband were confiscated, and she is asked if she has retained anything for the benefit of herself, she can contend that she has not; it being understood: *nothing that pertains to another.*"

"When a crime is secret, the culpability of the crime may be denied; it being understood: *publicly.*"

(The Father STOZ, Jesuit, *Of the Tribunal of the Penitency.*)

OF REBELLION.

I.

"The rebellion of a priest against the king is not a crime of *less majesty*, FOR A PRIEST IS NOT THE SUBJECT OF A MONARCH."
(EMMANUEL SA, Jesuit. *Aphorisms on the word.* CLERICUS.)

II.

"Nobody is so incapacitated that he can be ignorant when tyranny constitutes the danger of the State; in similar case, all laudable measures can be taken to throw off the yoke of tyranny."

The citations would be too very numerous; but the Jesuits have always preached this principle, and yet preach it, in the *Religious Universe.*

SIMONY.

1.

"If we administer a sacrament or holy thing, by a lustful pleasure, and this to recompense and not plainly to a title of pure gift, you will commit simony and sacrilege. This is in the case of that of a benefice to the brother as the price of the honor of his sister, because after having slept with the sister, it will be a benefice to the brother for gratitude, you will only incur the fault of *irreverence.*"

(FILLICIUS, Jesuit. *Moral Questions,* Vol. II, Chap. VII, page. 616.)

II.

According to the FATHER ARSDEKIN, a Swedish Jesuit, "Simony and astronomy are lawful things."

(See his *Tripartite Theology,* 1744, Vol. II, Treatise V, Chapter XII.)

III.

"You cannot buy a benefice with money; but you can say, '*If you will concede a benefice to me, I will remember you eternally.* But to avoid sinning and fulfill your promise, you must see to it that you do not oblige yourself interiorly to anything determined. Do not commit simony but make this agreement: *Concede to me your suffrage that I may be made Provincial, and I will stipulate on my part that you shall be prior;* because it is a compact, and the permutation of spiritual things that are not prohibited in the matter of benefices."

(Claudio Lacroix, Jesuit. *Commentaries of Busenbaum.*)

OF PROBABILITIES.

I.

"The doctrine of probabilities, we learn that we can, with all security of conscience, defer in all cases to the decision of many, or of such, only one doctor; and that his authority is valid to decide for us, to embrace an opinion that for which is conceded sufficient probability; although the contrary opinion can be at the proper time the most probable and sure."

(Peter Nicolo, Jesuit.)

II.

"It is permitted to a confessor that he may follow the opinion of the penitent and be careless of his own, and this is likely when the probable opinion which the penitent follows will incline to the detriment of the other. Example, if we do not treat, we do not restore."

(N. Balder, Jesuit. *Disputes upon Moral Theology*, Book IV, page 402.)

RELIGIOUS DOGMA.

I.

" It is difficult to determine the moment when the obligation begins, of the love of God."

(JUAN DE CARDENAS. *Crisis Theologica*, Page 241.)

II.

CLADIUS AGUAVIVA, fifth General of the Jesuits, attacked the bull against the doctrine of Moline, saying to Pope Paul, "If that it is to be made a similar affront to the Society, it will be difficult to answer, *that we do not intend invective and injuries against the Holy See*."

III.

Question. What shall we see in Paradise? *Answer.* The very sacred humanity of Christ, the adorable body of the Virgin Mary, and of the other saints among thousands and thousands of other beauties. *Question.* Will our utmost senses enjoy the pleasure that is our own? *Answer.* Yes, and the most admirable eternal enjoyment and without anything fastidious. *Question.* Can we see, hear, smell, taste and touch, and enjoy all the pleasures that we can receive? *Answer.* Yes, there is no doubt; the joyful hearing the song of harmony; receive the smell of savors; for the lust, nothing will fail of the pleasure of smell and perfumes, and can the pleasure of delicate touch. *Question.* If in the intelligence of speech in Paradise, tell me in what language? *Answer.* It is likely that it will be in Hebrew, for it will be the language that God has taught some men, and Jesus Christ has spoken; also can speak any other language, but the blessed will have the most perfect intelligence. *Question.* With what clothing will the blessed be covered? *Answer.* With a garment of glory and light, that will shine from all parts of the body and significant of those who have suffered the most for God."

(G. POMEY, Jesuit. *Theological Catechism*, Leon, 1675.)

IV.

The FATHER HARDUIN has pretended that *the Æniad and the Odes of Horace* were composed by some monks of the 14th century. Following him Eneas is Jesus Christ, Lalajea, the lover of Horace is no other than the Christian religion. He also thinks that all the preceding Councils of Trent never existed.

V.

"The Christian religion, evidently *is believable, but it is not evident that it is true*, because its teaching is confused, or it teaches confused things; and the most times, those that *pretend that the Christian religion is evidently true, are obliged to confess that it is evidently false; concluding that there does not exist any religion evidently true*. Why, or whence is the Christian religion the most true among so many that exist? The oracles of the prophets were created by the inspiration of God. And if I deny to you that which has been prophesied? *Yes, I maintain that the miracles attributed to Jesus Christ are not true.*"

(*Philosophical Thesis* of the Jesuits of Caen, maintained in the Royal College of Bourbon.)

What man will dare to take a step more in doubt and impiety?

VI.

"The sentiment of love to God is not obligatory."
(FATHER SIMON, Jesuit.)

VII.

"If a man who has made on the day of the Passover an unworthy communion, is he obliged to receive the sacrament again? *Answer.* He is not obliged; for he has complied with the obligation that is imposed by the Church. The law that ordains the communion only obliges the substance of the act; and the sacrilegious communion is sufficient."

(GEORGE GOBAT, Jesuit. *Moral Works*, Douai, 1700, Book I, Treatise IV, page 253.)

VIII.

In an exorcism that was made in Paris by Father GOTON, confessor of Henry IV, asked the Devil, "if before he seduced Eve, did the serpent have feet?"

It appears to us that all the pretended ingenuity of the *good fathers* is calculated, in their policy that make us believe at times that they are most sensible; and at others that they are impotent; and in effect that they can make us to fear an Order that writes that the blessed in heaven are covered with flesh and clothed with petticoats, and that they discuss if the serpent had feet or not. The Jesuits laugh at us; and during their hilarity, *the rattlesnake is coiled at our feet, climbing to strike us in the heart!*

IX.

"A son that was drunk, and in his intoxication killed his father, *we can rejoice at the assassination that he has committed*, because of the immense property which he will be the heir to; because we are to suppose that this parricide was not premeditated; and that he had for his object great riches; it was laudable in the extreme; or at the least, it was not certainly bad; we here conclude that it is not a reprehensible doctrine."

(GEORGE GODAT, Jesuit. *Moral Works*, Douai, 1700, Vol. II, Page 229.)

X.

"Inasmuch as all the world knows of purgatory," says LACROIS positively to BELLARMINE and GIMENIUS, "there exists another beautiful meadow, which is adorned with all classes of flowers, illumined in clear day, and exhales a delicious odor, an enchanted place, where the souls do not suffer the pains of the senses. This place is for the less guilty, a very moderate purgatory, and as a sanitary prison, where they can abide without any dishonor."

"It will not be so bad the sight of the other purgatory, where nobody, according to these brethren, has remained ten consecutive years. Aided by this, we can follow his doctrine, that all sins are venial, and will make hell less to be feared."

(Life of GAUDIS LACROIS, Jesuit,

XI.

"Mary preferred to be eternally condemned in hell, deprived of the sight of her son, and to see the demons, if he had been conceived in original sin."

(Father OQUATE, Jesuit. Sermon pronounced in Alcala in the year 1600.)

XII.

NICOLAS ORLANDINI, Jesuit, assures us that St. Ignatius carried to heaven the souls of his companions; and that having been detained a moment to speak with him, made prediction *"that every Christian that was seen in the habit of the Jesuits had the privilege of entering heaven with his reason."*

XIII.

ANTONIO SIRMON, who died in 1643, said in his *"Defense of Virtue,"* "That it is lawful to work by fear and hope."

XIV.

"If Peter is dead for legitimately defending himself, we can swear that he is not dead *unjustly.*"

"If a shopkeeper, having appraised a low price for your goods, you can use a false weight; and in conscience, *deny with an oath,* before the tribunals, that you used a false weight; it being understood *with damage to the buyer.*"

(Father GOBAT, Jesuit. *Moral Works*, Book II, page 319.)

PARODY OF THE PARADISE OF MAHOMET.
BY THE JESUIT ENRIQUEZ.

In a ridiculous book of the *"Occupation of the Saints"* we are assured by Enriquez: (Chapter 73.)

I.

"That the men and women are pleasantly occupied with feasts, masquerades and balls."

II.

(*Chapter* 74.) "That the angels are disguised as women, and appear to the saints with sumptuous dresses of ladies, with their hair curled, and with chemises and petticoats of muslin."

III.

(*Chapter* 58.) "That each blessed one in heaven has a particular habitation; and that Jesus Christ abides in a magnificent palace; having there large streets, beautiful and grand squares, castles and citadels."

IV.

(*Chapter* 62.) "That the supreme pleasure consists *in kissng and embracing the bodies of the blessed; and that they bathe in fountains after this, where they sing as nightingales.*"

V.

(*Chapter* 65.) "*That the women have blonde hair; they are adorned with rubies and jewels, in the same manner as here below.*"

This ray of madness, and we can pardon the Jesuits of their writings if they do not take other pages. Has not the Father Enriquez ridiculed the holy things as much or more than Voltaire? Our readers can judge.

For the Council of the Jesuits exposed in Trebeiis, the famous tunic of Jesus, and by their own Council exhibited in Our Lady *a nail* without producing as much as the tunic of Trebeiis, *have satisfied with usury the first costs.*

INSTRUCTIONS FOR THE CATHOLIC APOSTOLIC SOCIETY OF THE SANFEDISNAS, (OR THE JESUIT ORDER OF THE HOLY FAITH.)

(BY THE CATECHISM AND ADJOINED OATH OF THE SACRILEGIOUS SECT OF THE SANFEDISTAS, [THE SAME AS THE PAOLOTTI (PAULIST FATHERS) AN ORGANIZATION WITHIN [THE SOCIETY OF THE JESUITS.] WE CAN TRULY SEE TO WHAT EXTREME SUPERSTITION AND FANATICISM WILL LEAD. FREE MEN OF THE WORLD! BE ON THE ALERT!! BE AS EAGER AS THE ARGONAUTS OF THE FABLE, AND DO NOT BE BETRAYED BY HYPOCRISY. DESIRE THAT GOD SHALL TEAR AWAY THE MASK THAT COVERS THE ENEMIES OF LIBERTY, THAT THEY MAY APPEAR AS THEY ARE; THIS IS WITH ALL THE OTHER EVIL DEFECTS THAT THEY HAVE.)

OATH.

DICTATED BY THE CARDINAL JOSE ALBANI.

I, N. de N., in the presence of God Omnipotent, Father, Son and Holy Spirit, of Mary, always the Immaculate Virgin, of all the Celestial Court of Heaven, and of thee, honored father, I swear to let my right hand be cut off, my throat cut, and die of hunger or in the most atrocious torments; and pray Almighty God that he will condemn me to the pains of hell, before that I should betray or injure one of the illustrious fathers and brothers of the Catholic Apostolic Society in which I am in this moment become enrolled, or without scrupulously observing its laws, or do not give assistance to my needy brethren. I swear to firmly maintain the holy cause which I have embraced. I will not guard consideration for a single individual of the Society of the Liberals, whatever may be his birth, parentage or fortune. I will not have pity for the cries of the children nor the aged; and will spill unto the last drop of blood of the infamous liberals, without regard to sex, age or condition. I swear, in fine, implacable hatred to the enemies of our holy Roman Catholic Religion, one and true!

PASSWORDS AND COLLOQUY OF RECOGNITION.

Salutation. "Viva!" (Halloo!)
Answer. "Viva Pues!" (Halloo then!)
Question. We have a beautiful day?
Ans. To-morrow I hope it will be better.
Ques. I am pleased that this street is so bad?
Ans. In a short time it will be repaired.
Ques. In what manner?
Ans. With the bones of the Liberals.
Ques. How are you called?
Ans. South.
Ques. From whence cometh the light?
Ans. From Heaven.
Ques. What do you think of doing to-day?
Ans. To always persevere in separating the wheat from the chaff.
Ques. What is the length of your crook?
Ans. It is sufficient to pull down.
Ques. What tree produced it?
Ans. A laurel planted in Palestine, grown in the Vatican, under whose bower are covered all the faithful.
Ques. Do you propose to travel?
Ans. Yes.
Ques. Whither?
Ans. Unto the shores of felicity and religion on board of the little bark of the fisherman.

THE FOLLOWING IS FOR THE INITIATES OF THE SUPERIOR CLASS.

Ques. "Viva!" (Halloo!) You will be welcome; tell me as follows who you are?
Ans. A brother of yours.
Ques. Are you a man?
Ans. Yes, certainly; and consent that my hand may be cut off and my throat cut, and die of hunger in the most atrocious torments, if I at any time injure or betray one of my brethren.

Ques. How shall I know that you are a man faithful to your God and to his Prince?

Ans. With these words. Faith, Hope and Indissoluble Union.

Ques. Who admitted you among the Sanfedistas? (Holy Fathers of the Faith.)

Ans. A venerable man in gray hair.

Ques. What was done to receive you?

Ans. I was made to kneel upon my knee on the cross and to place my hand upon the Holy Eucharist, and I was armed with the BLESSED STEEL.

Ques. In what place was you received?

Ans. In the bends of the Jordan, in a place not contaminated by the enemies of the Holy Religion and its Princes, in the same hour in which was born our Divine Redeemer.

Ques. What were your colors?

Ans. With the yellow and black my head was covered, (colors of the Austrian flag) and my heart with the white and yellow. (Colors of the Papal flag.)

Ques. What is your duty?

Ans. To hope in the name of God and of the true Roman Catholic Church.

Ques. From whence cometh the wind?

Ans. From Palestine and the Vatican; that will disperse all the enemies of God.

Ques. What are the ties that bind you?

Ans. The love of God, of Country and of Truth.

Ques. How do you sleep?

Ans. Always in peace with God and with the hope of exciting war with the enemies of his holy name.

Ques. What do you call your passwords?

Ans. The first ALPHA, the second ARK of NOAH, the third IMPERIAL EAGLE, the fourth KEYS OF HEAVEN.

ALL. Have courage, brethren, and persevere. (1)

---

(1) Subterranean Rome, by Carlos Didier, pages 349, 351.)

CEREMONY OF INDUCTION AND EXTREME OATH OF THE JESUITS.

[When a Jesuit of the minor rank is to be elevated to command, he is conducted into the Chapel of the Convent of the Order, where there are only three others present, the principal or Superior standing in front of the altar. On either side stands a monk, one of whom holds a banner of yellow and white, which are the Papal colors, and the other a black banner with a dagger and red cross above a skull and crossbones, with the word INRI, and below them the words IUSTUM, NECAR, REGES, IMPIOS. The meaning of which is: *It is just to exterminate or annihilate impious or heretical Kings, Governments or Rulers.* Upon the floor is a red cross upon which the postulant or candidate kneels. The Superior hands him a small black crucifix, which he takes in his left hand and presses to his heart, and the Superior at the same time presents to him a dagger, which he grasps by the blade and holds the point against his heart, the Superior still holding it by the hilt, and thus addresses the postulant.]

SUPERIOR.

My son, heretofore you have been taught to act the dissembler: among Roman Catholics to be a Roman Catholic, and to be a spy even among your own brethren; to believe no man, to trust no man. Among the Reformers, to be a Reformer; among the Huguenots, to be a Huguenot; among the Calvinists, to be a Calvinist; among the Protestants, generally to be a Protestant; and obtaining their confidence to seek even to preach from their pulpits, and to denounce with all the vehemence in your nature our Holy Religion and the Pope; and even to descend so low as to become a Jew among the Jews, that you might be enabled to gather together all information for the benefit of your Order as a faithful soldier of the Pope.

You have been taught to insidiously plant the seeds of jealously and hatred between communities, provinces and states that were at peace, and incite them to deeds of blood, involving them in war with each other, and to create revolutions and civil wars in countries that were independent and prosperous, cultivating the arts and the sciences and enjoying the blessings of peace. To take sides with the combatants and to act secretly in concert with your brother Jesuit, who might be engaged on the other side, but openly opposed to that with which you might be connected; *only that the Church might be the gainer in the end, in the conditions fixed in the treaties for peace and that the end justifies the means.*

You have been taught your duty as a spy, to gather all statistics, facts and information in your power from every source; to ingratiate yourself into the confidence of the family circle of Protestants and heretics of every class and character, as well as that of the merchant, the banker, the lawyer, among the schools and universities, in parliaments and legislatures, and in the judiciaries and councils of state, and to "be all things to all men," for the Pope's sake, whose servants we are unto death.

You have received all your instructions heretofore as a novice, a neophyte, and have served as a coadjutor, confessor and priest, but you have not yet been invested with all that is necessary to command in the Army of Loyola in the service of the Pope. You must serve the proper time as the instrument and executioner as directed by your superiors; *for none can command here who has not consecrated his labors with the blood of the heretic; for "without the shedding of blood no man can be saved."* Therefore, to fit yourself for your work and make your own salvation sure, you will, in addition to your former oath of obedience to your Order and allegiance to the Pope, repeat after me

THE EXTREME OATH OF THE JESUITS.

I, M—— N——, Now, in the presence of Almighty God, the Blessed Virgin Mary, the blessed Michael the Archangel, the blessed St. John the Baptist, the holy Apostles St. Peter and St. Paul and all the saints and sacred hosts of heaven, and to you, my ghostly father, the Superior General of the Society of Jesus, founded by St. Ignatius Loyola, in the Pontificate of Paul the Third, and continued to the present, do by the womb of the Virgin, the matrix of God, and the rod of Jesus Christ, declare and swear, that his holiness the Pope is Christ's Vicegerent and is the true and only Head of the Catholic or Universal Church throughout the earth; and that by virtue of the keys of binding and loosing, given to his Holiness by my Saviour, Jesus Christ, he hath power to depose heretical kings, princes, states, commonwealths and governments, all being illegal without his sacred confirmation and that they may safely be destroyed. Therefore, to the utmost of my power, I shall and will defend this doctrine and His Holiness' right and custom against all usurpers of the heretical or Protestant authority whatever, especially the Lutheran Church of Germany, Holland, Denmark, Sweden and Norway, and the now pretended authority and churches of England and Scotland, and branches of the same now established in Ireland and on the Continent of America and elsewhere; and all adherents in regard that they be usurped and heretical, opposing the sacred Mother Church of Rome. I do now renounce and disown any allegiance as due to any heretical king, prince or state named Protestants or Liberals or obedience to any of their laws, magistrates or officers.

I do further declare that the doctrines of the churches of England and Scotland, of the Calvinists, Huguenots and others of the name Protestants or Liberals to be damnable, and they themselves damned and to be damned who will not forsake the same.

I do further declare, that I will help, assist and advise all or any of his Holiness' agents in any place wherever I shall be, in Switzerland, Germany, Holland, Denmark, Sweden, Norway, England, Ireland, or America, or in any other kingdom or territory I shall come to, and do my uttermost to extirpate the heretical Protestants or Liberals' doctrines and to destroy all their pretended powers, regal or otherwise.

I do further promise and declare, that notwithstanding I am dispensed with, to assume any religion heretical, for the propagating of the Mother Church's interest, to keep secret and private all her agents' counsels from time to time, as they may entrust me, and not to divulge, directly or indirectly, by word, writing or circumstance whatever; but to execute all that shall be proposed, given in charge or discovered unto me, by you, my ghostly father, or any of this sacred convent.

I do further promise and declare, that I will have no opinion or will of my own, or any mental reservation whatever, even as a corpse or cadaver, (*perinde ac cadaver,*) but will unhesitatingly obey each and every command that I may receive from my superiors in the Militia of the Pope and of Jesus Christ.

That 1 will go to any part of the world whithersoever I may be sent, to the frozen regions of the North, the burning sands of the desert of Africa, or the jungles of India, to the centres of civilization of Europe, or to the wild haunts of the barbarous savages of America, without murmuring or repining, and will be submissive in all things whatsoever communicated to me.

I furthermore promise and declare that I will, when opportunity presents, make and wage relentless war, secretly or openly, against all heretics, Protestants and Liberals, as I am directed to do, to extirpate and exterminate them from the face of the whole earth; and that I will spare neither age, sex or condition; and that I will hang, burn, waste, boil, flay, strangle and bury alive these infamous heretics, rip up the stomachs and wombs of their women and crush their infants' heads against the walls, in order to annihilate forever their execrable race. That when the same cannot be done openly, I will secretly use the poisoned cup, the strangulating cord, the steel of the poinard or the leaden bullet, regardless of the honor, rank, dignity, or authority of the person or persons, whatever may be their condition in life, either public or private, as I at any time may be directed so to do by any agent of the Pope or Superior of the Brotherhood of the Holy Faith, of the Society of Jesus.

In confirmation of which, I hereby dedicate my life, my soul and all my coporeal powers, and with this dagger which I now receive, I will subscribe my name written in my own blood, in testimony thereof; and should I prove false or weaken in my determination, may my brethren and fellow soldiers of the Militia of the Pope cut off my hands and my feet, and my throat from ear to ear, my belly opened and sulphur burned therein, with all the punishment that can be inflicted upon me on earth and my soul be tortured by demons in an eternal hell forever!

All of which I, M—— N——, do swear by the blessed Trinity and blessed Sacrament, which I am now to receive, to perform and on my part to keep inviolably; and do call all the heavenly and glorious host of heaven to witness these my real intentions to keep this my oath.

In testimony hereof I take this most holy and blessed Sacrament of the Eucharist, and witness the same further, with my name written with the point of this dagger dipped in my own blood and sealed in the face of this holy convent.

[He receives the wafer from the Superior and writes his name with the point of his dagger dipped in his own blood taken from over the heart.]

SUPERIOR.

You will now rise to your feet and I will instruct you in the Catechism necessary to make yourself known to any member of the Society of Jesus belonging to this rank.

In the first place, you, as a Brother Jesuit, will with another mutually make the ordinary sign of the cross as any ordinary Roman Catholic would; then one crosses his wrists, the palms of his hands open, the other in answer crosses his feet, one above the other; the first points with forefinger of the right hand to the center of the palm of the left, the other with the forefinger of the left hand points to the center of the palm of the right; the first then with his right hand makes a circle around his head, touching it; the other then with the forefinger of his left hand touches the left side of his body just below his heart; the first then with his right hand draws it across the throat of the other, and the latter then with his right hand makes the motion of cutting with a dagger down the stomach and abdomen of the first. The first then says *Iustum;* the other answers *Necar;* the first then says *Reges*. The other answers *Impios*. [The meaning of which has already been explained.] The first will then present a small piece of paper folded in a peculiar manner, four times, which the other will cut longitudinally and on opening the name JESU will be found written upon the head and arms of a cross three times. You will then give and receive with him the following questions and answers.

Ques. From whither do you come?

Ans. From the bends of the Jordan, from Calvary, from the Holy Sepulchre, and lastly from Rome.

Ques. What do you keep and for what do you fight?

Ans. The Holy faith.

Ques. Whom do you serve?

Ans. The Holy Father at Rome, the Pope, and the Roman Catholic Church Universal throughout the world.

Ques. Who commands you?

Ans. The Successor of St. Ignatius Loyola, the founder of the Society of Jesus or the Soldiers of Jesus Christ.

Ques. Who received you?

Ans. A venerable man in white hair.

Ques. How?

Ans. With a naked dagger, I kneeling upon the cross beneath the banners of the Pope and of our sacred Order.

Ques. Did you take an oath?

Ans. I did, to destroy heretics and their governments and rulers, and to spare neither age, sex nor condition. To be as a corpse without any opinion or will of my own, but to implicitly obey my superiors in all things without hesitation or murmuring.

Ques. Will you do that?

Ans. I will.

Ques. How do you travel?

Ans. In the bark of Peter the fisherman.

Ques. Whither do you travel?

Ans. To the four quarters of the globe.

Ques. For what purpose?

Ans. To obey the orders of my General and Superiors and execute the will of the Pope and faithfully fulfill the conditions of my oath.

Ques. Go ye, then, into all the world and take possession of all lands in the name of the Pope. He who will not accept him him as the Vicar of Jesus and his Vicegerent on earth, let him be accursed and exterminated.

PART SECOND.

PART SECOND.

INTRODUCTION.

At the close of the long and bloody civil war of the rebellion, the crowning act of infamy that stirred the heart of the nation to its lowest depths, was the assassination of Abraham Lincoln, the "Martyr President," who had guided the Ship of State through the stormy seas (whose crimsoned waves were incarnadined by the blood of patriots and that of the would-be destroyers of the Union) to the haven of national peace and the assured integrity of the whole Republic. Those in arms, who had in vain sought to divide the Union and cleave American Nationality in twain, were fast surrendering to the victorious troops of the patriot army of the Nation. Victor and vanquished alike rejoiced at the termination of the fratricidal strife, one to exult over the successes of "Liberty and Union, now and forever inseparable," and the other with vain regrets for a "Lost Cause," and to mourn for the loss of those who had fought and died in vain. The South was just beginning to return to reason, seeing the fruitlessness of her efforts in a wrong direction, and was disposed to make the best terms possible with the North in the restoration of peace and tranquility within her borders. The victorious armies were still in possession of the re-conquered territory, and general preparations were being made for evacuation and disbandment and return to their homes. It was at this time, that, on the night of the fourteenth of April, 1865, that the deadly bullet of the assassin did its fatal work and the morning of the fifteenth closed the earthly career of the greatest man and the best beloved President that ever assumed the duties of the Executive of the Nation.

The South was struck dumb with terror and astonishment

at an act committed at a time when no possible benefit could be derived from it, or help the Lost Cause, and lay helpless, crushed, at the feet of her now maddened victors, whose arms were raised ready to strike in terrible, merciless vengeance, against what they deemed a treacherous and perjured but suppliant and conquered foe. The South, in her agony of horror and fear, protested against the terrible crime, and he who had been before most bitterly cursed, derided and maligned, with all the intensity of sectional animosity and hatred, at the beginning and during the war, was now claimed by them to have been "THE SOUTH'S BEST FRIEND." It was the darkest and most perilous hour of the nation, when its pent up wrath seemed about to be let loose and the annihilation of the vanquished was deemed most certain. But He who rules the whirlwind and rides upon the storm commanded as in the days of old, "Peace! Be still, and the winds and the waves they obeyed Him."

When the Grand Funeral March of the Nation was commenced, and due preparation had been made by the hundreds of cities and towns for the reception of the remains of the Immortal Lincoln, the many hundreds of representatives of the people of the Pacific States and Territories sojourning in New York City, assembled at the Metropolitan Hotel and organized a meeting for the purpose of expressing their detestation of so horrible a crime, their sympathy to the family of the murdered President and to the nation, and to take the necessary steps towards paying a proper respect for his memory by marching in procession, in a division by themselves, along with their fellow citizens of the other States and Territories.

The Hon. George Barstow, ex-Speaker of the Assembly of the State of California, was chosen President of the meeting; the Hon. Richard McCormick, then Secretary of the Territory of Arizona, was chosen Secretary, and Major Edwin A. Sherman, then of the State of Nevada, was selected as Marshal of the Division of the Pacific States and Territories. Gen. John B. Frisbie and others presented resolutions which were unanimously adopted, and the meeting then adjourned subject to the orders of the Marshal, to meet at the corner of Wall and Nassau streets and to take the place assigned them in the procession. On the 24th of April the remains of the martyr President reached New York City and after having been viewed by more than a hundred thousand people of all classes, sexes and conditions, on the morning of the next day the grandest mournful pagent that the world ever saw was displayed in the great metropolis of the nation, and which having begun at the Capitol, was to be continued in length for more than a thousand miles, until rest was found at last in the cemetery at Oak Ridge, at Springfield, Illinois, the home of the illustrious dead.

On the morning of the day of the funeral procession in New York City, and shortly before taking our places in line, the Marshal of the division immediately in front of our own stepped up to us and asked, "Are you an American?" to which we answered "Yes." He then enquired, "Are you a Roman Catholic?" To which we answered emphatically, "*No!*" He then said: "The South had nothing to do with the assassination of Abraham Lincoln, but he was the victim of a Jesuit plot, which had long been planned to murder him; that it was known in Europe and our own country, and the conspiracy was wider spread than people had any idea of." At that time we considered it to be but one of a thousand rumors then afloat, but said, "If this be true as you say, I am willing to unite with you and with any body of true men who can be relied upon, and if it occupies the remainder of my life, I will leave not a stone unturned nor let any opportunity whatever escape me, but I will ferret the whole thing out from the beginning, but what I will get at the truth of the matter." For eighteen long years, after an immense amount of time and expense, both in traveling and correspondence, like a tireless detective, pursuing every thread and following up every track and trail, we at last have satisfactorily proven to ourself that the statement then made to us was true, and that Abraham Lincoln fell the victim of the Papal power is as certain as that the sun shines, and we are also convinced that our readers who will peruse the following pages will as readily and promptly come to the same conclusions.

We are fortified with actual sworn statements of fact, as will be seen, the assertions of distinguished statesmen, and following the rules of evidence, circumstantial and positive, there is no room whatever left for doubt, while a nest of foul, slimy and venomous serpents is uncovered, and we will leave it to our readers to say whether the title at the beginning of this book, :'The Engineer Corps of Hell; or Rome's Sappers and Miners," is appropriate or not.

San Francisco, August 24th, 1883.

EDWIN A. SHERMAN.

CHAPTER I.

PRELIMINARY OUTLINE.

In the year 1809 four men were born who were destined by an Almighty Providence to wield an influence and power in the world, in defense of civil and religious liberty, whose efforts were crowned with success, but as in all previous history, the sacrifice upon the altar of freedom had to be consecrated in its own blood.

One of these, and the chief of whom we have to speak, was Abraham Lincoln, the *Martyr President* of the United States, who was born February 12th, 1809, in Hardin County, Kentucky; the second the Rev. Charles Chiniquy, the American Luther, (and the client of Lincoln,) born July 30th, 1809, at Kamouraska, in Canada; the third, Alesandro Gavazzi, born ——, 1809, at Bologna, in Italy, who was the gallant champion, reformer and chaplain of Garibaldi's army for the liberation of Italy, at the same time that Abraham Lincoln was President of our own country and fighting for the preservation of liberty and the Union; and William E. Gladstone, the Prime Minister of England, born Dec. 29, 1809, and these four having the same common enemy to contend against, in their struggle for the principles of civil and religious liberty—the Jesuit emissaries and auxiliaries of the Papal power at Rome.

After so many years of patient research and investigation, we submit the following statement in the same manner to our readers, as a lawyer would present the opening of his case at the beginning of a suit in court, to an intelligent and impartial jury, and as follows, with the accompanying evidence to substantiate its truthfulness.

It appears that for a considerable length of time a controversy had sprang up and been maintained in the bosom of the Roman Catholic Church, in the diocese of Illinois, prior to the year 1856, and which was carried on for several years between Bishop O'Regan, of Chicago, on the one hand, with all the power of the episcopacy and tyranny of the hierarchy of the Papacy, and on the other by the Rev. Charles Chiniquy, then a Priest of that church at St. Anne's, Kankakee County, in said State, who resisted the arbitrary usurpations and tyrannical measures put forth by Bishop O'Regan.

It is not our purpose to go into a general detail of this controversy, as the Rev. Charles Chiniquy, now a Presbyterian Minister, in his admirable work of "Fifty Years in the Church of Rome," soon to appear, has given the fullest account of all these matters, to which our readers are referred, two chapters of which have been kindly furnished by him, which also become a part of the evidence contained herein in proof of the statement made. Suffice it to say in brief, however, that a general Roman Catholic colonization scheme for the taking possession of the Mississippi Valley had been determined upon by the late Pope Pius IX, in 1850, and a large emigration of people of that faith from the continent of Europe and from Canada was put in motion, and under the leadership of Father Chiniquy, colonies were planted in various places, but chiefly in the State of Illinois, and under the direct authority from Rome, with separate and specific command, in method and detail, but in spiritual matters subject to the rule of the Bishop of the diocese. Father Chiniquy, partly with his own money and that of his fellow colonists, bought the land and laid out a town called St. Ann's, in Kankakee county, built a church, established a school, and became at the same time pastor, teacher and manager of the affairs of his colony and exercised a truly paternal care over his entire flock, who were chiefly agricultural in their avocations and pursuits. While so engaged, he seems to have excited the envy and jealousy of some of his fellows in the priesthood, who were not pleased with his success and his indomitable perseverance, energy and industry, which was a standing rebuke to those who had less of piety in their composition, and who were more disposed to gratify their appetites and lethargy, than to cultivate the moral virtues of temperance and sobriety, or imitate the example of St. Paul, who labored with his own hands rather than be a charge to others.

A portion of these colonists who were artizans settled in the city of Chicago, where they could obtain employment at their professions and trades. Here they bought a lot and erected a church, supplied the altar with the necessary adornments in the best style, and with rich and costly vestments for the officiating priests. This neatness and elegance excited the envy of the Irish portion of the Roman Catholic population of that city and their priests, which extended even to the Bishop, their fellow countryman, who in the exercise of his arbitrary power, not only stripped the French Roman Catholic Chapel of priests' vestments, but actually robbed them of the church itself. On a Sunday morning when they came to attend church, the Frenchmen found no church there. *It had been stolen bodily!* They followed up the tracks of the trucks upon which it had been hauled away, and found it in another part of the city, still on wheels, but occupied by Irish Roman Catholics and an Irish priest celebrating mass. Their indignation knew no bounds. They protested against these outrages, not only to their Irish brethren of the same faith, to the priests, and lastly to the Bishop himself, but in vain. They were met by contumely, insult and abuse. They called upon Father Chiniquy, who not only appealed to the Pope, but also to Emperor Napoleon III, in nearly the following language:

"SIRE: My grandfather was a Captain in the French Navy, and for gallant services was in part awarded lands in Canada, which by the misfortunes of war was ceded by treaty to Great Britain. Upon retiring from the service of France he settled upon his estates in Canada, where my father and myself were born. I am thus with other Canadians who have come to this country a British subject by birth, an American citizen by adoption, but French still in blood and Roman Catholic in religion. I therefore, on the part of our people, humbly implore your Majesty to aid us by interceding with His Holiness Pope Pius IX, to have these outrages and wrongs righted."

The Emperor, Napoleon III, did intercede with the Pope, who sent out his Nuncio Bedini, who found things as stated. Bishop O'Regan was removed, and another Bishop who did not prove to be much better, was appointed in his place. It was during these times of trial, abuse and tyranny when the machinery of the courts was used to endeavor to force subjection of matters personal and temporal to Papal ecclesiastical law, to deprive American citizens of their just rights and free will and to make them complete subjects and vassals of Rome. Having failed to accomplish this by many tedious, expensive and harassing law-suits, then there was concocted one of the most damnable conspiracies that was ever hatched by devils to destroy the character of one of the noblest and fearless men that ever contended for the rights of man in any cause or anywhere on the face of God's earth. When the whole Papal power was united here in America against one man to crush and destroy him, and he was making the fight alone and single handed in a cause which involved the rights of every American citizen; when they had exhausted his financial resources and he was overwhelmed in debt, to complete his ruin, if it were possible, they resorted to infamy of the blackest dye to rob him of his good name by falsely charging him with crime, confirming with perjured oaths and damning their treacherous, cowardly souls forever. It was at this point in the darkest hour of his gloom and sorrow that his deliverer was to appear upon the scene to champion his cause and bring him off victorious in the contest; and that champion whose voice and arm was never lifted in vain to help the weak, down-trodden and oppressed, was ABRAHAM LINCOLN!

Before entering into the details of this conspiracy, it is but due to the memory of the "Martyr President," Abraham Lincoln, to positively and emphatically deny the false statement made by Roman Catholic journals, that he was ever a Roman Catholic in belief or baptized in that faith by any priest while in infancy, youth or manhood.

The *Catholic Monitor* of San Francisco, in its tirade and abuse of the Hon. Robert T. Lincoln, Secretary of War, because he very properly refused to permit a Roman Catholic Church to be erected upon the U. S. Military Reservation at the Presidio, among other things, said: *"that such narrow and bigoted views could only emanate from a degenerate son of a great father* OVER WHOSE HEAD WERE POURED THE BAPTISMAL WATERS OF THE CATHOLIC FAITH."

The only waters of that sort which ever were poured over Abraham Lincoln's head was on the night of April 14th, 1865, when Ford's Theater in Washington was the cathedral, and when the sacrament was administered by Wilkes Booth as the officiating priest, and he was baptized in his own blood and consecrated with a vengeance. It is time that an indignant protest should go forth from the American people against this shameless lying which would rob our country of the fair fame of Washington and Lincoln, whose glorious names are wantonly and insultingly attached to institutions which they warned their countrymen of and fought against. But there is so much lying that the Papists when cornered in one lie will seek refuge in another, as will be seen by the following:

"Father Larmer, a Catholic priest of Chicago, publishes a card in which he denies the recent statement about Abraham Lincoln being a Roman Catholic, he says: 'When I read the assertion in the *Univers* I was then Missionary Superintendent of a district which included seven counties in Illinois, Hancock being one of them, where the Bishop Le Fevre and the Abbe St. Cyr had labored as early missionaries. In the center of Hancock County there is a small town named Fountain Green. Near it was a Catholic Church, and early American settlers from Maryland and Kentucky located in the neighborhood, among whom was a branch of the Lincoln family and, others named Cameron and Geddings. *Consequently it was at John Lincoln's, or " Old Johnny Lincoln's"* (as he was familiarly named by the old settlers), *that these priests stopped. John was a brother of President Lincoln, not his father, and this John Lincoln joined the Catholic Church with his wife.* ABRAHAM LINCOLN WAS NOT A CATHOlic, nor had he ever lived in the district which Bishop Lefevre and the priest of St. Cyr attended.'"

So far as Abraham Lincoln not being a Roman Catholic is concerned, Father Larmer tells the truth; *but Abraham Lincoln never had a brother John.* His only brother's name was *Thomas*, who died in infancy, and his father and mother were *Baptists*, to which denomination in early life Abraham Lincoln more particularly leaned.

This denial of these false assertions of our martyred President ever having been baptized or being a Roman Catholic, is necessary, in the beginning, to establish his status and relationship to that institution.

CHAPTER II.

The plot against Chiniquy and his defense by Abraham Lincoln, his attorney, resulting in his triumphant success over the foul designs and perjury of the priests and their enemies.

After some five years and more of controversy with and resistance to the outrageous tyranny of Bishop O'Regan, Father Chiniquy now found himself confronted with a new and more deadly attempt for his destruction.

A plot had been concocted by the Bishop and other Irish Jesuit priesthood in the city of Chicago against the fearless French Canadian priest, and the trouble had extended so far that the laity was mainly divided into two hostile camps of Irish and French Catholics, and a religious war of races, in which the Protestant community of that section were silent spectators, though their sympathy was warmly extended to the latter, whom they looked upon as being grievously oppressed and abused by their Irish co-religionists, who were largely in preponderance and with an Irish Bishop at their head.

Two profligate French priests who were jealous of Father Chiniquy's success and influence over his people, were chosen as the tools of the Bishop to carry out his hellish designs. One of them by the name of LeBelle, caused a man by the name of Spinks to swear out a warrant against Father Chiniquy for seduction and rape with his (LeBelle's) own married sister at Chicago, and to ruin his reputation forever, if possible, by falsely charging him with this heinous crime, while the expense of the suit would have to be borne by the State, and the District Attorney, and associate counsel would be aided by the power and influence of Bishop O'Regan and his Jesuit auxiliaries.

It was at this juncture in the hour of his great distress that Father Chiniquy, by the advice of an unknown friend, in addition to his other counsel, secured the legal services of Abraham Lincoln. His enemies, fearing that he might be acquitted if the trial took place at Kankakee, where Chiniquy was well and favorably known, caused a change of venue to be taken to Urbana, Champaign County, Illinois. Chiniquy was arrested by the Sheriff and was taken to the place of trial. Judge Norton, of Joliet (now deceased), was the principal counsel on the part of the State against Chiniquy, while his counsel for the defense was Judge Osgood, of Joliet, now deceased. Mr. J. W. Paddock, of Kankakee (now deceased), and Abraham Lincoln.

Says Judge Osgood, also confirmed by Judge Norton: "Upon the trial of the cause against Father Chiniquy, the Roman Church had supœnaed five Catholic priests as witnesses! They attended court dressed as priests, wearing long, black robes, looking very dignified, and presenting an air of great condescension upon their part to appear in court, which they seemed to attempt to overawe by their presence and to give a sanctimonious air of truth to their false evidence to be given upon the stand when called for. Upon the convening of court in the morning there came an awkward lull in business arising from the tardiness of a juror. The parties, lawyers and attendants were all in proper place ready to go on, and nothing could be done in the absence of the tardy juror. Judge David Davis sat on the bench, a jolly, fat, good-natured person, weighing about three hundred pounds. Mr. Lincoln had angular features, long, bony fingers, and presented a comical appearance at the bar, for he was ever joking his brethren of the bar. Judge Jesse O. Norton was opposing counsel, a neat, tasty, tidy, ministerial appearing person of the Presbyterian faith, who never joked, and his dignity was blighted by the slightest 'smutty' allusion. The eleven jurors were common country farmers, honest, plain and blunt. The court-room was densely packed with country folks, who came to hear the distinguished array of counsel. While this pause for the absent juror was continuing, the five priests emerged from a side door and marched down the room in solemn and dignified procession and all took a seat in a row on a long bench provided for witnesses. Of course, their appearance attracted much attention. They were dressed alike, sat very prim, looking neither to the right or to the left; their hands were on their knees and their feet were in a straight line. For a minute a pin could have been heard to fall, so quiet was the room, and the audience seemed under a spell. At this moment, Mr. Lincoln seeing the effect they had produced, and quickly divining their purpose and determined to destroy it and their influence, which he conceived could be done at that point in no other way, leaned over the bar table towards Judge Norton, and with his hand to his mouth, as if to prevent his words being heard by anyone but Judge Norton, he spoke in a whisper voice (but a loud whisper that could be heard by every person in the room), 'Norton! Oh, Norton!' (and pointing his long arm and fingers at the row of priests at the same time, and making a quizzical expression of the face at the same time), 'I want to ask you a question in confidence.' 'What is it?' says Judge Norton. Says Lincoln, '*What has the ⸺ fellers got peckers for anyhow?*' It was nearly a minute before the point to the question was seen by the people. But as soon as it was seen, the jury, the lawyers, the crowd and court broke out into immoderate laughter. Norton was terribly shocked; the priests never smiled—they looked a picture of disgust. Every few minntes thereafter some one would break out afresh in laughter, and then it would run through the house. Judge Davis' sides fairly shook in the merriment. THE PRIESTS WERE TERRIBLY OFFENDED, AND THEIR EYES SHOWED A MALIGNITY OF INTENTION OF REVENGE TO BE GRATIFIED IN THE FUTURE WHICH THEIR TONGUES DARED NOT UTTER."

In 1862 a number of gentlemen in Washington (who were Democrats, but friends of Lincoln) sent him word they would call upon him and pay their respects. When they entered his room they announced the visit was purely a social call. They had no offices to ask for, no government policy to discuss, but they wanted to see him as they had seen him in Illinois. Mr. Lincoln was delighted at the spirit of the visit. He said it was the first visit he had had from friends. All previous callers had come for office for themselves or friends, or to discuss State matters, etc. He forgot he was President for the time, and his friends remained until twelve o'clock at midnight, telling stories and recounting court scenes in Illinois.

Mr. Lincoln told of this scene at Urbana, and he said "it was the most ludicrous thing he had ever seen in court." But this is a digression.

When the tardy juror arrived, the business of the court was proceeded with. The counsel for the prosecution called for their witnesses, and Father LeBelle took the stand and swore to a mass of perjured evidence against Chiniquy in his attempt of seduction and rape of his own (LeBelle's) sister. The evidence direct seemed overwhelming and conclusive in statement. Upon cross-examination by Lincoln, much of its effect was destroyed, but still it was feared by Lincoln that the minds of the jury were against the cause of his client and that he might be brought in guilty. The press had been poisoned, and advanced opinions of probable conviction and condemnation of Chiniquy were published in the journals everywhere for the very purpose of influencing the jury in securing that conviction.

The court adjourned in the afternoon until the next morning. In Chicago the newsboys were selling extra supplies of the papers, declaring the hoped for conviction by Bishop O'Regan and his coadjutors in advance. Fortunately however for Chiniquy, a French Canadian by the name of Terrien bought one of the papers and took it home to his wife. When she read the paper she said, "Chiniquy is innocent, and I know it." "I heard the whole thing as it was planned in the priest LeBelle's house by him with his sister, and he promised to give her two eighty-acre tracts of land if she would swear that Chiniquy had made dishonorable proposals to her and attempts upon her person." At first she refused, and denied positively that Chiniquy had ever done anything of the kind, and that she would be guilty of perjury and damn her own soul if she should swear to anything of the kind, for it was absolutely false. After much urging and pressing on the part of the priest LeBelle, and she still refused, he said: "Mr. Chiniquy will destroy our holy religion and our people if we do not destroy him. If you think that the swearing that I ask you to do is a sin, *you will come to confess to me and I will pardon it in the absolution I will give you.*"

"*Have you the power to forgive a false oath?*" replied Mrs. Bossy to her brother. "*Yes,*" he answered; "*I have that power;* for Christ has said to all his priests, 'What you shall bind on earth shall be bound in heaven; and what you shall loose on earth shall be loosed in heaven.'" Mrs. Bossy then said: "*If you promise that you will forgive me that false oath, and if you give me the 160 acres of land that you promised, I will do what you want.*" The priest LeBelle then said, "*All right!*"

When Narcisse Terrien heard this from his wife he said, "If it be so, we cannot allow Mr. Chiniquy to be condemned. Come with me to Urbana." But his wife being quite ill, said to her husband, "You know well that I cannot go. But Miss Philomena Moffat was with me then; she knows every particular of that wicked plot as well as I do. She is well, go and take her to Urbana. There is no doubt that her testimony will prevent the condemnation of Mr. Chiniquy."

Upon that her husband and Miss Moffat started at once, and arrived in the night at Urbana, sought Mr. Lincoln and revealed to him the whole diabolical plot, of which he went immediately and informed Chiniquy. In the meantime the priests watched the trains and examined the hotel registers and found that Mr. Terrien and Miss Moffat had arrived. The priest LeBelle met her coming from Mr. Lincoln's room, a colloquy ensued, and he offered her a large sum of money to leave immediately and return to Chicago and not appear in court. She positively refused, informed him that Mr. Lincoln knew all. Fearing the evil consequences that would result when the hellish scheme would be made public, he went and informed the other priests, and they left before daylight the next morning. The suit was withdrawn by consent of the court and counsel, but not until Mr. Lincoln, with words of burning eloquence and melting pathos, described the long and malicious persecution of his client by his enemies, and with the most bitter invective that the human mind can conceive or the tongue can utter, denounced the infernal machinations of Bishop O'Regan and his accomplices, and rising to his full height, declared, "that while an Almighty Ruling Providence permitted him to see the light of day and breathe the pure air of heaven, and so long as he had a brain to think, a heart to feel and a hand to execute his will, he would devote them all against that infernal power that was the enemy of all free government and of the free institutions of his country, that polluted the temples of justice with its presence and attempted to use the machinery of the law to oppress and crush the innocent and helpless.

It was for holding these perjured priests up to derision and thwarting their aims and projects in the beginning of this trial, and the declarations made when the infamous suit was withdrawn and the full knowledge he possessed of the rascality of that priesthood, which will stop at nothing to carry out its infernal designs, that he brought upon himself that relentless and merciless hatred which continued until it bore fruit in the then near future, the details of which will be found in another chapter; but before entering upon them we will direct the attention of our readers to the next two chapters following, from Father Chiniquy himself.

CHAPTER III.

[CHAPTER XLII OF "FIFTY TWO YEARS IN THE CHURCH OF ROME," BY REV. CHARLES CHINIQUY.]'

Public Acts of Simony—Thefts and Brigandage of Bishop O'Regan—General Cry of Indignation—I determine to resist him to his face—He Employs again Spink, to send me to Gaol, and he fails—drags me as a Prisoner to Urbana in the Spring of 1856, and he fails again—*Abraham Lincoln Defends Me*—My dear Bible becomes more than ever my Light and my Counsellor.

A month had hardly elapsed since the ecclesiastical retreat, when all the cities of Illinois were filled with the most strange and humiliating clamors against our Bishop. From Chicago to Cairo, it would have been difficult to go to a single town without hearing from the lips of the most respectable people, or reading in big letters in some of the most influential papers, that Bishop O'Regan was a thief, a Simoniac, a perjurer, or even something worse. The bitterest complaints were crossing each other over the length and breadth of Illinois, from almost every congregation. "He has stolen the beautiful and costly vestments we bought for our church!" cried the French Canadians of Chicago. "He has swindled us out of a fine lot given us to build our church, and sold it for fifty thousand dollars, and pocketed the money for his own private purposes, without giving us any notice," complained the Germans. "His thirst for money is so great," said the whole Catholic people of Illinois, "that he is selling even the bones of the dead to fill his treasury!"

I had not forgotten the bold attempt of the Bishop to wrench my little property from my hands, at his first visit to my colony. The highway thief who puts the dagger on the breast of the traveler, threatening to take away his life if he does not give him his purse, does not look more infamous to his victim than that Bishop appeared to me that day. But my hope that this was an isolated and exceptional case in the life of my superior, and I did not whisper a word of it to anybody. I began to think differently, however, when I saw the numerous articles in the principal papers of the State, signed with the most respectable names, accusing him of theft, Simony and lies. My hope at first was that there were many exaggerations in these reports; but as they came thicker day after day, I thought that my duty was to go to Chicago and see by myself to what extent those rumors were true. I went directly to the French Canadian Church, and to my unspeakable dismay, I found that it was too true that the Bishop had stolen the fine church vestments, which my countrymen had bought for their own priest in their great solemnities, and he had transferred them to his Cathedral of St. Mary, for his own personal use. The indignation of my poor countrymen knew no bounds. It was really deplorable to hear with what supreme disgust and want of respect they were speaking of their Bishop. Unfortunately, the Germans and the Irish were still ahead of them in their unguarded, disrespectful denunciations. Several were speaking of prosecuting the bishop before the civil courts, to force him to disgorge what he had stolen. And it was with the utmost difficulty that I succeeded in preventing some of them from mobbing and insulting him publicly in the streets, and even in his own palace. The only way I could find to appease them was to promise that I would speak to his Lordship, and tell him that it was the desire of my countrymen to have those church vestments restored to them.

The second thing I did was to go to the cemetery, to see for myself to what extent it was true or not the Bishop was selling the very bones of his dead diocesans, in order to make money.

On my way to the Roman Catholic graveyard, I met a great number of cartloads of sand, which, I was told by the carters, had been taken from the cemetery; but I did not like to stop them, except when I was at the very door of the consecrated spot. There I found three carters which were just leaving the grounds. I asked, and obtained from them the permission to search in the sand which they were carrying, in order to see if there were not some bones. I could not find any in the first cart, and my hope was that it would be the same with the two others. But, to my horror and shame, I found the inferior jaw of a child in the second, and part of the bones of an arm, and almost the whole foot of a human being, in the third cart. I politely requested the carters to show me the very place where they had dug that sand, and they complied with my prayer. To my unspeakable regret and shame, I found that the Bishop had told an unmitigated falsehood, when, to appease public indignation against his sacrilegious traffic, he had published that he was selling only the sand which was outside the fence, on the very border of the lake. It is true, that to make his case good, he had ordered the old fence to be taken away, in order to make a new one, many feet inside of the first one. But this miserable and shameful subterfuge rendered his crime still greater than it had at first appeared. What added to the gravity of that public iniquity is, that the Bishop of Chicago had got that piece of land from the city for a burial-ground, only after they had made a solemn oath to use it only for burying the dead. Every load of that ground sold, then, was not only an act of Simony, but was the breaking of a solemn oath! No words can express the shame I felt, after convincing myself of the correctness of what the press of Chicago, and the whole State of Illinois, had published against our Bishop about this sacrilegious traffic.

Slowly retracing my steps to the city from the cemetery, I went directly to the Bishop to fulfill the promise I had made to the French Canadians, to try to obtain the restoration of their fine church vestments. But I was not long with him without seeing that I would gain nothing but his enmity, by pleading the cause of my poor countrymen. However, I thought my duty was to do all in my power to open the eyes of the Bishop to the pit he was digging for himself and for us and all Catholics by his conduct. "My Lord," I said, "I will not surprise your Lordship when I tell you that all true Catholics of Illinois are filled with sorrow by the articles they find every day in the press against our Bishop."

"Yes, yes," he abruptly replied; "the good Catholics must be sad indeed to read such disgusting diatribes against their superior, and I presume you are one of those who are sorry. But, then, why do you not prevent your insolent and infidel countrymen from writing those things? I see that a great part of those libels are signed by French Canadians."

I answered: "It is to try, as much as it is in my power, to put an end to these scandals that I am in Chicago to-day, my Lord."

"Very well, very well," he replied; "as you have the reputation of having a great influence over your countrymen, make use of that influence to stop them in their rebellious conduct against me, and I will then believe that you are a good friend."

I answered: "I hope to succeed in what your Lordship wants me to do. But there are two things to be done in order to secure my success."

"What are they?" quickly asked the Bishop.

"The first is, that your Lordship give back the fine church vestments which you have taken from the French Canadian congregation of Chicago; the second is, that your Lordship abstain absolutely, from this day, to sell the sand of the burial-ground, which covers the tombs of the dead."

Without answering a word, the Bishop struck his fist violently on the table, and crossed the room with a quiet step two or three times, then turning towards me and pointing his finger to my face, he exclaimed in an indescribable accent of rage, "Now I see the truth of what Mr. Spink told me! You are not only my bitterest enemy, but you are at the head of my enemies—you take sides with them against me! You approve of their rebellious writings! I will never give back those church vestments. They are mine, as the French Canadian Church is mine! Do you not know that the ground on which the churches are built, as well as the churches themselves, and all that belongs to the Church, belong to the Bishop? Was it not a burning shame to see such fine church vestments in a poor, miserable church of Chicago, where the Bishop of that important city was covered with rags? It was in the interest of episcopal dignity that I ordered those rich and splendid vestments, which are mine by the law, to be transferred from that small and insignificant congregation to my Cathedral of St. Mary. And if you had an ounce of respect for your Bishop, Mr. Chiniquy, you would immediately go to your countrymen and put a stop to their murmurs and their slanders against me, by telling them simply that I have taken what was mine from that church, which is mine also, to the cathedral, which is altogether mine. Tell your countrymen to hold their tongues, respect their Bishop when he is in the right, as I am to-day."

I had, many times, considered the infamy and injustice of the law which the Bishops have got passed all over the United States, making every one of them a corporation, with the right of possessing personally all the Church properties of the Roman Catholics. But I had never understood the infamy and tyranny of that law so clearly as in that hour. It is impossible to describe with ink and paper the air of pride and contempt with which that Bishop in effect told me, "All those things are mine, I do what I please with them. You must be mute and silent when I take them away from your hands. It is against God himself that you rebel, when you refuse me the right of dispossessing you of all those properties which you have purchased with your own money, and which have not cost me a cent!"

In that moment I felt that the law, which makes every Bishop the only master and proprietor of all the religious goods, houses, churches, lands and money of their people as Catholics, is simply diabolical, and that the church which sanctions such a law is anti-Christian. Though it was at the risk and peril of everything dear to me that I should openly protest against that unjust law, there was no help, for I felt constrained to do so with all the energy I possessed:

"I answered: " My Lord, I confess that this is the law in the United States; but this is a human law, *directly opposed to the Gospel*. I do not find a single word in the Gospel which gives such a power to the Bishop. Such a power is an abusive, not a Divine power, which will, sooner or later, destroy our Holy Church in the United States, as it has already mortally wounded it in Great Britain, France and many other places. When Christ said in the Holy Gospel, that he had not enough of ground to lay his head, he condemned in advance the pretentions of the Bishops who lay their hands on our church properties as their own. Such a claim is a usurpation, and not a right, my Lord. Our Saviour, Jesus Christ, protested against that usurpation, when asked by a young man to meddle in his temporal affairs with his brothers; he answered that 'He had not received such a power.' The Gospel is a long protest against that usurpation. In every page it tells us that the Kingdom of Christ is not of this world. I have myself given fifty dollars to help my countrymen to buy those fine church vestments. They belong to them, not to you!"

My words, uttered with an expression of firmness which the Bishop had not seen in any of his priests, fell upon him at first as an electric shock. They so puzzled him that he looked at me a moment as if he wanted to see whether it were a dream or a reality, that one of his priests had the audacity to hold such language in his presence. But, recovering soon from his stupor, he interrupted me by striking his fist again on the table, and saying with anger: "You are half a Protestant, your words smell of Protestantism. The Gospel! the Gospel! that is your great power of strength against the laws and regulations of our Holy Church! If you think, Mr. Chiniquy, that you will frighten me with your big words about the Gospel! you will see your mistake at your own expense. I will make you remember that it is the '*Church*' you must obey, and it is through your Bishop that the Church rules you!"

"My Lord," I answered, "I want to obey the Church; but it is a Church founded on the Gospel; a Church that respects and follows the Gospel, that I want to obey."

These words threw him in a real fit of rage. He answered: "I am too busy to hear your impertinent babblings any longer. Please let me alone; and remember that you will soon hear from me again, if you cannot teach your people to respect and obey their superior."

The Bishop kept his promise. I heard of him very soon after, when his agent, Peter Spink, dragged me again a prisoner before the criminal court of Kankakee, accusing me falsely of crimes which his malice alone could have invented! My Lord O'Regan had determined to interdict me; but not being able to find any cause in my private or public life as a priest to ground such a sentence, he had pressed that land speculator Spink to prosecute me again, promising to base his sentence of interdict on the condemnation which he had been told would be passed against me by the criminal court of Kankakee. But the Bishop, with Peter Spink, were again to be disappointed, for the verdict of the court given the thirteenth of November, eighteen hundred and fifty-five (1855) was again in my favor.

My heart filled with joy at this new great victory my God had given me over my merciless persecutors. I was blessing Him when my two lawyers, Messrs. Osgood and Paddock, came to me and said: "Our victory, though great, is not so decisive as we expected, for Mr. Spink has just made an oath that he has no confidence in this Kankakee court, and he has appealed, by a *change of venue*, to the court at Urbana, in Champaign County. We are sorry that we have to tell you that you must remain a prisoner, under bail, in the hand of the Sheriff, who is bound to deliver you to the Sheriff of Urbana, the nineteenth of May, next Spring."

I nearly fainted when I heard this. The ignominy of being again in hands of the Sheriff for so long a time—the enormous expense, far beyond my means, to bring my fifteen or twenty witnesses to such a long distance—nearly one hundred miles; the new oceans of insults, false accusations, perjuries with which my enemies were to overwhelm me again, and the new risk of being condemned, though innocent, at that distant court—all those things crowded in my mind to crush me down. For a few minutes I was obliged to sit, for I would surely have fallen to the ground had I continued to stand on my feet. A kind friend had to bring me some water and wash my forehead to prevent me from fainting. It seemed to me for a moment that my God had forsaken me, and that He was to let me fall powerless into the hands of my foes. But I was mistaken. That merciful God was near me in that dark hour to give me one of the marvelous proofs of His paternal and loving care.

The very moment I was leaving the court, with a heavy heart, a gentleman, a stranger, came to me and said: "I have followed your suit from the beginning. It is more formidable than you suspect. Your persecutor, Spink, is only an instrument in the hands of the Bishop. The real persecutor is the land-shark who is at the head of the diocese, and who is destroying our holy religion by his private and public scandals. As you are the only one among his priests who dare to resist him, he is determined to get rid of you; he will expend all his treasures and use the almost irresistible influence of his position to crush you down.

"The misfortune for you is, *that when you fight a Bishop,, you fight all the Bishops of the world.* They will unite all their treasures and influence to Bishop O'Regan's to silence you, though they hate and despise him. There was no danger of any verdict against you in this part of Illinois, where you are too well known for the perjured witnesses they have brought to influence your judges. But when you are among strangers, mind what I tell you, the false oaths of your enemies may be accepted as gospel truths by the jury, and then, though innocent, you are lost. Though your two lawyers are expert men, you will want something better at Urbana. *Try to secure the services of Abraham Lincoln of Springfield, If that man defends you, you will surely come out victorious from this deadly conflict."*

I answered: "I am much obliged to you for your sympathetic words; but would you please allow me to ask your name?"

"Be kind enough to let me keep my *incognito* here," he answered; "the only thing I can say is, that I am a Catholic like you, and one who, like you, cannot bear any longer the tyranny of our American Bishops. With many others, *I look to you as our deliverer, and for that reason I advise you to engage the services of Abraham Lincoln"*

"But," I replied, "who is that Abraham Lincoln? I never heard of that man before."

He answered me: *"Abraham Lincoln is the best lawyer and the most honest man in Illinois."*

I went immediately with that stranger to my two lawyers, who were consulting with each other only a few steps distant, and asked them if they would have any objection that I should ask the services of Abraham Lincoln to help them to defend me at Urbana.

They both answered: "Oh! if you can secure the services of Abraham Lincoln, by all means do it; we know him well. *He is one of the best lawyers and one of the most honest men we have in our State."*

Without losing a moment, I went to the telegraph office with that stranger, and I telegraphed to Abraham Lincoln, to ask him if he would defend my honor and my life (though I was a stranger to him) at the next May term of the court of Urbana.

About twenty minutes later I received the answer: " *Yes, I will defend your honor and your life at the next May term of the court of Urbana.* A. LINCOLN."

My unknown friend then paid the telegraph operator, pressed my hand, and said: "May God bless and help you, dear Father Chiniquy; continue to fight fearlessly against our mitered tyrants, and God will help you to the end." He then took a train to go north, and soon disappeared, as a vision from heaven. I have never seen him since, though I have not let a day pass without asking my God to bless him. Two or three minutes later, Spink came to the telegraph office to telegraph to Lincoln, asking his services at the next term of the court at Urbana, but it was too late!

Before being dragged to Urbana, I had to renew the Easter (1856), the oil which is used for the sick in the ceremony which the Church of Rome calls the Sacrament of Extreme Unction, and in the baptism of the children. I sent my little silver box to the Bishop by a respectable young merchant of my colony called Dorion; but he brought it back without a drop of oil, with a most abusing letter from the Bishop, for my not having sent five dollars to pay for the holy oil. It was just what I expected. I knew that it was his use to make his priests pay five dollars for that oil, which is not worth more than two or three cents. This act of my Bishop was one of the evident cases of simony of which he was guilty every day. I took his letter with my little silver box to the Archbishop of St. Louis, my Lord Kenrick, before whom I brought my complaint against the Bishop of Chicago, the 9th April, 1856. That high dignitary told me that many priests of the Diocese of Chicago had already brought the same complaints before him, and exposed the infamous conduct of their Bishop. He agreed with me that the rapacity of Bishop O'Regan, his thefts, his lies and his acts of simony were public and intolerable, but he had no remedy for them. He said: "The only thing I advise you to do is, to write to the Pope directly.— prove your charges against that guilty Bishop as clearly as possible. I will myself write to His Holiness, to corroborate all you have told me, for I know it is true. My hope is that it will attract the attention of the Pope. He will probably send some one from Rome to make an inquiry, and then that wicked man will be forced to offer his resignation. If you succeed as I hope in your praiseworthy efforts to put an end to such scandals, you will have well deserved the gratitude of the whole Church, for that unprincipled dignitary is the cause that our holy religion is not only losing her prestige in the United States, but is becoming an object of contempt wherever these public crimes are known."

I was, however, forced to postpone my writing to the Pope, for a few days after my coming from St. Louis to my colony I had to deliver myself again into the hands of the Sheriff of Kakakee, who was obliged by Spink to take me prisoner and deliver me as a criminal into the hands of the Sheriff of Champaign County, the 19th of May, 1856.

It was then that I met Mr. Abraham Lincoln for the first time. He was a giant in stature, but I found him still more a giant in the noble qualities of his mind and his heart. It was impossible to converse five minutes with him without loving him. There was such an expression of kindness and honesty in that face, and such an attractive magnetism in the man, that after a few moments' conversation one felt as tied to him by all the noblest affections of the heart.

When pressing my hand, he told me: "You were mistaken when you telegraphed that you were unknown to me. I know you by reputation, as the stern opponent of the tyranny of your Bishop and the fearless protector of your countrymen in Illinois. I have heard much of you from two friends, and last night your lawyers, Messrs. Osgood and Paddock, have acquainted me with the fact that your Bishop employs some of his tools to get rid of you. I hope it will be an easy thing to defeat his projects and protect you against his machinations."

He had then asked me how I had been induced to desire his services. I answered by giving him the story of that unknown friend, who had advised me to have Mr. Abraham Lincoln for one of my lawyers, for the reason that "he was the best lawyer and the most honest man in Illinois."

He smiled at my answer, with that inimitable and unique smile which we may call the "Lincoln smile," and he replied: "That unknown friend would probably have been more correct had he told you that Abraham Lincoln was the ugliest lawyer of the country," and he laughed outright.

I spent six long days at Urbana as a criminal, in the hands of the Sheriff, at the feet of my judges. During the greater part of the time all that human language can express of abuse and insult was heaped on my poor head. God only knows what I suffered in those days. But I was providentially surrounded as by a strong wall when I had Abraham Lincoln for my defense, "the best lawyer and the most honest man of Illinois," and the learned and honest David Davis for my Judge, the last Vice-President of the United States, and the first its most honored President,

I never heard anything like the eloquence of Abraham Lincoln when he demolished the testimonies of the two perjured priests, Lebel and Carthumel, who, with ten other false witnesses, had sworn against me. I would have surely been declared innocent after that eloquent address, and the charge of the learned Judge Davis, had not my lawyer by a sad blunder *left a Roman Catholic on the jury*. Of course, that Irish Roman Catholic wanted to condemn me, when the eleven intelligent and honest Protestants were unanimous in voting "Not guilty."

The Court having, at last, found that it was impossible to persuade the jury to give a unanimous verdict, discharged them. But Spink again forced the Sheriff to keep me prisoner, by obtaining from the Court the permission to begin the prosecution, *de nova*, at the term of the Fall, the 19th of October, 1856.

Humanly speaking, I would have been one of the most miserable of men, had I not my dear Bible, which I was meditating and studying day and night in those dark days of trial.

But though I was still in the desolate wilderness, far away yet from the promised land, my Heavenly Father never forsook me. He many times let the sweet manna fall from heaven to feed my desponding soul and cheer my fainting heart. More than once I was fainting with spiritual thirst. He brought me near the Rock from the side of which the living waters were gushing to refresh and renew my strength and courage.

Though the world did not suspect it, I knew from the beginning that all my tribulations were coming from my unconquerable attachment and unfaltering love and respect for the Bible as the root and source of every truth given by God to man, and I felt assured that my God knew it also. That assurance supported my courage in the conflict. Every day my Bible was becoming dearer to me. I was then trying to walk in its marvelous light, and from its divine teachings I wanted to learn my duties and my rights. I like to acknowledge that it was the Bible which gave me the power and the wisdom I was in need of, fearlessly to face so many faces. That power and wisdom I felt were mine. My dear Bible enabled me to remain calm in the very lion's den, and it gave me from the beginning of that terrible conflict the assurance of the final victory, for every time I bathed my soul in its divine light I heard my merciful Heavenly Father's voice, "Fear not, I am with thee!

CHAPTER IV.

[CHAPTER LIV OF "FIFTY-TWO YEARS IN THE CHURCH OF ROME," BY REV. CHARLES CHINIQUY.]

Address from my People, asking me to remain—Address of the People to the Bishop—I am again dragged as a Prisoner by the Sheriff to Urbana—Perjury of the Priest LeBelle—Abraham Lincoln's anxiety about the Issue of the Prosecution—My distress—Night of desolation—The rescue—Miss Philomene Moffat sent by God to save me—LeBelle's confession and distress—Spink withdraws his suit—My innocence acknowledged—Noble words and conduct of Abraham Lincoln—The oath of Miss Philomene Moffat.

The Sabbath afternoon after the three drunken priests nailed their unsigned, unsealed, untestified and consequently null sentence of excommunication to the door of our chapel, the people had gathered from every part of our colony into the large hall of the court-house of Kankakee City to hear several addresses on their duties of the day, and they unanimously passed the following resolution:

"*Resolved*. That we, French Canadians of the County of Kankakee, do hereby decide to give our moral support to Rev. C. Chiniquy, in the persecution now exerted against him by the Bishop of Chicago, in violation of the laws of the Church, expressed and sanctioned by the Councils."

After this resolution had been voted, Mr. Bechard, who is now one of the principal members of the Parliament of Canada, and who was then a merchant in Kankakee City, presented to me the following address, which had also been unanimously voted by the people:

"DEAR AND BELOVED PASTOR: For several years we have been witnesses of the persecutions of which you are the subject, on the part of the bad priests, your neighbors, and on the part of the unworthy Bishop of Chicago; but we also have been the witnesses of your sacradotal virtues—of your forbearance or their caluminous blows—and our respect and affection for your person has but increased at the sight of all those trials.

"We know that you are persecuted, not only because you are a Canadian priest, and that you like us, but also because you do us good in making a sacrifice of your own private property to build school-houses and to feed our teachers at your own table. We know that the Bishop of Chicago, who resembles more an angry wolf than a pastor of the Church, having destroyed the prosperous congregation of Chicago by taking away from them their splendid church, which they had built at the cost of many sacrifices, and giving it to the Irish population, and having discouraged the worthy population of Bourbonnois Grove in forcing on them drunken and scandalous priests, wants to take you away from among us, to please Spink, the greatest enemy of the French population. They even say that the Bishop, carrying iniquity in its extreme bounds, wanted to interdict you. But as our Church cannot and is not willing to sanction evil and calumny, we know that all those interdicts, based on falsehoods and spite, are null and void.

"We therefore solicit you not to give way in presence of

the perfidious plots of your enemies and not to leave us. Stay among us as our pastor and our father, and we solemnly promise to sustain you in all your hardships to the end, and to defend you against our enemies. Stay among us, to instruct us in our duties by your eloquent speeches, and to enlighten us by your pious examples. Stay among us, to guard us against the perfidious designs of the Bishop of Chicago, who wants to discourage and destroy our prosperous colony, as he has already discouraged and destroyed other congregations of the French Canadians, by leaving them without a pastor or by forcing on them unworthy priests."

That stern and unanimous determination of my countrymen to stand by me in the impending struggle is one of the greatest blessings which God has ever given me. It filled me with a courage which nothing could hereafter shake. But the people of St. Anne did not think that it was enough to show to the Bishop that nothing could ever shake the resolution they had taken to live and die free men. They gathered in a public and immense meeting on the Sabbath after the sham excommunication, to *adopt* the following address to the Bishop of Chicago, a copy of which was sent to every Bishop of the United States and Canada and to Pope Pius IX :

"To His Lordship, Anthony O'Regan, Bishop of Chicago : We, the undersigned, inhabitants of the parish of St. Anne, Beaver settlement, seeing with sorrow that you have discarded our humble request, which we have sent you by the four delegates, and have persisted in trying to drive away our honest and worthy priest, who has edified us in all circumstances by his public and religious conduct, and having, contrary to the rules of our Holy Church and common sense, struck our worthy pastor, Mr. Chiniquy, with excommunication, having caused him to be announced as a schismatic priest, and having forbidden us to communicate with him in religious matters, are hereby protesting against the unjust and iniquitous manner in which you have struck him, refusing him the privilege of justifying himself and proving his innocence.

"Consequently, we declare that we are ready at all times as good Catholics, to obey all your orders and ordinances that are in accordance with the laws of the Gospel and the Church, but that we are not willing to follow you in all your errors of judgments, in your injustices and covetous caprices. Telling you, as St. Jerome wrote to his Bishop, that as long as you will treat us as your children, we will obey you as a father; but as long as you will treat us as our master, we shall cease to consider you as our father. Considering Mr. Chiniquy as a good and virtuous priest, worthy of the place he occupies, and possessing as yet all his sacradotal powers, in spite of your null and ridiculous sentence, we have unanimously decided to keep him among us as our pastor; therefore praying your Lordship not to put yourself to the trouble of seeking another priest for us. More yet: we have unanimously decided to sustain him and furnish him the means to go as far as Rome, if he cannot have justice in America.

"We further declare: that it has been dishonorable and shameful for our Bishop and for our holy religion to have seen, coming under the walls of our chapel, bringing the orders of the Prince of the Church of a representative of Christ, three men covered with their sacradotal garments, having their tongues half paralyzed by the effects of brandy, and who, turning their backs to the church, went in the house and barn of one of our settlers and there emptied their bottles. Then from there, taking their seats in their buggies, went towards the settlement of L'Erable, singing drunken songs and hallooing like wild Indians. Will your Lordship be influenced by such a set of men, who seem to have for their mission to degrade the sacrados and Catholicism.

"We conclude, in hoping that your Lordship will not persist in your decision, given in a moment of madness and spite; that you will reconsider your acts, and that you will retract your unjust, null and ridiculous excommunication, and by these means avoid the scandal of which your precipitation is the cause. We then hope that, changing your determination, you will work to the welfare of our holy religion, and not to its degradation, in which your intolerant conduct would lead us, and that you will not persist in trying to drive our worthy pastor, Rev. Charles Chiniquy, from the flourishing colony that he has founded at the cost of the abandonment of his native land, of the sacrifice of the high position he had in Canada.; that you will bring peace between you and us, that we shall have in the kind Bishop of Chicago not a tyrant, but a father, and that you will have in us, not rebels, but faithful children, who will help you to embellish and make your Christianity by our virtues and our good examples. Subscribing ourselves the obedient children of the Church.

"THEOPILE DORIEN,   J. B. LEMOINE, N. P.,
"DET. VANIER,   OLIVER SENECHALL,
"J. B. BELANGER,   BASILIQUE ALLAIR,
"CAMILE BETOURNEY,   MICHEL ALLAIN,
"STAN'LAS GAGNE,   JOSEPH GRISI,
"ANTOINE ALLAIN,   JOSEPH ALLARD,
"And five hundred others."

This address, singed by more than five hundred men, all heads of families, and reproduced by almost the whole press of the United States, fell as a thunderclap on the head of the heartless destroyer of our people. But it did not change his destructive plans. It had just the contrary effect. As a tiger, mortally wounded by the sure shots of the hunters, he filled the country with his roaring, hoping to frighten us by his new denunciations. He published the most lying stories to explain his conduct, and to show the world that he had good reasons for destroying the French congregation of Chicago, and trying the same experiment on St. Anne.

In order to refute his false statements, and show more clearly to the whole world the reasons I had, as a Catholic priest, to resist him, I addressed the following letter to his Lordship:

"ST. ANNE, KANKAKEE COUNTY, ILL.,
Sept. 25, 1856.

"RT. REV'D O'REGAN: You seem to be surprised that I have offered the holy sacrifice of Mass since our last interview. Here are some of my reasons for so doing.

"1st. You have not suspended me; far from it, you have given me fifteen days to consider what I should do, threatening only to interdict me after that time, if I would not obey your orders.

"2d. If you have been so ill-advised as to suspend me, for the crime of telling you that my intention was to live the life of a retired priest in my little colony, sooner than to be exiled at my age, your sentence is ridiculous and null; and if you were as expert in the pure Canonica as in the art of pocketing our money, you would know that you are yourself suspended *ipso facto* for a year, and that I have nothing to fear or to expect from you now.

"3d. When I bowed down before the altar of Jesus Christ, twenty-four years ago, to receive the priesthood, my intention was to be the minister of the Catholic Church, but not a slave of a lawless tyrant.

"4th. Remember the famous words of Tertullian, '*Nimia potestas, nulla potestas,*' for the sake of peace, I have, with many others, tolerated your despotism till now; but my patience is at an end, and for the sake of our Holy Church, which you are destroying, I am determined with many to oppose an insurmountable wall to your tyranny.

"5th. I did not come here, you know well, as an ordinary missionary; but I got from your predecessor the permission to form a colony of my emigrating countrymen. I was not sent here in 1851 to take care of any congregation. It was a complete wilderness; but I was sent to form a colony of Catholics. I planted my cross in a wilderness. In a great part with my own money, I have built a chapel, a college and a female academy. I have called from everywhere my countrymen—nine-tenths of them came here only to live with me, and because I had the pledged word of my Bishop to do that work. And as long as I live the life of a good priest I deny you the right to forbid me to remain in my colony, which wants my help and my presence.

"6th. You have never shown me your authority (but once) except in the most tyrannical way. But now, seeing that the more humble I am before you the more insolent you grow, I have taken the resolution to stand by my right as a Catholic priest and as an American citizen.

"7th. You remember, that in our second interview you forbade me to have the good preceptors we have now for our children, and you turned into ridicule the idea I had to call them from Canada. Was that the act of a Bishop or of a mean despot?

"8th. A few days after you ordered me to live on good terms with R. R. LeBelle and Carthavel, though you were well acquainted with their scandalous lives, and twice you threatened me with suspension for refusing to become the friend of those two rogues! Was that the deed of a Bishop? And you have so much made a fool of yourself before the four gentlemen I sent to you to be the witnesses of your iniquity and my innocence, that you have acknowledged before them that one of your principal reasons for turning me out of my colony was, that I had not been able to keep peace with three priests whom you acknowledged to to be depraved and unworthy priests! Is not that surpassing wickedness and tyranny anything recorded in the blackest pages of the most daring tyrants? You want to punish by exile a gentleman and a good priest, because he cannot agree to become the friend of three public rogues! I thank you, Bishop O'Regan, to have made that public confession in the presence of unimpeachable witnesses. I do not want to advise you to be hereafter very prudent in what you intend to do against the reputation and character of the priest of St. Anne. If you continue to denounce as you have done since a few weeks, and to tell the people what you think fit against me, I have awful things to publish of your injustice and tyranny.

"As Judas has sold our Saviour to his enemies, so you

have sold me to my enemy of L'Erable. But be certain that you shall not deliver up your victim as you like.

"For withdrawing a suit which you have incited against my honor, and which you shall certainly lose, you drag me out from my home and order me to the land of exile, and you cover that iniquity with the appearance of zeal for the public peace, just as Pilate delivered his victim into the hands of his enemies to make his peace with them.

"Shame on you, Bishop O'Regan! For the sake of God, do not oblige me to reveal to the world what I know against you. Do not oblige me, in self-defence, to strike, in you, my merciless persecutor. If you have no pity for me, have pity on yourself, and on the Church which that coming struggle will so much injure.

"It is not enough for you to have so badly treated my poor countrymen of Chicago—your hatred against the French Canadians cannot be satisfied except when you have taken away from them the only consolation they have in this land of exile—to possess in their midst a priest of their own nation whom they love and respect as a father! My poor countrymen of Chicago, with many hard sacrifices, had built a fine church for themselves and a house for their priest. *You have taken their church from their hands and given it to the Irish;* you have sold the house of their priest, after turning him out; and what have you done with the $1,500 you got as its price? Public rumor says that you are employing that money to support the most unjust and infamous suit against one of their priests. Continue a little longer, and you may be sure that the cursing of my poor countrymen against you will be heard in heaven, and that the God of Justice will give them an avenger.

"You have, at three different times, threatened to interdict and excommunicate me if I would not give you my little personal properties! and as many times you have said in my teeth, that I was a bad priest, because I refused to act according to your rapacious tyranny!

"The impious Ahab, murdering Naboth to get his fields,

is risen from the dead in your person. You cannot kill my body, *since I am protected by the glorious flag of the United States;* but you do worse, you try to destroy my honor and my character, which are dearer to me than my life. In a moral way you give my blood to be licked by your dogs. But remember the words of the prophet to Ahab, 'In this place where the dogs have licked the blood of Naboth, they shall lick thy blood also.' For every false witness you shall bring against me, I shall have a hundred unimpeachable ones against you. Thousands and thousands of religious Irish and generous Germans and liberty and fair-play-loving French Canadians will help me in that struggle. I do not address you these words as a threat, but as a friendly warning.

"Keep quiet, my Lord; do not let yourself be guided by your quick temper; do not be so free in the use of suspense and interdicts. These terrible arms are two-edged swords, which very often hurt more the imprudent who make use of them than those whom they intend to strike.

"I wish to live in peace with you. I take my God to witness, that to this day I have done everything to keep peace with you. But the peace I want is the peace which St. Jerome speaks of when, writing to his Bishop, he tells him:

"'It is no use to speak of peace with the lips, if we destroy it with our works. It is a very different way to work for peace, from trying to submit every one to an abject slavery. We, also, we want peace. Not only we desire it, but we implore you instantly to give it. However, the peace we want is the peace of Christ—a true peace, a peace without hatred, a peace which is not a masked war, a peace which is not to crush enemies, but a peace which unites friends.

"'How can we call peace what is nothing but tryanny? Why should we not call everything by its proper name? Let us call hatred—what is hatred? And let us say that peace reigns only when a true love exists. We are not the authors of the troubles and divisions which exist in the Church. A father must love his children. A bishop, as well as a father, must wish to be loved, but not feared. The old proverb says, "*One hates whom he fears*," and we naturally wish for the death of the one we hate. If you do not try to crush the religious men under your power they will submit themselves to your authority. Offer them the kiss of love and peace and they will obey you. But liberty refuses to yield as soon as you try to crush it down. The best way to be obeyed by a free man is not to deal with him as with a slave. We know the laws of the Church, and we do not ignore the rights which belong to every man. We have learned many things, not only from long experience, but also from the study of books. The king who strikes his subjects with an iron rod, or who thinks that his fingers must be heavier than his father's hand, has soon destroyed the kingdom even of the peaceful and mild David. The people of Rome refused to bear the yoke of their proud king.

"'We have left our country in order to live in peace. In this solitude our intention was to respect the authority of the pontiffs of Christ (we mean those who teach the true faith). We want to respect them not as our masters, but as our fathers. Our intention was to respect them as Bishops, not as usurpers and tyrants who want to reduce us to slavery by the abuse of their power. We are not so vain as to ignore what is due to the priests of Christ, for to receive them is to receive the very One whose Bishops they are. But let them be satisfied with the respect which is due to them. Let them remember that they are fathers, not masters, of those who have given up everything in order to enjoy the privileges of a peaceful solitude. May Christ who is our mighty God grant that we should be united, not by a false peace, but by a true and loyal love, lest that by biting each other we destroy each other.'

[Letter of St. Jerome to his Bishop.]

"You have a great opinion of the episcopal power, and so have I. But St. Paul and all the Holy Fathers that I have read, have also told us many things of the dignity of the priest (after Christus Sacerdos). I am your brother and equal in many things; do not forget it. I know my dignity as a man and as a priest, and I shall sooner lose my life than to surrender them to any man, even a Bishop. If you think you can deal with me as a carter with his horse, drawing him where he likes, you will very soon see your error.

"I neither drink strong wines nor smoke, and the many hours *that others spent in emptying their bottles and smoking their pipes*, I read my dear books—I study the admirable laws of the Church and the Gospel of Christ. I love my books and the holy laws of our Church, because they teach me my rights as well as my duties. They tell me that many years ago a general council, which is something above you, has annulled your unjust sentence, and brought upon your head the very penalty you intended to impose upon me. They tell me that any sentence from you, coming (from your own profession) from bad and criminal motives, is null, and will fall powerless at my feet.

"But I tell you again, that I desire to live in peace with you. The false reports of LeBelle and Carthevel have disturbed that peace; but it is still in your power to have it for yourself and to give it to me. I am sure that the sentence you say you have preferred against me is coming from a misunderstanding, and your wisdom and charity, if you can hear their voice, can very easily set everything as they were two months ago. It is still in your power to have a warm friend, or an immovable adversary in Kankakee County. It would both be equitable and honorable in you to extinguish the fires of discord which you have so unfortunately enkindled, by drawing back a sentence which you would never have proffered if you had not been deceived. You would be blessed by the Church of Illinois, and particularly by the 10,000 French Canadians who surround me, and are ready to support me at all hazards.

"Do not be angry from the seeming harsh words which you find in this letter. Nobody could tell you these sad truths, though every one of your priests, and particularly those who flatter you the most, repeat them every day.

"By kind and honest proceedings you can get everything from me, even the last drop of my blood; but you will find me an immovable rock if you approach me as you have always done (but once) with insults and tyrannical threats.

"You have not been ordained a Bishop to rule over us according to your fancy, but you have the eternal laws of justice and equity to guide you. You have the laws of the Church to obey as well as her humblest child, and as soon as you do anything against these imperishable laws you are powerless to obtain your object. It is not only lawful, but a duty to resist you. When you strike without a legitimate or a canonical cause; when you try to take away my character to please some of your friends; when you order me to exile to stop a suit which you are inciting against me; when you punish me for the crime of refusing to obey the orders you gave me to be the friend of three public rogues; when you threaten me with excommunication, because I do not give you my little personal properties, I have nothing to fear from your interdicts and excommunication.

"What a sad lot for me, and what a shame for you, if by your continual attacks at the doors of our churches or in the public press, you oblige me to expose your injustice. It is yet time for you to avoid that. Instead of striking me like an outcast, come and give me the paternal hand of charity, instead of continuing that fratricidal combat. Come and heal the wounds you have made and already received. Instead of insulting me by driving me away from my colony to the land of exile, come and bless the great work I have begun here for the glory of God and the good of my people. Instead of destroying the college and the female academy, for the erection of which I have expended my last cent, and whose teachers are fed at my table, come and bless the three hundred little children who are daily attending our schools.

"Instead of sacrificing me to the hatred of my enemies, come and strengthen my heart against their fury.

"I tell you again, that no consideration whatever will induce me to surrender my right as a Catholic priest *and as an American citizen.* By the first title you cannot interdict me, as long as I am a good priest, for the crime of wishing to live in my colony and among my people. *By the second title, you cannot turn me out from my home.*

"C. CHINIQUY."

It was the first time that a Roman Catholic priest with his whole people had dared to speak such language to a Bishop of Rome on this continent. Never yet had the unbearable tyranny of those haughty men received such a public rebuke. Our fearless words fell as a bombshell in the camp of the Roman Catholic hierarchy of America.

With very few exceptions, the press of the State of Illinois, whose columns had so often echoed the cries of indignation raised everywhere against the tyranny of Bishop O'Regan, took sides with me. Hundreds of priests, not only from Illinois, but from every corner of the United States, addressed their warmest thanks to me for the stand I had taken, and asked me, in the name of God and for the honor of the Church, not to yield an inch of my rights. Many promised to support us at the court of Rome, by writing themselves to the Pope, to denounce not only the Bishop of Illinois, but several others, who, though not so openly bad, were yet trampling under their feet the most sacred rights of the priests and the people. Unfortunately those priests gave me a saddening knowledge of their cowardice by putting in their letters "*Absolutely confidential.*" They all promised to help me when I was storming the strong fortress of the enemy, provided I would go alone in the gap, and that they would keep themselves behind thick walls, far from shot and shell.

However, this did not disturb me, for, my God knows it, my trust was not in my own strength, but in his protection. I was sure that I was in the right, that the Gospel of Christ was on my side, that all the canons and laws of the councils were in my favor.

My library was filled with the best books on the canons and the laws passed in the great councils of my Church. It was written in big letters in the celebrated work, "*Histoire du droit canonique.*" There is no arbitrary power in the Church of Christ. (Vol. III, page 139.)

The Council of Augsburg, held in 1548 (Can. 24), had declared that, "no sentence of excommunication will be passed, except for great crimes."

The Pope St. Gregory had said: "That censurers are well when not inflicted for great sins or for faults which have not been clearly proved."

"An unjust excommunication does not bind before God those against whom it has been hushed. But it injures only the one who has proffered it."

(Eccl. Laws, by HERICOURT, C. XXII, No. 50.)

"If an unjust sentence is pronounced against any one he must not pay any attention to it; for, before God and his Church, an unjust sentence cannot injure anybody. Let, then, that person do nothing to get such an unjust sentence repealed, for it cannot injure him."

(St. Gelace—The Pope—*Canoni bin est.*)

The canonists conclude, from all the laws of the Church on that matter, "That if a priest is unjustly interdicted or excommunicated he may continue to officiate without any fear of becoming irregular."

(Eccl. Laws, by HERICOURT, C. XXII, No. 51.)

Protected by these laws, and hundreds of others too long to enumerate, which my Church had passed in every age, strengthened by the voice of my conscience, which assured me that I had done nothing to deserve to be interdicted or excommunicated; sure, besides, of the testimony brought by our four delegates that the Bishop himself had declared that I was one of his best priests, that he wanted to give me my letters to go and perform the functions of my ministry in Cahokia. Above all, knowing the unanimous will of my people that I should remain with them and continue the great and good work so providentially trusted to me in my colony, and regarding this as an indication of the Divine will, I determined to remain, in spite of the fulminations of the Bishop of Chicago. All the councils of my Church were telling me that he had no power to injure me, and that all his official acts were null.

But if he were spiritually powerless against me, it was not so in temporal matters. His power and his desire to injure us had increased with his hatred, since he had read our letters and seen them in all the papers of Chicago.

The first thing he did was to reconcile himself to the priest LeBelle, whom he had turned out ignominiously from his diocese some time before. That priest had since that obtained a fine situation in the diocese of Michigan. He invited him to his palace, and petted him several days. I felt that the reconciliation of those two men meant nothing good for me. But my hope was, more than ever, that the merciful God who had protected me so many times against them, would save me again from their machinations. The air was, however, filled with the strangest rumors against me. It is said everywhere that Mr. LeBelle was to bring such charges against my character that I would be sent to the penitentiary.

What were the new iniquities to be laid to my charge? No one could tell. But the few partisans and friends of the Bishop, Messrs. LeBelle and Spink were jubilant and sure that I was to be forever destroyed.

At last the time arrived when the Sheriff of Kankakee had to drag me again as a criminal and a prisoner to Urbana, and deliver me into the hands of the Sheriff of that city. I arrived there on the 20th of October with my lawyers, Messrs. Osgood and Paddock, and a dozen witnesses. Mr. Abraham Lincoln had preceded me only by a few minutes from Springfield. He was in the company of Judge David Davis, to-day (1883) Vice-President of the United States, when I met him.

The jury having been selected and sworn, the Rev. Mr. LeBelle was the first witness called to testify and say what he knew against my character.

Mr. Lincoln objected to that kind of testimony, and tried

to prove that Mr. Spink had no right to bring his new suit against me by attacking my character. But Judge Davis ruled that the prosecution had that right in the case that was before him. Mr. LeBelle had, then, full liberty to say anything he wanted, and he availed himself of his privilege. His testimony lasted nearly an hour, and was too long to be given here. I will only say that he began by declaring that " Chiniquy was one of the vilest men of the day—that every kind of bad rumors were constantly circulating against him. He gave a good number of those rumors, though he could not positively swear if they were founded on truth or not, for he had not investigated them. But he said that there was one of which he was sure, for he had authenticated it thoroughly. He expressed a great deal of apparent regret that he was forced to reveal to the world such things, which were not only against the honor of Chiniquy, but, to some extent, involved the good name of a dear sister, Madame Bossy. But as he was to speak the truth before God, he could not help it—the sad truth was to be told. " *Mr. Chiniquy*, he said, "*had attempted to do the most infamous things with my own sister, Madame Bossy.* She herself has told me the whole story under oath, and she would be here to unmask the wicked man to-day before the whole world, if she were not forced to silence at home from a severe illness."

Though every word of that story *was a perjury*, there was such a color of truth and sincerity in my accuser, that his testimony fell upon me and my lawyers and all my friends as a thunderbolt. A man who has never heard such a calumny brought against him before a jury in a court-house packed with people, composed of friends and foes, will never understand what I felt in this the darkest hour of my life. My God only knows the weight and the bitterness of the waves of desolation which then passed over my soul.

After that testimony was given there was a lull and a most profound silence in the court-room. All the eyes were turned upon me, and I heard many voices speaking of me, whispering, "The villain!" Those voices passed through my soul as poisoned arrows. Though innocent, I wished that the ground would open under my feet and bring me down to the darkest abysses, to conceal me from the eyes of my friends and the whole world.

However, Mr. Lincoln soon interrupted the silence by addressing to LeBelle such cross-questions that his testimony, in the minds of many, soon lost much of its power. And he did still more destroy the effect of his (LeBelle's) false oath, when he brought my twelve witnesses, who were among the most respectable citizens of Bourbonnais, formerly the parishioners of Mr. LeBelle. Those twelve gentlemen swore that Mr. LeBelle was such a drunkard and vicious man that he was so publicly my enemy on account of the many rebukes I had given to his private and public vices, that they would not believe a word of what he said, even upon his oath.

At ten P. M. the Court was adjourned, to meet again the next morning, and I went to the room of Mr. Lincoln with my two other lawyers, to confer about the morning's work. My mind was unspeakably sad. Life had never been such a burden to me as in that hour. I was tempted, with Job, to curse the hour when I was born. I could see in the face of my lawyers, though they tried to conceal it, that they were also full of anxiety.

"My dear Mr. Chiniquy," said Mr. Lincoln, "though I hope, to-morrow, to destroy the testimony of Mr. LeBelle against you, I must concede that I see great dangers ahead. *There is not the least doubt in my mind that every word he has said is a sworn lie;* but my fear is that the jury thinks differently. I am a pretty good judge in these matters. I feel that our jurymen think that you are guilty. There is only one way to perfectly destroy the power of a false witness—it is by another direct testimony against what he has said, or by showing from his very lips that he has perjured himself. I failed to do that last night, though I have diminished, to a great extent, the force of his testimony. Can you not prove an alibi, or can you not bring witnesses who were there in the same house that day, who would flatly and directly contradict what your remorseless enemy has said against you?"

I answered him: "How can I try to do such a thing when they have been shrewd enough not to fix the very date of the alleged crime against me?"

"You are correct, you are perfectly correct, Mr. Chiniquy," answered Mr. Lincoln, "as they have refused to precise the date, we cannot try that. *I have never seen two such skillful rogues as those two priest. There is really a diabolical skill in the plan they have concocted for your destruction. It is evident that the Bishop is at the bottom of the plot.* You remember how I have forced LeBelle to confess that he was now on the most friendly terms with the Bishop of Chicago since he has become the chief of your accusers. Though I do not give up the hope of rescuing you from the hands of your enemies, I do not like to conceal from you that I have several reasons to fear that you will be declared guilty and condemned to a heavy penalty, or to the penitentiary, *though I am sure you are perfectly innocent.* It is very probable that we will have to confront that sister of LeBelle to-morrow. Her sickness is probably a feint, in order not to appear here except after the brother will have prepared the public mind in her favor. At all events, if she does not come, they will send some justice of the peace to get her sworn testimony, which will be more difficult to rebut than her own verbal declarations. That woman is evidently in the hands of the Bishop and her brother priest, ready to swear anything they order her, and I know nothing so difficult as to refute such female testimonies, particularly when they are absent from the court. The only way to be sure of a favorable verdict to-morrow is, that *God Almighty would take our part and show your innocence!* Go to Him and pray, for He alone can save you."

Mr. Lincoln was exceedingly solemn when he addressed those words to me, and they went very deep into my soul.

I have often been asked if Abraham Lincoln had any religion? But I never had any doubt about his profound confidence in God, since I heard those words falling from his lips in that hour of anxiety. I had not been able to conceal my deep distress. Burning tears were rolling on my cheeks when he was speaking, and there was on his face the expression of friendly sympathy which I will never forget. Without being able to say a word, I left him to go to my little room. It was nearly eleven o'clock. I locked the door and fell on my knees to pray, but I was unable to say a single word. The horrible sworn calumnies thrown at my face by a priest of my own Church were ringing in my ears; my honor and my good name so cruelly and forever destroyed; all my friends and my dear people covered with an eternal confusion; and more than that, the sentence of condemnation which was probably to be hurled against me the next day in the presence of the whole country, whose eyes were upon me! All those things were before me, not only as horrible phantoms, but as heavy mountains, under the burdens of which I could not breathe. At last the fountains of tears were opened and it relieved me to weep; I could then speak and cry: "Oh! my God! have mercy upon me! thou knowest my innocence! hast thou not promised that those who trust in Thee cannot perish! Oh! do not let me perish when Thou art the only One in whom I trust! Come to my help! Save me!"

From eleven P. M. to three in the morning I cried to God, and raised my supplicating hands to his throne of mercy. But I confess to my confusion, it seemed to me in certain moments, that it was useless to pray and to cry, for though innocent, I was doomed to perish. I was in the hands of my enemies. My God had forsaken me.

What an awful night I spent! I hope none of my readers will ever know by their own experience the agony of spirit I endured. I had no other expectation than to be forever dishonored and sent to the penitentiary the next morning! But God had not forsaken me! He had again heard my cries, and was once more to show me His infinite mercy!

At three o'clock A. M. I heard three knocks at my door and I quietly went to open it. "Who was there? *Abraham Linham Lincoln, with a face beaming with joy!*"

I could hardly believe my eyes. But I was not mistaken. It was my noble-hearted friend, the most honest lawyer of Illinois!—one of the noblest men Heaven had ever given to earth. It was Abraham Lincoln who had been given me as my protector! On seeing me bathed with tears, he exclaimed, "*Cheer up, Mr. Chiniquy, I have the perjured priests in my hands. Their diabolical plot is all known, and if they do not fly away before the dawn of day they will surely be lynched. Bless the Lord, you are saved!*"

The sudden passage of extreme desolation to an extreme joy came near killing me. I felt as suffocated, and unable to utter a single word. I took his hand, pressed it to my lips, and bathed it with tears of joy. I said: "May God forever bless you, dear Mr. Lincoln. But please tell me how you can bring me such glorious news!"

Here is the simple but marvellous story, as told me by that great and good man whom God had made the messenger of his mercies towards me:

"As soon as LeBelle had given his perjured testimony against you yesterday," said Mr. Lincoln, "one of the agents of the Chicago press telegraphed to some of the principal papers of Chicago: 'It is probable that Mr. Chiniquy will be condemned, for the testimony of the Rev'd Mr. LeBelle seems to leave no doubt that he is guilty.' And the little Irish boys, to sell their papers, filled the streets with the cries: 'Chiniquy will be hung! Chiniquy will be hung!' The Roman Catholics were so glad to hear that, that ten thousand extra copies have been sold. Among those who bought those papers was a friend of yours, called Terrien, who went to his wife and told her that you were to be condemned, and when the woman heard that she said, 'It is too bad, *for I know Mr. Chiniquy is not guilty.*' 'How do you know that?' said the husband. She answered: '*I was there when the priest LeBelle made the plot, and promised to* give his sister two eighties of good land if she would swear a false oath—and accuse him of a crime which that woman said he had not even thought of with her.'

"'If it be so,' said Terrien, "we cannot allow Mr. Chiniquy to be condemned. Come with me to Urbana.'

"But that woman being quite unwell, said to her husband, 'You know well I cannot go; but Miss Philomena Moffat was with me then. She knows every particular of that wicked plot as well as I do. She is well; go and take her to Urbana. There is no doubt that her testimony will prevent the condemnation of Mr. Chiniquy.'

"That Narcisse Terrien started immediately, and when you were praying God to come to your help, He was sending your deliverer at the full speed of the railroad cars. Miss Moffat has just given me the details of that diabolical plot. I have advised her not to show herself before the Court is opened. I will then send for her, and when she will have given, under oath, before the Court, the details she has just given me, I pity Spink with his perjured priests. As I told you, I would not be surprised if they were lynched, for there is a terrible excitement in town among many people, who from the beginning suspect that the priests have perjured themselves to destroy you.

"Now your suit is gained, and to-morrow you will have the greatest triumph a man ever got over his confounded foes. But you are in need of rest as well as myself. Goodbye."

After thanking God for that marvellous deliverance, I went to bed and took the needed rest.

But what was the priest LeBelle doing in that very moment? Unable to sleep after the awful perjury he had just made, he had watched the arrival of the trains from Chicago with an anxious mind, for he was aware, through the confessions he had heard, that there were two persons in that city who knew his plot and his false oath; and though he had the promises from them that they would never reveal it to anybody, he was not without some fearful apprehension that I might, by some way or other, become acquainted with his abominable conspiracy. Not long after the arrival of the trains from Chicago, he came down from his room to see in the book where the travelers register their names, if there were any newcomers from Chicago, and what was his dismay when he saw the first name entered was " *Philomena Moffat!*" That very name Philomena Moffat, who some time before had gone to confess to him that she had heard the whole plot from his own lips, when he had promised one hundred and sixty acres of land to persuade his sister to perjure herself in order to destroy me. A deadly presentiment chilled the blood in his veins! "Would it be possible that this girl is here to reveal and prove my perjury before the world?"

He immediately sent for her, when she was just coming from meeting Mr. Lincoln.

"Miss Philomena Moffat here! he exclaimed, when he saw her. "What are you coming here for this night?" he said.

"You will know it, sir, to-morrow morning," she answered.

"Ah! wretched girl! you come to destroy me?" he exclaimed.

She replied: "I do not come to destroy you, for you are already destroyed. Mr. Lincoln knows everything."

"Oh! my God! my God!" he exclaimed, in striking his forehead with his hands. Then taking a big bundle of bank-notes from his pocket-book, he said: "Here are one hundred dollars for you if you take the morning train and go back to Chicago."

"If you would offer me as much gold as this house could contain I would not go," she replied.

He then left her abruptly, ran to the sleeping-room of Spink, and told him: "Withdraw your suit against Chiniquy; we are lost; he knows all."

Without losing a moment, he went to the sleeping-room of his co-priest, Carthumel, and told him, "Make haste—dress yourself and let us take the morning train; we have no business here, Chiniquy knows all our secrets."

When the hour of opening the Court came, there was an immense crowd, not only inside, but outside its walls. Mr. Spink, pale as a man condemned to death, rose before the Judge and said: " Please the Court, allow me to withdraw my prosecution against Mr. Chiniquy. I am now persuaded that he is not guilty of the faults brought against him before this tribunal."

Abraham Lincoln, having accepted that reparation in my name, made a short but one of the most admirable speeches I have ever heard, on the cruel injustices I had suffered from my merciless persecutors, and denounced the rascality of the priests who had perjured themselves, with such terrible colors, that it had been very wise on their part to fly away and disappear before the opening of the Court. For the whole city was ransacked for them by hundreds, who blamed me for forgiving them and refusing to have my revenge for the wrong they had done me. But I really thought that my enemies were sufficiently punished by the awful public disclosures of their infernal plot. It seemed that the dear Saviour who had so visibly protected me, was to be obeyed, when he was whispering into my soul, "Forgive them and love them as thyself."

Was not Spink sufficiently punished by the complete ruin which was brought upon him by the loss of that suit? *For having gone to Bishop O'Regan to be indemnified for the enormous expenses of such a long prosecution, at such a distance,* the Bishop coldly answered him: "*I had promised to indemnify if you would put Chiniquy down, as you promised me. But as it is Chiniquy who has put you down, I have not a cent to give you.*"

Abraham Lincoln had not defended me only with the zeal and talent of the ablest lawyer I have ever known, but as the most devoted and noblest friend I ever had. After giving more than a year of his precious time to my defense, and that he had pleaded during two long sessions of the

Court at Urbana without receiving a cent from me, I considered that I was owing him a great sum of money. My two other lawyers, who had not done the half of his work, had asked me a thousand dollars each, and I had not thought that too much. After thanking him for the appreciable services he had rendered me, I requested him to show me his bill, assuring him that, though I would not be able to pay the whole cash, I would pay him to the last cent, if he had the kindness to wait a little for the balance.

He answered me with a smile and an air of inimitable kindness, which was peculiar to him: " My dear Mr. Chiniquy, I feel proud and honored to have been called to defend you. But I have done it less as a lawyer than as a friend. The money I should receive from you would take away the pleasure I feel at having fought your battle. Your case is unique in my whole practice. *I have never met a man so cruelly persecuted as you have been, and who deserve it so little. Your enemies are devils incarnate. The plot they had concocted against you is the most hellish one I ever knew.* But the way you have been saved from their hands, the appearance of that young and intelligent Miss Moffat, who was really sent by God in the very hour of need, when, I confess it again, I thought everything was nearly lost, is one of the most extraordinary occurrences I ever saw. It makes me remember what I have too often forgotten, and what my mother often told me when young—that our God is a prayer-hearing God. This good thought sown into my young heart by that dear mother's hand, was just in my mind when I told you, ' Go and pray, God alone can save you.' But I confess to you that I had not faith enough to believe that your prayer would be so quickly and so marvelously answered by the sudden appearance of that interesting young lady last night. Now let us speak of what you owe me. Well!—well—how much do you owe me? *You owe me nothing; for I suppose you are quite ruined.* The expenses of such a suit, I know, must be enormous. Your enemies want to ruin you. *Will I help them to finish your* ruin, when I hope I have the right to be put among the most sincere and devoted of your friends?"

"You are right," I answered him; "you are the most devoted and noblest friend God ever gave me, and I am nearly ruined by my enemies. But you are the father of a pretty large family; you must support them. Your traveling expenses in coming twice here for me from Springfield; your hotel bills during the two terms you have defended me must be very considerable. It is not just that you should receive nothing in return of such work and expenses."

"Well! well!" he answered, "I will give you a promissory note which you will sign;" taking then a small piece of paper, he wrote:

"URBANA, May 23, 1856.

"Due A. Lincoln fifty dollars, for value received."

He handed me the note, saying, "Can you sign that?"

After reading it, I said, "Dear Mr. Lincoln, this is a joke. It is not possible that you ask only fifty dollars for services which are worth at least two thousand dollars."

He then tapped me with the right hand on the shoulders and said: "Sign that; it is enough. I will pinch some rich men for that and make them pay the rest of the bill, and he laughed outright.

I signed the note, which I paid to him six months later; and that note is still in my hands, as a precious relic of the noblest man God ever put at the head of the great Republic. I thought it was my duty to go and express my respect every year to Abraham Lincoln at "the White House" in Washington, when he was President, and four times I went there to renew the assurance of my gratitude for what he had done, and every time he gave me the most touching proofs of his kindness and friendship. He especially invited me to be with him, and he put me at his right hand, the nearest to him, when the deputies of whole Northern States came to tell him that he was unanimously selected to continue to direct the helm of this great country during the next four years.

I would have many interesting things to say of that good and great man were I not prevented by the short limits of this chapter. Suffice it to say, *that it was by his advice* that I requested Miss Philomena Moffat, who is now one of the most respectable ladies of Chicago, under the name of Mrs. Philomena Schwartz, to give under oath the facts which she told to Mr. Lincoln on the night of —— October, eighteen hundred and fifty-six. Here is her solemn oath:

"STATE OF ILLINOIS, } ss.
  Cook County, }

"Philomena Schwartz, being first duly sworn, deposes and says: That she is of the age of twenty-three years, and resides at 484 Milwaukie Avenue, Chicago; that her maiden name was Philomena Moffat; that she knew Father LeBelle, the Roman Catholic priest of the French Catholics of Chicago during his lifetime, and knows Rev. Father Chiniquy; that about the month of May, A. D. 1854, in company with Miss Eugenia Bossey, the housekeeper of her uncle, the Rev'd Mr. LeBelle, who was then living at the parsonage on Clark street, Chicago, while we were sitting in the room of Miss Bossey, the Rev. Mr. LeBelle was talking with his sister, Mrs. Bossey, in the adjoining room, *not suspecting that we were there hearing his conversation through the door which was partly opened*; though we could neither see him nor his sister, *we heard every word of what they said* together, the substance of which is as follows—Rev. Mr. LeBelle in substance to Mrs. Bossey, his sister:

"'You know that Mr. Chiniquy is a dangerous man, and he is my enemy, having already persuaded several of my congregation to settle in his colony. *You must help me to put him down, by accusing him of having tried to do a criminal action with you.*'

"Madame Bossey answered: '*I cannot say such a thing against Mr. Chiniquy, when I know it is absolutely false.*'

"Rev. Mr. LeBelle replied: 'If you refuse to comply with my request, *I will not give you the one hundred and sixty acres of land I intended to give you*, you will live and die poor.'

"Madame Bossey answered: 'I prefer never to have that land, and I like better to live and die poor, *than to perjure myself to please you.*'

"The Rev. Mr LeBelle several times urged his sister, Mrs. Bossey, to comply with his desires, but she refused. At last, weeping and crying, she said: '*I prefer never to have an inch of land than to damn my soul by swearing to a falsehood.*'

"The Rev. Mr. LeBelle then said:

"'Mr. Chiniquy will destroy our holy religion and our people if we do not destroy him. If you think that the swearing I ask you to do is a sin, *you will come to confess to me, and I will pardon it in the absolution I will give you.*

"'Have you the power to forgive a false oath?' replied Mrs. Bossey to her brother, the priest.

"'*Yes*,' he answered, '*I have that power;* for Christ has said to all his priests, "What you shall bind on earth shall be bound in heaven, and what you shall loose on earth shall be loosed in heaven."'

"Mrs. Bossey then said: '*If you promise that you will forgive that false oath and if you give me the one hundred and sixty acres of land you promised, I will do what you want.*'

"'The Rev'd Mr. LeBelle then said: '*All right!*'' I could not hear any more of that conversation, for in that instant Miss Eugenia Bossey, who had kept still and silent with us, made some noise and shut the door.

"Affiant further states: That some time later I went to confess to Rev. Mr. LeBelle, and I told him that I had lost my confidence in him. '*I lost my confidence in you since I heard your conversation with your sister, when you tried to persuade her to perjure herself in order to destroy Father Chiniquy.*'

"Affiant further says: That in the month of October, A. D. 1856, the Rev'd Mr. Chiniquy had to defend himself, before the civil and criminal court of Urbana, Illinois, in an action brought against him by Peter Spink; some one wrote from Urbana to a paper of Chicago, that Father Chiniquy was probably to be condemned. The paper which published that letter was much read by the Roman Catholics, who were glad to hear that that priest was to be punished. Among those who read that paper was Narcisse Terrien. He had lately been married to Miss Sara Chaussey, *who told him that Father Chiniquy was innocent; that she was present with me when Rev'd Mr. LeBelle prepared the plot with his sister, Mrs. Bossey, and promised her a large piece of land if she would swear falsely against Father Chiniquy.* Mr. Narcisse Terrien wanted to go with his wife to the residence of Father Chiniquy, but she was unwell and could not go. He came to ask me if I remembered well the conversation of Rev'd Mr. LeBelle, and if I would consent to go to Urbana to expose the whole plot before the court, and I consented.

"We started that same evening for Urbana, where we arrived late at night. *I immediately met Mr. Abraham Lincoln, one of the lawyers of Father Chiniquy, and told all that I knew about that plot.*

"That very same night the Rev'd Mr. LeBelle, having seen my name on the hotel register, came to me much excited and troubled, and said: 'Philomena, what are you here for?'

"I answered him: 'I cannot exactly tell you that; but you will probably know it to-morrow at the court-house!'

"'Oh, wretched girl!' he exclaimed, 'you have come to destroy me.'

"'I do not come to destroy you,' I replied, 'for you are already destroyed!'

"Then drawing from his portmonnaie-book a big bundle of bank-notes, which he said were worth one hundred dollars, he said: 'I will give you all this money if you will leave by the morning train and go back to Chicago.'

"I answered him: 'Though you would offer as much gold as this room can contain, I cannot do what you ask.'

"He then seemed exceedingly distressed, and he disappeared. The next morning Peter Spink requested the Court to allow him to withdraw his accusations against Father Chiniquy, and to stop his prosecutions, having, he said, found out that he, Father Chiniquy, was innocent of the things brought against him, and his request was granted. *Then the innocence and honesty of Father Chiniquy was acknowledged by the Court after it had been proclaimed by Abraham Lincoln*, who was afterwards elected President of the United States.

"(Signed) PHILOMENA SCHWARTZ.

"I, Stephen R. Moore, a Notary Public in the County of Kankakee, in the State of Illinois, and duly authorized by law to administer oaths, do hereby certify that, on this 21st day of October, A. D. 1881, Philomena Schwartz personally appeared before me, and made oath that the above affidavit by her subscribed is true, as therein stated. In witness whereto, I have hereunto set my hand and notarial seal.

"STEPHEN R. MOORE,
"Notary Public."

CHAPTER V.

FURTHER LITIGATION—BISHOP FOLEY A RELUCTANT WITNESS, ETC.

It is necessary for our purpose to give the intelligent reader further information concerning Father Chiniquy in the defense of himself and his people, before taking up our line of argument and evidence concerning Abraham Lincoln. The following appeared in the *Kankakee Times*, City of Kankakee, Illinois:

THE CHURCH OF ROME AND LIBERTY OF CONSCIENCE.

"In one of your past issues you told your readers that the Rev. Mr. Chiniquy had gained the long and formidable lawsuit instituted by the Roman Catholic Bishop to dispossess him and his people of their Church property. But you have not yet given any particulars about *the startling revelations the Bishop having to make before the Court* in reference to the still existing laws of the Church of Rome against those whom they call heretics. Nothing however is more important for every one than to know precisely what those laws are."

"As I was present when the Roman Catholic Bishop Foley of Chicago was ordered to read in Latin and translate into English those laws, I have kept a correct copy of them, and I send it to you with the request to publish it."

"The Rev. Mr. Chiniquy presented the works of St. Thomas and St. Liguori to the Bishop, requesting him to say, under oath, if those works were or were not among the highest theological authorities in the Church of Rome all over the world. After a long and serious opposition on the part of the Bishop to answer, the Court having said he (the Bishop) *was bound to answer*, the Bishop confessed that these theological works were looked upon as among the highest authorities, and that they were taught and learned in all the colleges and universities of Rome as standard works. Then the Bishop was requested to read in Latin and translate into English the following laws and fundamental principles of action against the heretics as explained by St. Thomas and Liguori:

[We omit the Latin and give the translation by the Bishop.]

"An excommunicated man is deprived of *all* civil communication with the faithful, in such a way that if he is not tolerated they can have no communication with him, as it is in the following verse:

"'It is forbidden to kiss him, pray with him, salute him, *to eat or to do any business with him.*'"

[St. Liguori, vol IX, page 162.]

"Though heretics must not be tolerated because they deserve it, we must bear them till, by a second admonition, they may be brought back to the faith of the Church. But those who, after a second admonition, remain obstinate in their errors, must not only be excommunicated, *but they must be delivered to the secular power to be exterminated.*"

"Though the heretics who repent must always be accepted to penance as often as they have fallen, they must not, in consequence of that, always be permitted to enjoy the benefits of this life. * * * * When they fall again, they are admitted to repent; *but the sentence of death must not be removed.*

[St. Thomas, vol. IV, page 91.]

"When a man is excommunicated for his apostacy, *it follows from that very fact that all those who are his subjects are released from the oath of allegiance by which they were bound to obey him.*"

[St. Thomas, vol. IV, page 94.]

The next document of the Church of Rome brought before the Court was the act of the Council of Lateran, A. D. 1215:

"We excommunicate and anathematize every heresy that exalts itself against the holy, orthodox and Catholic faith, *condemning all heretics by whatever name they may be known*—for though their faces differ, they are tied together by their tails. Such as are condemned, are to be delivered over to the secular powers *to receive due punishment. If laymen, their goods must be confiscated.* If priests, they shall be first degraded from their respective orders, *and their property applied to the use of the Church in which they have officiated.* Secular powers of all ranks and degrees are to be *warned*, induced and, *if necessary, compelled by ecclesiastical censures*, TO SWEAR *that they will exert themselves to the utmost in the defense of the faith*, AND EXTIRPATE ALL HERETICS DENOUNCED BY THE CHURCH WHO SHALL BE FOUND IN THEIR TERRITORIES. And when any person shall assume government, whether it be spiritual or temporal, *he shall be bound to abide by this decree.*"

"If any temporal lord, after having been admonished to clear his territory of heretical depravity, the metropolitan and the bishops of the province shall unite in excommunicating him. Should he remain contumacious a whole year, the fact shall be signified to the Supreme Pontiff, *who will declare his vassals released from that time*, AND WILL BESTOW HIS TERRITORY ON CATHOLICS, TO BE OCCUPIED BY THEM, ON THE CONDITION OF EXTERMINATING THE HERETICS AND PRESERVING THE SAID TERRITORY IN THE FAITH."

"Catholics who shall assume the cross *for the extermination of heretics*, shall enjoy the same indulgencies, and be protected by the same privileges as are granted to those who go to the help of the holy land. We do decree further: that *all who may have dealings with heretics*, and especially such as receive, defend or encourage them, shall be excommunicated. HE SHALL NOT BE ELIGIBLE TO ANY PUBLIC OFFICE. HE SHALL NOT BE ADMITTED AS A WITNESS. HE SHALL NEITHER HAVE THE POWER TO BEQUEATH HIS PROPERTY BY WILL NOR SUCCEED TO ANY INHERITANCE. HE SHALL NOT BRING ANY ACTION AGAINST ANY PERSON, BUT ANY ONE CAN BRING AN ACTION AGAINST HIM. SHOULD HE BE A JUDGE, HIS DECISION SHALL HAVE NO FORCE, NOR SHALL ANY CAUSE BE BROUGHT BEFORE HIM. SHOULD HE BE AN ADVOCATE, HE SHALL NOT BE ALLOWED TO PLEAD. SHOULD HE BE A LAWYER, NO INSTRUMENTS MADE BY HIM SHALL BE HELD VALID, BUT SHALL BE CONDEMNED WITH THEIR AUTHOR."

"*The Roman Catholic Bishop swore that these laws had never been repealed, and* (of course), *that they were still the laws of his Church.* He had to swear that, every year, *he was bound, under pain of eternal damnation,* to say, in the presence of God, and to read in his Brevarium (his prayer-book), that '*God himself had inspired*' what St. Thomas had written about the manner that the heretics should be treated by the Roman Catholics."

"I will abstain from making any remarks upon these startling revelations of that Roman Catholic high authority. But I think it is the duty of every citizen to know what the Roman Catholic bishops and priests understand by liberty of conscience. The Roman Catholics are as interested as the Protestants to know precisely what the teachings of their Church are on that subject of liberty of conscience, and hear the exact truth, as coming from such a high authority, that there is no room left for any doubt.

"Vox Populi."

A copy of the above having come into our hands, and after much inquiry as to the author of this communication, we learned that it was the Hon. Stephen R. Moore, an eminent lawyer of Kankakee, Illinois, who also had become one of the Rev. C. Chiniquy's counsel, and to whom we addressed letters asking for the fullest information that could be obtained, who kindly furnished all that was possible to be obtained of him in relation to the same, and of Lincoln's connection with suits brought against Chiniquy.

The following extracts from his letters are here given:

"KANKAKEE, ILL., May 15,
and June 3, 1882.

"MR. EDWIN A. SHERMAN, San Francisco, Cal.—DEAR SIR: * * * You ask, 'What Judge was upon the bench at the time the suit was brought (you mean trial), when Bishop Foley was required to translate from the works of St. Thomas Aquinas and St. Liguori? who were Chiniquy's attorney, etc.?'

"Judge Charles H. Wood: Chiniquy's attorneys were Judge Wm. Osgood (formerly associate counsel with Lincoln and Paddock) and myself.

"You ask me to give you the facts in regard to the examination of Bishop Foley, when we made him make the translations.

"We knew that he was the head of authority of the Church in Illinois. We knew that he would not dare deny the authority of the books as binding on the Church. If Mr. Chiniquy would swear to the books being authority, it would be denied by all Catholics, when they could not deny it when the proof came from the Bishop.

"We wanted to show, also, *that it was authority in the Church to-day,* as well as at the time they were published. This could only be done by forcing the Bishop to be a witness. We knew he would go away from the jurisdiction of the Court, so he could not be served with process if he knew what we wanted. Our statute allows any person, whether officer or not, to serve a subpœna. We got the process, and in my possession on the evening before the trial, and I took the evening train for Chicago. I found a friend in Chicago to go with me. I knew that if I sent up my name he would refuse to see me. My friend sent up his card, with request to see the Bishop. This was about nine o'clock at night. After a long delay, he came to the library. He was much astonished when he saw me, and looked at his card to assure himself that no mistake had occurred. I introduced my friend, who politely read the process, commanding him to appear upon the next day at Kankakee and testify in the case, at the same time tendering him his witness fees, being five cents per mile and one dollar for the day's services. He indignantly refused the money, and *declared he would not attend. He thought the courts had no power over him. He recognized no authority but the authority of the Church.* I assured him that he must do as he thought best; but he must take the consequences. It would be a contest between him and the Court, *and I had never seen the Court fail to enforce the orders of the Court.*

"He sent for the attorney for his diocese, Hon. B. G. Caulfield, and after the interview, *he had no difficulty in concluding to obey the process of Court.*

"When he went on the witness-stand we wanted Judge Osgood to handle him, but he declined. I had my subject well in hand and was quite familiar with the original, and after he made a few attempts to evade me, he came down to the work and made a good witness He never forgave me for it, however. He really felt that his high position had been lowered. *It was the first time that any lawyer had done such a thing.*"

Upon the criminal trial brought against Chiniquy, at which Father LeBelle committed perjury, Mr. Moore says:

"Mr. Lincoln told a story there that has never been in print, which convulsed Judge Davis with laughter. I got the story from Osgood and Norton. Father Chiniquy never mentioned it. The story is a little harsh to polite ears, but was quite characteristic of Mr. Lincoln, and no ladies were present when he got it off. He never offended ladies;

but some latitude was permissible in those days, when only men were in court.

[This story referred to, has already been given in Chapter II, when Lincoln asked that peculiar question of Judge Norton about the priests who attended as witnesses.]

"The lawyers then engaged in these matters have all closed the record (all dead). Peter Spinks is still alive, living somewhere in Minnesota, quite infirm, full of trouble, poor, and very bitter toward Father Chiniquy. He is very deaf, and practically lost his memory. Father LeBelle died a few years after that trial, at Kalamazoo, Michigan. (This is now my recollection.) *He died under a cloud, either by his own hand or by violence. It is generally believed that he took poison.*

"Father Chiniqny, in his book to be published soon, 'Fifty-two Years in the Romish Church,' devotes a chapter or two to the period of these Urbana law-suits, and I went to Chicago during the past year and got the affidavit of the lady who heard Father LeBelle try to make his sister falsely testify against Chiniquy [which has already been given in the last chapter].

"My dear sir, I could write you a volume of incidents in the life of Father Chiniquy, growing out of the fight which the Roman Catholic Church has made on him. They have been intensely interesting to me. I would not know where to begin. His life has been a battle since I first knew him in 1857. And in all the conflicts he has trusted in the FATHER with a trust that few men knew anything of, *and in no single instance has* GOD *failed to succor him.* Sometimes it looked as if defeat must come; but in it all was God, and He led him through trying times to signal victory. The world to-day would not believe Father Chiniquy's life. A faithful biography of him, showing the providences of God in his life and work, would be received with doubt if not downright disbelief. You would have to be with him for a quarter of a century, as I have been, and know him in his severest trials, to know the trusting confidence he has in his

Father, and see the wonderful care with which God has preserved him in his life and work.

"I have the honor to be, very respecfully, your obedient servant, STEPHEN R. MOORE."

We have deemed it thus necessary to give the main facts and the causes which brought Abraham Lincoln into the contest in defense of Father Chiniquy against the warfare waged against him by the Papal power, showing the status and honorable reputation of Father Chiniquy and the damnable conspiracy formed against him.

There is one thing, however, that is not fully stated, in regard to the settlement between Chiniquy and Lincoln in relation to the due-bill of fifty dollars which Chiniquy gave to Lincoln, as related in the last chapter, and which should fully appear in his forthcoming work of "Fifty-two Years in the Romish Church."

Father Chiniquy, in his oral statement to us, in addition to what has already been given, describes the scene between Lincoln and himself as follows, and which we believe to be true:

While Lincoln was writing the due-bill, the relaxation of the great strain upon Father Chiniquy's mind and the great kindness and generosity of his defender and benefactor in charging him so little for such great service and the forebodings of what might be in store for Lincoln in the future, caused him to break out in sobs and tears. Mr. Lincoln, as he had just finished writing the due-bill, turned round to him and said: "Father Chiniquy, what are you crying for? You ought to be the most happy man alive. You have beaten your enemies and gained a glorious victory, and you will come out of all these troubles in triumph.

Said Father Chiniquy: "Mr. Lincoln, I am not weeping for myself, *but for you, sir, and your death; they will kill you, sir.* What you have said and done in Court, holding them up in derision and making the declarations you have in Court and defeating them in ignominy and shame, *there will* be no forgiveness for you, and sooner or later they will take your life. And let me say further, that were I a Jesuit as they are, and some one of them been in my place and I in theirs, *it would be my sworn purpose to either kill you myself or find the man to do it, and you will be their victim!"*

At this Mr. Lincoln's countenance changed to a most peculiar visage, expressing determination, and with a sarcastic smile accompanying it, said: "Father Chiniquy, is that so?"

"It is," answered Father Chiniquy.

"Then," said Mr. Lincoln, as he spread out the due-bill for my signature, *"please sign my death-warrant!"*

Father Chiniquy signed the due-bill, which he shortly afterwards paid, and kindly loaned to us in the year 1878, still in our possession, and which we had laid on a lithographic stone by Wm. T. Galloway & Co. of San Francisco, and several thousand certified copies of it struck off for our brethren and friends.

It eventually *proved to be* the death-warrant of Abraham Lincoln, as we shall endeavor to show in the following chapters, and that as previously stated in Part First—"*In whatever place of the Catholic world a Jesuit is insulted or resisted, no matter how insignificant he may be, he is sure to be avenged—* AND THIS WE KNOW."

CHAPTER VI.

THE PAPAL CONSPIRACY AGAINST THE UNITED STATES AND THE REPUBLIC OF MEXICO — NATURALIZED CITIZENS ABSOLVED FROM THEIR ALLEGIANCE TO THE UNION BY ROMAN CATHOLIC BISHOPS AND PRIESTS — ARCHBISHOP HUGHES SENT TO EUROPE — PRESIDENT LINCOLN'S DECLARATIONS, ETC., ETC.

Great political events almost immediately following these lawsuits, as related in the previous chapters, soon drew Mr. Lincoln into a more active political life, and he was obliged to leave the affairs of Father Chiniquy in the hands of his associate and other counsel who succeeded him, in contesting the abuses and wanton attacks of the Romish hierarchy in the State of Illinois. Cardinal Bedini, the Papal Nuncio, had arrived with full power from Pope Pius IX. Bishop O'Regan was removed and sent elsewhere and another and more politic successor was chosen to fill his place; and he in turn was succeeded by Bishop Foley and others, who continued the litigation begun against Chiniquy to rob him and his people of their property, which they had purchased with their own money and acquired by their own industry.

Abraham Lincoln, however, from that time, was frequently the recipient of anonymous letters, filled with personal abuse and threats of vengeance and the declarations to take his life. He however gave them no particular attention, but destroyed them as soon as received, and directed his thoughts and actions to the great political questions of the day which were then agitating the public mind.

For twenty years Abraham Lincoln and Stephen A. Douglas had been invariably opposed to each other at the bar and in the forum, and they were the champions of their respective parties in the political arena. In 1857, among other questions, in which that of Intervention or Non-intertion on the part of Congress in the Territories was discussed, was that of subduing the "Mormon Rebellion." Mr. Douglas was in favor of ending the difficulty by annulling the Act establishing the Territory of Utah. Mr. Lincoln took issue with him on that point, and declared himself in favor of coercing the Mormon population into obedience to the United States Government and its laws, which declaration a few years afterwards found force in executive statement, when President, in December, 1864. He said: *"When an individual, in a Church or out of it, becomes dangerous to the public interest, he must be checked."* He understood the Mormon hierarchy in its governmental organization and its attitude towards free government of the people and the national authority to be precisely like that of Rome; but by reason of its strength and remote position it had assumed an open, bold, belligerant attitude in arms against the United States Government, and that it must be suppressed.

In 1858 the great Senatorial contest between Lincoln and Douglas was fought before the people, and in that contest the whole political power of the Roman Catholic Bishops and priesthood in Illinois was wielded in favor of Stephen A. Douglas (whose wife was of that faith, and she having been educated at the Convent in Georgetown, District of Columbia), and against their declared foe, Abraham Lincoln. So united were they in their opposition and concentrating their entire influence, money and strength to defeat Mr. Lincoln, that out of the whole Democratic vote cast, the Lecompton and Administration Democratic vote was only 5,091 votes out of 127,031, while Stephen A. Douglas received 121,940 votes, and Abraham Lincoln 126,084 votes, and the latter had a plurality over Douglas of 4,144 votes, and was fairly elected; but owing to an unjust and unequal districting of the State, the Douglas party secured the Legislature and his re-election to the United States Senate.

The current of political events, however, bore Mr. Lincoln along until he was on the 18th of May, 1860, nominated by the National Republican Convention for the office of President of the United States. This act brought him directly to the front as the leader of a great national political party only four years of age in its organization.

Immediately upon his nomination for the Presidency, Rome commenced its work of conspiracy in an open manner, as it had previously intrigued and plotted in the dark against Abraham Lincoln and against the American Union. The National Democratic party was split in twain in Hibernia Hall, at Charleston, South Carolina. The conspiracy in its political action was complete. With that great party divided the rending of the Union was to be assured, and to this end even Stephen A. Douglas with all of his great popularity and statesmanship could not save it, and he went down with his party to political disaster and defeat. The election on the 6th of November, 1860, gave Abraham Lincoln to the Republic, as the Saviour of the Union and the Redeemer of that race which for centuries had been held in bondage.

States had seceded, formed a new Confederacy, seized forts, arsenals, mints, cannon, arms and munitions of war, and with armies ready for hostilities on the field of battle, before Lincoln was inaugurated President. The emissaries of Rome, both North and South, were incessantly fanning the sparks of sectional strife which was soon to burst out in flame and not to be extinguished until flooded with rivers of the best blood of the nation. The repeated threats of assassination which Lincoln had continued to receive since his masterly defense of Chiniquy now poured in upon him from every quarter. Undaunted by these cowardly missives, Lincoln commenced his journey, February 11, 1861, from his home to which he was destined never to return alive. General Scott, Seward and others, fearful of what might occur, prepared for his peaceful inauguration at Washington. The celebrated Pinkerton with his detective force accompanied him on his journey to the Capitol of the nation. The plots for his then assassination ripened thick and fast, but through the kind providence of an Almighty God, he was then preserved to the nation to perform his mighty work. The chief plot of all, to take his life, was concocted in the then Roman Catholic city of Baltimore. It is said that "statesmen laid the plan, bankers endorsed it, and adventurers were to carry it into effect." This statement was true only in part. Rome was the head which planned it, and the Jesuits with their instruments were to execute it. But before proceeding direct to the Capitol he had accepted the invitation to raise the American flag on Independence Hall at Philadelphia, on Washington's birthday, and to visit the Legislature of Pennsylvania. Mr. Lincoln was warned that by delaying his immediate departure for Washington he would imperil his own safety, for there was positive reliable information in regard to his contemplated assassination.

Mr. Lincoln heard the officer's statement, and said in reply, "I have promised to raise the American flag on Independence Hall at Philadelphia to-morrow morning, and to be publicly received by the Pennsylvania Legislature in the afternoon of the same day. *Both of these engagements,*" said he, with emphasis, "*I will keep if it costs me my life!*"

Those engagements he faithfully kept, and in his closing remarks at Independence Hall, said: "The Declaration of Independence gave liberty not alone to the people of this country, but hope for the world for all future time. It was that which gave promise that in our time the weight should be lifted from the shoulders of all men, and that all should have an equal chance. This is the sentiment embodied in the Declaration of Independence. Now, my friends, can this country be saved upon that basis? If it can, I will consider myself one of the happiest men of the world if I can save it. *But if this country cannot be saved without giving up this principle, I was about to say, I would rather be assassinated on* THIS *spot than surrender it.*" And then he added solemnly, as he drew his tall form to its fullest height, "*I have said nothing but what I am willing to live by, and, in the presence of Almighty God, to die by!*"

[Contrast this with the pastoral letter sent out to be read in all the Roman Catholic Churches by the Fourth Roman Catholic Provincial Council, which met at Cincinnati on March 20, 1882: "It reviews the progress of religion, *and holds that all men are not created equal, but some should obey others.*" "Negroes have no rights which the white man is bound to respect," said the Roman Catholic Chief Justice of the United States Supreme Court—Judge Taney in his Dred Scott Decision.]

Mr. Lincoln then slowly but steadily raised the flag, amidst the booming of cannon and the cheers of the many thousands who had assembled to hear him and witness it.

> "*Aye, sure,* would the *priests and princes of earth,*
> Greet the fall of thy flag with a joyous ' hurrah.'
> Even now scarce suppressing demoniac mirth,
> They would hail thy decadence with a fiendish '*ha! ha!*'"
> —(MAYNE REID.)

Lincoln then left Philadelphia for Harrisburgh, where he was received by the Legislature of Pennsylvania with all the honors due to his exalted station, and in the evening left for Washington, arriving twelve hours sooner than he was expected, thus escaping the assassination intended by the conspiracy formed in Baltimore against him.

["For a long time it was believed that an Italian barber of that city was the Orsini who undertook to slay President Lincoln on his journey to the Capitol in February, 1861, and it is possible he was one of the plotters; but it has come out on a recent trial of an Irishman named *Byrne*, in Richmond, that he (*Byrne*) was the Captain of the band that was to take the life of Mr. Lincoln. This *Byrne* used to be a notorious gambler of Baltimore, and emigrated to Richmond shortly after the 19th of April, of bloody memory. He was recently arrested in Jeff. Davis' capital on a charge of keeping a gambling-house and of disloyalty to the Chief Traitor's pretended government. *Wigfall testified to Byrne's loyalty to the rebel cause, and gave in evidence that Byrne was the Captain of the gang who were to kill Mr. Lincoln,* AND UPON THIS EVIDENCE HE WAS LET GO."—*Providence Journal, April* 4, 1862.]

Abraham Lincoln having been duly inaugurated President on March 4, 1861, entered upon the duties of his office to undertake the mighty task before him.

A large portion of the Roman Catholic population of the North, with Archbishop Hughes at their head, were ostensibly true and loyal to the Union, and to their credit be it said, that, owing to their knowledge and experience of the principles and institutions of a free government of the people, that they to a certain degree were so, and under the first noble impulses of their nature they rallied promptly and volunteered their services in defense of the Government for the preservation of the Union. But as will be seen, their ardor did not last long, and their efforts were paralyzed by orders from Rome.

Scarcely had Abraham Lincoln assumed the duties and responsibilities of the executive of the nation, he found through reliable sources that he was to be confronted with a most formidable Papal conspiracy against the Union, in Europe as well as in the Canadian dominion, and that the entire Roman Catholic population of the South as well as the North, by their bishops and priests, were absolved from their allegiance to the United States Government and its President, Abraham Lincoln. In the North it was done secretly, at the South it was done openly.

An eminent Freemason of Charleston, South Carolina (now deceased), who remained loyal and true to the Union, but necessarily passive during the late War of the Rebellion, stated to us the facts that this absolving Roman Catholics from the allegiance to the Government of the United States was practiced every where. When the act of secession was passed Bishop Lynch of that State ordered a *Te Deum* to be celebrated in all the churches of his diocese, which was done. Further, that he consecrated the arms and flags of companies and regiments mustered into the rebel service. That the same was repeated on the fall of Fort Sumter, and he spoke exultingly of the result of the conflict. Father Ryan of Georgia did the same. About six weeks before the inauguration of Lincoln as President, the American flag was hauled down from the staff upon the State House at Baton Rouge, Louisiana, and the Pelican rebel flag was hoisted in its place, after having been previously consecrated with Roman Catholic ceremonies by Father Hubert; and, said the *Richmond Dispatch:* "By approval of the Roman Catholic Bishop of Louisiana, the Churches in his diocese at New Orleans and elsewhere were authorized and donated their bells for cannon in the Confederate service."

"Shortly after Gen. Phelps issued his proclamation at Ship Island in 1861, Jeff. Davis instructed his agents at Havana that 'they must create the impression with the

Spaniards that if the Federals subjugated the Confederacy, Mr. Lincoln would turn his army and navy against slavery AND THE ROMAN CATHOLIC RELIGION IN THE ISLAND OF CUBA." [See Rebellion Record.]

The Pope, with the Archbishop of Mexico, united in one object and purpose, entered into a coalition with Austria, Spain and France to not only indirectly destroy the American Union, but directly to destroy all forms of republican government on the American continent, and especially to establish upon the ruins of the Mexican Republic (then under President Juarez) an empire ruled and directed from the Vatican at Rome, as will be seen from the extract of a letter from Pope Pius IX to the Emperor Maximilian of October 18, 1864, which was captured with other papers, and may now be found at Washington:

"[Diplomatic Correspondence U. S., Part III, 1865, page 620]—

"Heretofore, and on more than one occasion, we have made complaints on this point, in public and solemn acts, protesting against the iniquitous law called that of reform, which overturned the most inviolable rights of the Church and outraged the authority of its pastors, against the usurpations of ecclesiastical property and the plunder of the Church; against the false maxims which directly attacked the holiness of the Catholic religion; finally, against many other outrages committed against sacred persons, but against the pastoral ministry and the discipline of the Church."

"Let no one obtain permission to teach and publish false maxims * * * *let instruction, public as well as private, be directed and superintended by ecclesiastical authority;* and, finally, let the chains be broken that have hitherto retained the Church dependent on the arbitrary control of the civil government."

This letter, of which the above is an extract, was sent in answer to certain acts of Emperor Maximilian, by which he confirmed several decrees of President Juarez in relation to religious toleration, public education, and in relation to the alienation of some Church property which had belonged to the intriguing treason-plotting Jesuits who had been expelled from that country.

Said Bancroft, the historian, in his eulogy of Abraham Lincoln, delivered February 12, 1866, before both houses of Congress, the President and Cabinet, the U. S. Supreme Court, the officers of the Army and Navy and the diplomatic Corps assembled:

"But the Republic of Mexico on our borders was, like ourselves, distracted by a rebellion, and from a similar cause."

"The monarchy of England had fastened upon us slavery which did not disappear with independence. In like manner the ecclesiastical policy established by the Council of the Indies in the days of Charles V and Philip II retained its vigor in the Mexican Republic. The fifty years of civil war under which she had languished was due to the bigoted system which was the legacy of monarchy, just as here the inheritance of slavery kept alive political strife and culminated in civil war. As with us there could be no quiet but through the end of slavery, so in Mexico there could be no prosperity until the crushing tyranny of intolerance should cease."

"It was the condition of affairs in Mexico *that involved the Pope of Rome in our difficulties so far that he alone among sovereigns recognized the Chief of the Confederate States as a President and his supporters as a people; and in letters to two great prelates of the Roman Catholic Church in the United States, gave Councils for peace when peace meant the victory of secession.* Yet events move as they are ordered. The blessing of the Pope of Rome on the head of the Duke Maximilian could not revive in the nineteenth century the ecclesiastical policy of the sixteenth; and the result is a new proof that there can be no prosperity in the State without religious freedom."

[On the 3d day of December, 1863, the Pope acknowledged the independence of the Southern Confederacy.]

When the Secession Convention of the Southern Confederacy met at Montgomery, Ala., Dec. 9, 1860, Mr. Memminger presented two flags in each of which was the cross, to take the place of the stars and stripes. One of them being sent by some Roman Catholic young ladies from Charleston, South Carolina. In his remarks he said: "But, sir, I have no doubt that there was another idea associated with it in their minds—*a religious one;* and, although we have not yet seen in the heavens the '*in hoc signo vinces*' written upon the labarum of Constantine, *yet the same sign has been manifested to us upon the tablets of the earth;* FOR WE ALL KNOW *that it has been by the aid of revealed religion that we have achieved over fanaticism the victory which we this day witness; and it is becoming, on this occasion,* THAT THE DEBT OF THE SOUTH TO THE CROSS SHOULD BE THUS RECOGNIZED."

This was the Latin or Papal cross, with the stars of the rebel States upon it, which had swallowed them all—the cross in blue, upon a field of blood. The objection to such a flag from Protestants and Jews caused them for awhile to adhere to the "stars and bars," copied after the "old flag;" but the secret compact and alliance of the chief conspirators with Rome must be kept, and the *cross must be in the flag somehow, and the stars on the cross must be retained;* but to silence the murmurings and objections of the Protestants and Jews the cross was made diagonal—a St. Andrew's cross—with the intention in the future to restore the Latin or Papal cross to its original place. It was this flag that was presented to the rebel army by Beauregard, the Roman Catholic General, and that floated at the mast-head of the *Alabama,* when commanded by the Jesuit, Raphael Semmes, which was sunk by the *Kearsarge,* and everywhere to go down in defeat before the heaven-born glory, the banner of the free, our own loved stars and stripes.

Said the *Mobile Register:* "When Admiral Semmes was

told by his physicians that his disease would prove fatal, and that a few hours, or at most days, would end his earthly career, he kindly thanked them, and requested a *reverend father of the Society of Jesus, his confessor, his bosom friend,* be sent for at once. In the meantime he arranged his earthly affairs quietly and satisfactorily. When the Father came, the Admiral received with marked devotion and happiness the sacrament," etc.

When President Lincoln found himself and the Union so thoroughly beset with difficulties and conspiracies, and having received reliable and authentic information of the Papal hierarchy in the South and elsewhere absolving Roman Catholics from their allegiance to the United States Government, he sent an invitation to Archbishop Hughes of New York, to come to Washington, where the following conversation between them took place:

Said Mr. Lincoln, "Archbishop Hughes, I have invited you here as the chief representative and episcopal dignitary of the Roman Catholic Church in the United States, for the purpose of a conference with you, the result of which, I trust, will be of benefit to the country and satisfactory to ourselves. The various religious denominations in the South have, in many places, openly declared their sympathy with the Rebellion, and through their representatives in their various conventions, conferences, etc., regard the division of the Union as a fixed fact. 'The Protestant Episcopal Church of the Confederate States' is already a separate institution, while the 'Methodist Episcopal Church South,' which years ago split off from the main body, has made its declarations in favor of its own section, but retains some organizations and authority in States that are not in revolt. The Southern Baptists and others have done the same, and as religious organizations, have become political, and declared in favor of secession. These Protestant religious societies, both clerical and laity, are purely local, and with no foreign spiritual head or Church government to direct or control them, and their pastors are chosen and accepted by the popular voice from among themselves. To a great extent, however, though they have gone in a wrong direction in national affairs, but they have followed out the American idea of self-government, and nine hundred and ninety-nine per cent. out of a thousand in numbers are native and to the manor born, and in no portion of the United States, as you are no doubt well aware, is the prejudice against the foreign-born population so great as it is in the South. Yet throughout the South, and in a great many places in the North, as I am reliably informed through authentic sources and in the public press, the bishops and priests of your Church, acting under an implied if not direct authority from the Pope, whose declared sympathy is with the Rebellion, have absolved all Roman Catholic citizens from their allegiance to the United States Government, encouraged them in acts of rebellion and treason, and have consecrated the arms and flags borne by the insurgent troops which have been raised to fight against the Union. Bishop Lynch of Charleston, South Carolina, Fathers Ryan of Georgia, and Hubert of Louisiana, and others, have been particularly active and conspicuous in this work."

"I have sent for you chiefly on the score of humanity. I do not want this war, which has been so wickedly begun for the destruction of the Union, to become a religious one. It is bad enough as it is, but it would become ten-fold worse should it eventually take that shape, and its consequences no one now living could foresee. There is an apparent coalition between the Pope and Jefferson Davis, at the head of the rebel government, and the acts of his bishops and priests in the South and elsewhere confirm this opinion. And if such be the case, the others in authority and the laity in the North must naturally be influenced and governed in their actions by what is sanctioned and directed by their Spiritual Head at Rome. Their loyalty to the Government of the United States would naturally wane; they would become neutral and passive if at last they did not become active sympathisers with the Rebellion, and they soon take up arms as auxiliaries against the Union. Your Church is a unit with a supreme head and not divisible. Its chief is a temporal sovereign, who wields the scepter over the States of the Church in his own country, and so far as he can do so by concordats, treaties or otherwise, enforces the establishment of the Roman Catholic Church as the religion of the State with other powers where he is able to, and looks with a jealous eye upon all governments where he does not command the secular arm, or where his authority in temporal affairs is disputed.

"Now what I desire to state to you is, the definition of the rights of an American citizen as towards his government so far as they apply to the matter in question. A native born American citizen has the inherent right of revolution within his own country. If he does not like to obey the laws of his government or wants to set up a new government, by exciting revolt and takes up arms to overturn it, he has the inherent right to do so within the limits of the territorial boundaries of his government, but not to destroy or segregate any portion of his common country from the rest, and he must take his chances of his treason and rebellion in the success or defeat of his object. Not so, however, with the naturalized foreign-born citizen, *he has no such right*. He cannot become a President or Vice-President under our own Constitution, and he is not accorded the same rights and privileges under the rebel government that he enjoys under that of the United States. Every naturalized citizen is bound by his oath in his renunciation of allegiance to every other power, prince or potentate on the face of the earth, and is sworn to support and defend the Constitution and Government of the United States against all its enemies whatsoever, either domestic or foreign. Now after having taken that oath, he cannot renounce it in favor of any other government within its territorial limits, and if found to be giving aid, sympathy or encouragement to its enemies, or is captured with arms in his hands fighting against the government which he has sworn to support, he is *liable to be shot or hung as a perjured traitor and an armed spy, as the sentence of a court martial may direct*, AND HE W'LL BE SO SHOT OR HUNG ACCORDINGLY, AS THERE WILL BE NO EXCHANGE OF SUCH PRISONERS. If a naturalized citizen finds that he cannot comply with his oath of naturalization, he must leave the country, or abide the consequences of his disaffection and disloyalty.

"The position in which the bishops and priests of your Church in the South have placed the naturalized citizens belonging to their faith, as well as themselves, is a perilous one, and their acts must be recalled and annulled by the Pope, or they and their followers must abide the results of their perjured and treasonable action."

Archbishop Hughes, nominally a Union man, and necessarily for policy's sake, if nothing else, compelled to be so from his official position in that Church, as a public man in the North, and himself a naturalized citizen, saw the status of himself and others in like condition, and feeling the full force of President Lincoln's argument, agreed to do what he could by his influence with the Pope to have the acts referred to annulled by the Pope, and this with other matters to prove his own loyalty and sincerity, went to Europe for that purpose as well as others with which he was entrusted with a special mission by President Lincoln, which he performed satisfactorily and received his personal thanks.

The effect was a simulated neutrality, but the evil had been done already, and as the war had to be fought out to the bitter end, there was that which could not have been the result of accident, but rather of design, among Roman Catholic troops who were engaged on both sides, and in battle, as a general rule, they were not, as organized bodies, arrayed against each other. In Northern cities they resisted the draft, created riots and performed acts of outrage, robbery and murder, which at last had to be suppressed by veteran troops sent from the field for that purpose.

But the war had come to an end. The original plan of the Jesuits and the Pope, both in the United States and Mexico, was to end in ignominious failure—the Union cause to triumph and the Republic of Mexico to be restored. Protestant blood on both sides had been caused to flow in rivers and drench the mountains and the plains, while the places of the victims of the internecine strife were to be filled with importations from Roman Catholic populations from abroad. During the long night of four years of sorrow and tears and death which swept every hearthstone in the land, Abraham Lincoln, ever trusting and ever confident of the coming dawn of liberty, of peace and the success of the cause of the Union, was in receipt of constant threats of assassination. In July, 1864, on being reminded that right must eventually triumph, admitted that, but expressed the opinion that he should not live to see it, and added: "*I feel a presentiment that I shall not outlast the Rebellion. 'When it is over, my work will be done!'*"

But that the great crime of his assassination might not be fixed upon the real Jesuit conspirators and murderers, the South was to be made to unjustly bear the stigma of the horrid deed, which was to forever rankle as a festering thorn in the restored Union and keep alive the smouldering embers of sectional hate between the North and the South, and to keep Protestant Americans forever apart, while the balance of power should be augmented and retained in the hands of the Papal hierarchy, "a sword whose blade should be everywhere, but with its hilt at Rome."

We have thus shown the outlines with some of the details of the general Papal conspiracy against the United States, and Abraham Lincoln as President, with Pope Pius IX at the head, and in our next chapter we shall review the circumstances connected with the assassination of Abraham Lincoln, and the deed itself.

CHAPTER VII.

WARNINGS OF THREATENED ASSASSINATION FROM EUROPE—THE ASSASSINATION—ARREST OF MRS. SURRATT AND PAYNE—CONFESSION OF MRS. SURRATT—FLIGHT OF JOHN SURRATT TO CANADA AND TO ROME, AND ENLISTMENT IN THE POPE'S ARMY—WILKES BOOTH'S LETTER, AND WONDERFUL MEMORY OF MATTHEWS—THE TRUE THEORY AND EVIDENCE OF THE ASSASSINATION—TRIBUTES OF THE NATIONS TO ABRAHAM LINCOLN, ETC.

We shall soon come to the scene of the great tragedy, which occurred at John T. Ford's Theatre at Washington City, on the night of April 14th, 1865. *Whenever Rome decides upon a funeral the corpse is sure to be ready!* The prophecy and warnings of Father Chiniquy and continually repeated threats of assassination received for nearly nine years by Abraham Lincoln were now to be fulfilled.

Says Gen. L. C. Baker, the eminent detective: "On one occasion I carried to Mr. Lincoln two anonymous communications, in which he was threatened with assassination. In a laughing, joking manner, he remarked: 'Well, Baker, what do they want to kill me for? If they kill me, they will run the risk of getting a worse man.'"

Was he not a worse man for the Union? [Andrew Johnson's nomination for Vice-President was distasteful to Lincoln, but he preferred him to Gen. W. S. Rosecrans, a Roman Catholic, whose name was suppressed by Stanton, the Secretary of War.] In reply to a letter of warning from Hon. John Bigelow, then American Consul to Paris, Mr. Seward, Secretary of State, wrote as follows:

"DEPARTMENT OF STATE,
Washington, July 15, 1864.

* * * "There is no doubt that, from a period *anterior* to the breaking out of the insurrection, plots and conspiracies for the purposes of assassination have been frequently formed and organized, and it is not unlikely that such a one has been reported to you, is now in agitation among the insurgents. If it be so, it need furnish no ground for anxiety. Assassination is not an American practice or habit, and one so vicious and so desperate cannot be engrafted into our political system. This conviction of mine has steadily gained strength since the civil war began. Every day's experience confirms it. The President during the heated season occupies a country house near the Soldiers' Home, two or three miles from the city. He goes to and from that place on horseback night and morning, unguarded. I go there unattended at all hours, by daylight and moonlight, by starlight and without any light."

Fatal, delusive confidence, and to be taken advantage of when the plot at last was fully ripe for execution. Our Consul in London was apprised of plots for the assassination of the President, Cabinet and distinguished Generals.

On March 17, 1865, Consul F. H. Morse, in his letter, among other things, repeats the language of his secret agent, speaking of the conspirators there in Paris:

"For I repeat again what I have already done to you before: They are bent on destruction, and will not stop at any object, even to the taking of life, so as to attain their ends; and, mark me, *Mr. Seward is not the only one they will assassinate.* I have heard some fearful oaths, and it is war to the teeth with them. I feel confident *that there is some secret understanding between them and the Emperor of this government*—at least, I am given to understand so. The death of the Duke de Morny has deprived them of an interview with the Emperor, which was to have taken place, if I am rightly informed, on Sunday last."

On the 14th day of April, 1865, President Lincoln had presided over a very harmonious meeting of his Cabinet, and invited all of them who felt so disposed to accompany him to the theater that evening; but for various reasons and excuses of other engagements, there was not one of them able to avail themselves of his invitation. However, Mr. Lincoln, accompanied by his wife, Major H. R. Rathbone and Miss Clara H. Harris, went to Ford's Theater in the evening, to witness the play of our "American Cousin."

The full description in all its details of the act of the assassination of Abraham Lincoln by John Wilkes Booth, is too familiar to our readers to be repeated here. We will briefly state, however, that "about ten o'clock of April 14, 1865, while the play of 'Our American Cousin' was progressing, a stranger, who proved to be John Wilkes Booth, an actor of some note, worked his way into the proscenium-box occupied by the Presidential party, and leveling a pistol close behind the head of Mr. Lincoln, he fired, and the ball was lodged deep in the brain of the President. The assassin then drew a dirk, assaulted Major Rathbone, who attempted to detain him, inflicting severe wounds, sprang from the box, flourishing the weapon aloft, and shouted, as he reached the stage: '*Sic semper tyrannus! the South is avenged!*' He dashed across the stage, and before the audience could realize the real position of affairs, the murderer had mounted a fleet horse in waiting in an alley in the rear of the theater, and galloping off, he escaped for a time. In his attempt to jump from the box to the stage his spur caught in the folds of the American flag, which caused him to break his leg, and which accident also eventually aided in his capture."

The foul deed at last had been accomplished, and the prophecy of Father Chiniquy was fulfilled. At just twenty-two minutes past seven o'clock on the morning of April 15, 1865, the soul of Abraham Lincoln returned to its Maker. The autopsy was held by the surgeons, and his body was borne through cities and towns to find a resting-place at last at his home in Springfield, Illinois.

The escape of the principal assassin, and the search for him and his accomplices in the crime, which was immediately followed up by Gen. Lafayette C. Baker, and the demands for vengeance and punishment of the conspirators now engrossed the attention of the people. As there were

Roman Catholics directly involved in the planning and execution of the plot, with the whole Jesuit organization behind them, officers in pursuit and search for the murderers were thrown off on a false scent, that they might make their escape. Some had been already arrested. Concerning these, says Gen. Baker, in his faithful report: "*I mention, as an exceptional and remarkable fact, that every conspirator in custody* IS BY EDUCATION *a Catholic.*"

Mrs. Surratt and her whole family were Roman Catholics, and before she moved to Washington City from Surrattsville she left her tavern to a trusty friend, *John Lloyd, who was also a Roman Catholic*, and aided Booth and Harold, as originally provided for in the conspiracy, in arming them and in making their escape. Says Gen. Baker: "Treason never found a better agent than Mrs. Surratt. She was a large, masculine, self-possessed female, mistress of her house, and as lithe a rebel as Belle Boyd or Mrs. Greenborough. She had not the flippancy and menace of the first, nor the social power of the second; but the Rebellion has found no fitter agent. At her country tavern at Surrattsville and Washington home Booth was made welcome."

Six weeks before the murder young Surratt had taken two splendid repeating carbines to Surrattsville and told John Lloyd to secrete them, and he did so. On Thursday, the day before the murder, John Surratt, who knew of and connived at the assassination, was sent northward by his mother, and in company with two disguised Jesuit priests, made his way to Canada, and of whose escape we shall speak of hereafter. On the very afternoon of the murder, Mrs. Surratt was driven to Surrattsville, and she told John Lloyd to have the carbines ready, because they would be called for that night. Harold was made quartermaster, and hired the horses. He and Atzerodt were mounted between eight o'clock and the time of the murder, and riding about the streets together. Lloyd, a few days before the murder, sent his wife away on a visit to Fort Fresh. She did not know why she was sent away, but swore it was so. Harold, three weeks before the murder, visited Port Tobacco, and said that "the next time the boys heard of him *he would be in Spain;*" he added, "*that with Spain there was no extradition treaty,*" which is well known as one of the most intense Roman Catholic Governments and countries on the globe, the birthplace of Ignatius Loyola, the founder of the Order of the Jesuits, where the Inquisition was first established and last destroyed. Harold said at Surrattsville that he meant to make a barrel of money, or his neck would stretch. Atzerodt said if he ever came to Port Tobacco again he would be rich enough to buy the whole place. Wilkes Booth told a friend to go to Ford's on Friday night and see the best acting in the world. Michael O'Laughlin and Sam. Arnold were to have been parties to it, but backed out of it in the end—O'Laughlin taking upon himself the crime to kill General Grant. "*They all, however, relied npon Mrs. Surratt, and took their cues from Wilkes Booth.*"

Now who controlled and directed Mrs. Surratt in this conspiracy? Was it Booth? *No!* IT WAS THE JESUIT PRIESTHOOD WHO WERE HER FATHER CONFESSORS, who like Father LeBelle with his sister in Chiniquy's case, *claimed to possess the power in the confessional to forgive the very crimes that they suggested and incited.*

The manner of the capture of Booth and Harold, and the tragic fate of the former, is too familiar to our readers to be repeated here. Our aim is to direct attention to the real originators and arch conspirators and plotters against the Union, the life of the Republic and of Abraham Lincoln, and to show the connection between them and the tools they employed.

The indictment of the prisoners and others—David E. Harold, George A. Atzerodt, Lewis Payne, *Michael O'Laughlin, John H. Surratt, Edward Spangler*, Samuel Arnold, *Mary E. Surratt* and Samuel Mudd—charged them with combining, confederating and conspiring together with one John H. Surratt, John Wilkes Booth, Jefferson Davis, George N. Saunders, Beverly Tucker, Jacob Thompson, William C. Cleary, Clement C. Clay, George Harper, George Young and others unknown, to kill Abraham Lincoln, President, Andrew Johnson, Vice-President, William H. Seward, Secretary of State, and Ulysses S. Grant, Lieut.-General in command of the Armies of the United States, under the direction of the said Abraham Lincoln, etc , and for having traitorously murdered the said Abraham Lincoln, then President of the United States, and traitorously assaulting with intent to kill and murder the said William H. Seward, then Secretary of State, etc, and with lying in wait with intent to kill and murder Andrew Johnson, Vice-President of the United States, etc., and Ulysses S. Grant, then being Lieut.-General in command of the Armies of the United States, etc. Of these prisoners, Harold, Atzerodt, Payne and Mrs. Surratt, on July 5, 1865, were found guilty by the Court and sentenced to be hanged, and President Johnson fixed the day of execution, the 7th day of July, 1865, or only two days thereafter. The sentence of Arnold, Mudd and O'Laughlin were at hard labor for life, and Spangler at hard labor for six years.

"Atzerodt had a room almost directly over Vice-President Johnson's and had all the materials and weapons for murder, but lost spirit or opportunity. Booth's coat was found there, and he had evidently occupied the same room. Atzerodt fled alone, and was found at the house of his uncle, in Montgomery County, Maryland."

There will ever be an unsatisfactory mystery about Andrew Johnson not meeting with the same fate of Lincoln on that eventful night. Payne had, as far as he was able, done his bloody work with William H. Seward, and having vainly tried to escape from Washington, was thrown from his horse, and returned in time to be taken prisoner at Mrs. Surratt's house when she was arrested. Why did not Atzerodt attempt the life of Johnson as agreed? By reason of Grant leaving the city in going to New York, O'Laughlin failed to kill him. Mrs. Surratt had faithfully performed her part of the conspiracy. Coarse and hard and calm, Mrs.

Surratt shut up her house after the murder and waited with her daughters until the officers came. She was imperturable, and rebuked her girls for weeping, and would have gone to jail like a statue, but that in her extremity Payne knocked at her door. He had come, he said, to dig a ditch for Mrs. Surratt, whom he well knew. But Mrs. Surratt protested that she had never seen the man at all.

"How fortunate, girls," she said, "that these officers are here; this man might have murdered us all."

"Her effrontery stamps her as worthy of companionship with Booth. Payne has been identified by a lodger of Mrs. Surratt's as having visited the house twice under the name of Wood."

"On the night before the execution Miss Surratt was with her mother several hours, as were also Rev. Fathers Wiget and Walter, and Mr. Brophy, who was also present that morning. She slept very little, if any, *and required considerable attention, suffering with cramps and pains the entire night, caused (it is said) by her nervousness.*" [Query: Was it not owing to something administered by the priests?]

"When being led out for execution she cast her eyes upward upon the scaffold for a few moments, with a look of curiosity combined with dread. One glimpse, and her eyes fell to the ground, and she walked along mechanically, her head drooping, and if she had not been supported would have fallen. She ascended the scaffold, and was led to an armchair, in which she was seated. An umbrella was held over her by the two *holy fathers* to protect her from the sun. During the reading of the order of the execution by General Hartranft, the priests held a small crucifix before her, which she kissed fervently several times."

"The alleged important after-discovered testimony which Aiken, counsel for Mrs. Surratt, stated would prove her innocence, was submitted to Judge Advocate General Holt, and after a careful examination, he failed to discover anything in it having a bearing on the case. This was communicated to President Johnson, *and he declined to interfere in the execution of Mrs. Surratt.*"

There are some things in connection with this summary justice inflicted upon these condemned instruments and tools while the chief conspirators remained in the background and went unpunished, that are subject to investigation. The shortness of time, *scarcely forty-eight hours from the time of receiving their sentences until being executed.* This may partly be explained on the ground of its being the action of a military court; but President Johnson being the Commander-in-Chief, could have granted a reprieve for a short time longer, and could have commuted the sentence of Mrs. Surratt to imprisonment for life on account of her sex, but '*dead men (and dead women) tell no tales.*' He not only refused to reprieve or commute her sentence, but that he might not be importuned to interfere, gave imperative orders that he would receive no one that day. In vain did Miss Surratt that morning apply to see him and plead for her mother's life during the whole forenoon, up to the last moment before the execution took place, but it was utterly useless, and with the exception of Mrs. Surratt's counsel, there was none to appeal for her.

That Mrs. Surratt was guilty of performing her part in the terrible drama there is not the least doubt, but the greatest criminals went unhung. Strict orders were given that no newspaper reporters should be admitted to the cells of the condemned, *that no further information or any confession or statement should be elicited from them*, and therefore whatever they had to say should be lodged in the breasts of their *spiritual advisers alone.* As a sow will eat her own progeny, so Rome was also interested in having no reprieve or commutation of sentence granted, and the Jesuit priesthood therefore made no extra exertions in their behalf, while the son of the murderess was concealed and found protection within her bosom. The priests who attended Mrs. Surratt performed their part well, and by means of the seal of confession, *by which felony is compounded and the ends of justice defeated* by it, perfect security is guaranteed to the criminal, no matter how great the crime, while priests placed in full knowledge of it, use that knowledge to advance the interests of the Papal power, and to conceal their own complicity and guilt.

A constant effort has been made from that time to cover the crime of Abraham Lincoln's assassination by throwing dust into the eyes of the American people, and attributing the cause to mental hallucination on the part of Wilkes Booth, who imagined Lincoln to be a Cæsar and himself a Brutus, destined to take his life. That his great love for the South and hatred of the North, and especially of Lincoln as President, was coupled with his idea, and acting under this inspiration, he became the chief conspirator and actor in this bloody drama; and the theory is made to appear as plausible as possible, to divert attention from the Brotherhood of Hell, which is governed and directed from their head at Rome.

It has been told to us, coming from what we believe to be true authority, that Booth, about three weeks before he committed the crime, was admitted to the Roman Catholic Church, and privately received the sacraments from no less a personage than Archbishop Spaulding himself, which he did to silence any conscientious scruples that he might have to taking Abraham Lincoln's life, and that he might have the whole influence and sympathy of persons of that faith in protecting and concealing him when the act was done to aid him in it. He certainly had that aid and influence in planning and accomplishing his hellish work and in making his escape, and it could not have been more cheerfully and faithfully rendered than it was, even if he had been a Jesuit priest himself. We believe the statement to be true; and as it was but a short time after that Archbishop Spaulding received a donation of funds for a specific purpose, which was to uniform and equip a military body in the same manner and style as the Papal Guard at Rome. The uniforms, muskets, cartridge-boxes and belts all bearing the Papal coat of arms, and consecrated by the Pope himself, were sent to Archbishop Spaulding at Baltimore; and when he died he was buried with military honors, and his remains escorted by the same military body-guard. The entire diocese of Archbishop Spaulding was rebel to the core and fierce in its hatred of Lincoln.

There is an old saying that "murder will out," and even Roman Catholics who will confess to their priest, will at some time thereafter when not apprehending danger to themselves, will tell and disclose more than is prudent, and thus give themselves away, as will appear from the following special dispatch from Philadelphia to the *Chicago Tribune* of December 3, 1882:

" A hitherto unpublished and very interesting story of Lincoln' assassination will appear in the *Press* to-morrow, and includes acts of the assassin just previous to his shooting the President, with his letter of justification, intrusted to JOHN MATTHEWS the actor, to JOHN F. COYLE, editor of the *National Intelligencer*. The story is told by JOHN J. FORD the theater manager and MR. MATTHEWS. After stating that it is morally certain that BOOTH *never thought of the murder until the day it was committed"* [TOO THIN.] MR. FORD said: "Until BOOTH came to the theater that morning he had no knowledge that the President intended visiting the theater in the evening. *That afternoon* he wrote the letter justifying his assassination. [NOTE.—*A long letter of over two hundred lines.*] This letter he gave to JOHN MATTHEWS, who is now engaged in New York. He was then playing at my theater. The letter was intended to be published in the *National Intelligencer*, and it was well towards night when he gave it to MATTHEWS. He was riding down Pennsylvania Avenue toward the National Hotel when he met MATTHEWS and handed him the letter.

" MATTHEWS DESTROYED THE LETTER *immediately after the shooting, and no one ever saw it but him.*"

Finding that all his plans for abduction had failed, and the end of the war was growing nearer and nearer, he at the very last moment determined to take the desperate chance of assassination. Booth was a very gifted young man, and was a great favorite in society in Washington. He was engaged, it was said, to a young lady of high character and position. I understand that she wrote to EDWIN BOOTH after the assassination, telling him that she was his brother's bethrothed, and would marry him even at the foot of the scaffold. "My God! my God! I have no longer a country! This is the end of Constitutional liberty in America." These were the words spoken with startling emphasis on the evening of the 14th of April, 1865, by JOHN WILKES BOOTH. He was passing down Pennsylvania Avenue, in Washington, and near the corner of Thirteenth street had met JOHN MATTHEWS, a fellow-actor and *a boyhood friend*, whom he thus addressed: "'He was as pale as a ghost when he uttered these words,' said MR. MATTHEWS to me a day or two since. There were quite a number of Confederate prisoners along the avenue as he spoke, and when he said 'This is an end to Constitutional liberty in America,' he pointed feelingly toward them. He looked at them after they had passed, and was thoughtful. He turned to me quickly and said: 'I want you to do me a favor.' 'Anything in my power, John,' I replied. He thrust his hand into his pocket and drawing out a letter, said: '*Deliver this to* MR. COYLE, *of the National Intelligencer, to-night, by eleven o'clock, unless I see you before that. If I do, I can attend to it myself.*' I took the letter, saw that it was sealed, put it into my pocket and walked on. BOOTH, who was on horseback, rode rapidly down the street, *and I never saw him again until he jumped from the box in Ford's Theater*, AFTER SHOOTING THE PRESIDENT. I was then playing at Ford's Theater, the piece being 'Our American Cousin.' Laura Keene was the star. BOOTH *almost ran against me*, as he leaped across the stage, on his way to the door. There was of course a great commotion, and I at once went to my dressing-room and picked up my wardrobe, passed under the stage out through the orchestra and the auditorium to the street, with the audience. *My room was directly oppo-*

site, at Mr. Peterson's, the house at which Mr. Lincoln died. I walked quickly across, locked the doors, and began at once to change my clothes. In picking up my coat, the letter which Booth had given me upon the street before the theater opened, dropped out of my pocket upon the floor. I had almost forgotten it in my excitement. I quickly picked it up, tore it open, and read it very carefully. 'My God!' thought I, '*this condemnation of my friend shall not be found in my possession!*' and I THREW IT INTO THE FIRE, *watched it until it burned to cinders, and then mixed the atoms with the coal-ashes.* In the excitement and horror which followed the shooting, the archangel could never have explained the possession of that letter. I did not then realize, however, by what a slender thread my life was hung. *My impulse when I read the letter was, that the evidence to condemn my friend should not remain with me.*" [NOTE.—*It will thus be seen that Matthews became an accessory to the murder of Lincoln after the fact by his own admission.*]

The correspondent asked Mr. Matthews: "Who else saw that letter besides yourself?" He answered: "*No other living man after it came into my possession. It was sealed and directed to Mr. Coyle, one of the editors of the National Intelligencer.*"

"Do you recall ITS CONTENTS?" "*Almost as vividly as though I had just committed them to memory.* It began:

"'WASHINGTON, D. C., April 14, 1865.

"'TO MY COUNTRYMEN: For years I have devoted my time, my energies and every dollar I possessed in the world for the furtherance of an object. I have been baffled and disappointed. The hour has come when I must change my plan. I know the vulgar herd will blame me for what I am about to do, but posterity I am sure will justify me. [Right or wrong, God judge me, not man. Be my motive good or bad, of one thing I am sure—the lasting condemnation of the North. I love peace more than life. I have loved the Union beyond expression. For four or five years I waited, hoped and prayed for the dark clouds to break, and for a restoration of our former sunshine. To wait longer would be a crime. My prayers have proved as idle as my life. God's will be done. I go to see and share the bitter end.] This war is a war with the Constitution and the reserved rights of the State. [It is a war upon Southern rights and institutions. The nomination of Abraham Lincoln, four years ago, bespoke war. His election forced it. I have held the South was right. In a foreign struggle, I too could say, "My country, right or wrong;" but in a struggle such as ours, where the brother tries to pierce the brother's heart, for God's sake, choose the right! When a country like this spurns justice from her side, she forfeits the allegiance of honest freemen, and should leave him untrammeled by any fealty soever, to act as his conscience may approve. People of the North, to hate tyranny, to love liberty and justice, to strike at wrong and oppression, was the teaching of our fathers. The study of our early history will not let me forget it, and may it never.]

"'I do not want to forget the heroic patriotism of our fathers who rebelled against the oppression of the mother country.

["'This country was formed by the white, not the black man, and looking upon African slavery from the same stand-point held by the noble framers of our Constitution, I have for one ever considered it one of the greatest blessings both for themselves and for us, that God ever bestowed upon a favored nation. Witness heretofore our wealth and power. Witness their elevation and enlightenment above their condition elsewhere. I have lived among it most of my life, and have seen less harsh treatment from master to man than I have beheld in the North from father to son. Yet Heaven knows no one would be willing to do more for the negro race than I, could I but see a way to still better their condition; but Lincoln's policy is only preparing the way for their annihilation. The South are not nor have they been fighting for the continuance of slavery.

The first battle of Bull Run did away with that idea. Their causes since for war have been as noble and greater far than those that urged our fathers on. Even should we allow they were wrong at the beginning of this conflict, cruelty and injustice have made the wrong become the right, and they stand now the wonder and admiration of the world as a noble band of patriotic heroes. Hereafter, reading of their deeds, Thermopylæ will be forgotten.]

["'When I aided in the capture and execution of John Brown (who was a murderer on our Western border, and who was fairly tried and convicted before an impartial judge and jury, of treason, and who, by the way, has since been made a god), I was proud of my little share in the transaction. for I deemed it my duty, and that I was helping our common country to perform an act of justice. But what was a crime in poor John Brown is now considered (by themselves) as the greatest and only virtue of the whole Republican party. Strange transmigration, vice to become a virtue simply because more indulge in it. I thought then as now, that the Abolitionists were the only traitors in the land, and that the entire party deserved the same fate as poor old John Brown. Not because they wished to abolish slavery, but on account of the means they have ever endeavored to use to effect that abolition. If Brown were living, I doubt whether he himself would set slavery against the Union. Most or nearly all the North do openly curse the Union if the South are to return and retain a single right guaranteed to them by every tie which we once revered as sacred. The South can make no choice. It is extermination or slavery for themselves (worse than death) to draw from. I know my choice] and hasten to accept it. [I have studied hard to discover on what grounds the right of a State to secede has been denied, when our very name United States and the Declaration of Independence provides for secession. But there is now no time for words I know how foolish I shall be deemed for undertaking such a step as this, where, on the one side, I have many friends and everything to make me happy, where my profession alone has gained me an income of more than twenty thousand dollars a year, and where my great personal ambition in my profession has such a great field for labor. On the other hand, the South have never bestowed upon me one kind word; a place now where I have no friends, except beneath the sod; a place where I must either become a private soldier or a beggar. To give up all the former for the latter, besides my mother and sster, whom I love so dearly. Although they so widely differ from me in opinion seems insane, but God is my judge, I love justice more than I do a country that disowns it; more than fame and wealth; more—Heaven pardon me if I am wrong—more than a happy home. I have never been upon a battlefield; but oh! my countrymen, could you see all the reality or effects of this horrid war as I have seen them in every State save Virginia, I know you would think like me and would pray the Almighty to create in the Northern mind a sense of right and justice, even should it possess no seasoning of mercy, and He would dry up the sea of blood between us that is daily growing wider. Alas! I have no longer a country. She is fast approaching her threatened doom. Four years ago I would have given a thousand lives to see her remain—as I had always known her—powerful and unbroken, and now I would hold my life as naught to see her what she was. Oh! my friends, if the fearful scenes of the past four years had never been enacted, or if what has been had been a frightful dream from which we could now awake, with what overflowing hearts could we bless our God and pray for continued favor. How I have loved the old flag can never now be known. A few years since and the entire world could boast of none so pure and spotless. But I have of late been seeing and hearing of the bloody deeds of which she had been made the emblem, and shudder to think how changed she has grown. Oh! how I have longed to see her break from the mist of blood and death circled around the folds, spoiling her beauty and tarnishing her honor. But no! Day by day she has been dragged deeper and deeper into cruelty and oppression till now (in my eyes) her once red stripes look like bloody gashes on the face of Heaven. I look now upon my early admiration of her glories as a dream. My love is now for the South alone, and to her side I go penniless.] Her success has been near my heart, and I have labored faithfully to further an object which would have more than proved my unselfish devotion. Heartsick and disappointed, I turn from the path which I had been following into a bolder and more perilous one. Without malice, I make the change. I have nothing in my heart except a sense of duty to my choice. If the South is to be aided it must be done quickly. It may already be too late. When Cæsar had conquered the enemies of Rome and the powers that were his menaced the liberties of the people, Brutus arose and slew him. The stroke of his dagger was guided by love for Rome. It was the spirit and ambition of Cæsar Brutus struck at.

> "Oh, then, that we could come by Cæsar's spirit,
> And not dismember Cæsar: but, alas,
> Cæsar must bleed for it."

"'I answer with Brutus—he who loves his country better than gold or life.   JOHN W. BOOTH.'

"Following Mr. Booth's signature," Mr. Matthews continued, "which was evidently written in great haste, were the names of Payne, Harold and Atzerodt, all in *Booth's* own handwriting, given as the men who would stand by him in executing his changed plans. Booth wrote John S. Clarke, the actor, his brother-in-law, a letter identical in many respects with the one he left with me, as justification for his act. The arguments were all the same, *the changes in the letter I destroyed being those which would naturally follow the change of plan from kidnapping to assassination.*"

"How did the fact that Booth had left such a letter become known?"

"When John was killed a diary was taken from his person containing the entry that he had left a letter to the *National Intelligencer.*"

"ABOUT THE TIME OF THE IMPEACHMENT OF PRESIDENT JOHNSON, the other Washington papers made an assault upon the *National Intelligencer, calling it the organ of John Wilkes Booth, and rather insinuated* THAT PRESIDENT JOHNSON *was in some way cognizant of the letter,* IF NOT OF THE KILLING, *before it occurred. I felt then compelled to speak out and announce that it was I who received the letter* AND DESTROYED IT. *I had,* AT THE TIME OF ITS DESTRUCTION, AS A CATHOLIC, TOLD THE REV. FATHER BOYLE OF WASHINGTON, ALL ABOUT THE LETTER, AND THE CIRCUMSTANCES UNDER WHICH I RECEIVED IT."

Now let us investigate and analyze this Jesuitical story.

If Booth only changed his mind after twelve o'clock at noon of the 14th of April, and having got his accomplices ready and prepared for their hellish work that evening, would he have taken the time to have carefully prepared such a lengthy letter? Common sense would answer, *No!* Would he have betrayed himself and his accomplices by attaching their names to such a letter after he had written it? Common sense would answer, *No!* Would it be possible for any man, an actor or anyone else, to memorize such a lengthy epistle in a very few moments while under such an excitement of so great a murder, and the victim the President of the United States, lying in a dying condition, surrounded by so many of his Cabinet, family, surgeons and others in the same house, and almost immediately under him, when at the same time he was excitedly anxious to destroy such a letter by burning it in the fire and endeavoring to destroy every vestige of it in the coal-ashes of a grate? Common sense again answers, *No! By telling Father Boyle of its destruction at the time, he made him also, as well as himself, an accessory to the crime after the fact, for that Catholic priest kept that knowledge to himself.*

Why was he "*compelled to speak out,*" and draw the fire

to himself at the time of the impeachment of PRESIDENT JOHNSON? Why so careful of Johnson's reputation and official position, and in what way in any manner could it relieve him? Does it not fasten suspicion and doubt upon Andrew Johnson's memory, and leave the impression that he (Johnson) knew of the existence of that letter beforehand, and of the intended assassination of Abraham Lincoln, while he himself might " have no hand in his death, yet would receive the benefit of his dying," by becoming President in his stead? Does it not show that Andrew Johnson had a personal interested motive in not granting a reprieve or commutation of the sentence of Mrs. Surratt? He as President could pardon notorious conspirators against the Union, who had stirred up the savage Indians to war and led them in brigades upon the battle-field, where the most hellish atrocities were perpetrated by them, but he could not commute the sentence or pardon a woman no worse than they.

The whole of this letter business being so faithfully committed to memory, bears the evidence of fraud and falsehood upon the face of it, and it is proven to our satisfaction that it is a Jesuitical performance, to divert attention from themselves, and yet every effort only draws it more closely to them. The letter of Wilkes Booth to his brother-in-law, John S. Clarke, written the November previous, was taken bodily, *verbatim et literatum*, as will be seen by examining it in " Raymond's Life of Lincoln," pages 794–5–6, with the exception of the date, and what follows, down to the words " Right or wrong, God judge me, and not man," etc., and all that appears in brackets (as stated to have been committed to memory by Matthews), down to the words " and to her side I go penniless," there the plagiarism ceases. The remainder of Booth's letter, and closing, is as follows:

"They say she has found that 'last ditch,' which the North have so long derided, and been endeavoring to force her in, forgetting that they are our brothers, and that it is impolitic to goad an enemy to madness. Should I reach her in safety and find it true, I will proudly beg permission to triumph or die in that same 'ditch' by her side.

"*A Confederate doing duty on his own responsibility.*

"J. WILKES BOOTH."

The *Philadelphia Press* of April 19, 1865, had the following:

"We have just received the following letter, written by John Wilkes Booth, and placed by him in the hands of his brother-in-law, J. S. Clarke. It was written by him in November last, and left with J. S. Clarke, in a sealed envelope, and addressed to himself in his own handwriting. In the same envelope were some United States bonds and oil stocks. This letter was opened by Mr. Clarke for the first time on Monday last, and immediately handed by him to Marshal Milward, who has kindly placed it in our hands. Most unmistakably it proves that he must for many months have contemplated seizing the person of the late President. It is, however, doubtful whether he imagined the black deed which has plunged the nation into the deepest gloom, and at the same time awakened it to a just and righteous indignation:

"'————, ————, 1864.

"'MY DEAR SIR: You may use this as you think best; but as *some* may wish to know *when, who* and *why*, and as I do not know how to direct it, I give it (in the words of your master)—'*To whom it may concern.*'"

Then follows the sentence, "Right or wrong," etc., as already stated. That Matthews remembered so thoroughly the contents of the letter delivered to him for *Coyle*, is preposterous under the circumstances. But that he perhaps with the aid of others, copied the letter to Clarke and added to it, is obvious, and the changes were made by himself to give it the coloring it bears. It is possible that Booth might have made use of some of the language quoted by Matthews, and if he did, there is one line exceedingly appropriate—"*The stroke of his dagger was guided* BY LOVE FOR

ROME"—and knowing that he had the aid and sympathy of all who bear allegiance to Rome. The *pretext* for the crime was to avenge the South, and to fasten an additional stigma upon her that was undeserved and unjust; to keep the North and South forever apart, and prevent a true reconciliation and solid peace being made between them that would insure the perpetuity of the Union. But Rome was foiled.

That there were others besides Spangler employed in and about Ford's Theater, who knew of the intended assassination of Lincoln, is evident, and how many priests were confessed to by them is a matter known only between them and the *holy fathers*, and it is possible that in time more will unmask themselves, as Matthews has done.

Before concluding this subject, let us turn our attention to the other conspirator, John H. Surratt.

When Father Chiniqui, who had repeatedly warned Lincoln against assassination, learned that the deed had been done, his sorrow knew no bounds. He had left the Roman Catholic Church with hundreds of his followers, and has since led out of that sink-hole of iniquity more than twenty-five thousand of his fellow Canadian countrymen to Protestantism. With his knowledge of Canada, where he was born and had spent most of his life, and where his personal influence was so great, he left no stone unturned to discover, if possible, the retreat of the conspirator, and to aid in bringing him to justice. John H. Surratt, by previous arrangement, had left Washington nearly forty-eight hours before the crime was committed, and was accompanied by two Jesuit priests in disguise, who saw him safely over the line to Canada, as an *avant courier of Wilkes Booth*, who was to have made his escape in that direction after having done the deed. Spangler having failed on his part to shut off the gas (through some difficulty or words with Withers, the leader of the orchestra, which prevented him), which would have completely covered the tracks of Booth in the sudden darkness, and no one would have known who committed the deed but the conspirators themselves, left Booth to be exposed to the glare of the light and to be recognized by all who knew him. He evidently had planned two routes of escape, one by the way of Canada and the other by the route he took. The breaking of his leg by his spur catching in the folds of the flag, which tripped him and retarded his movements, left him no alternative but to take the route he did. It is somewhat singular, too, that the theater proprietor and manager had no American flag for the President's box, and the one used belonged to one of the musicians, an Italian, named Saltavullo, who suggested to Mr. Withers that it be used to decorate the front part of the box, and it was accordingly raised.

"Edward Spangler died on the 19th of February, 1874, at the residence of Dr. Mudd, of Baltimore, a co-conspirator with whom he had suffered imprisonment. Before his death he made a confession, which has been communicated to Mr. Withers, in effect that the presence of the musician at the 'governor' prevented a fearful panic. He (Spangler) was hovering around the instrument with the intention of turning off the gas in the auditorium, the moment that Booth landed on the stage. The cover was up to facilitate that operation, and had he not been ordered away by Mr. Withers, who turned the cover down to sit upon it, the gas would have been turned off and nobody would know to a certainty who assassinated the President. Booth was not recognized at the time of his leap by the audience; but Miss Laura Keene, who stood at the wings, recognized him, and shouted to the audience, 'It is John Wilkes Booth!' At that time he was struggling with Mr. Withers at the rear of the stage. The turning off of the gas at the proper time, Mr. Withers believes, would have allowed the assassin to escape unrecognized and have led to further tragic results."

Says Gen. L. C. Baker, in his work, on page 563: "*During my visits to the prisoners, before their execution, Mrs. Surratt confessed to me her complicity with the conspirators, so far as the int.nded abduction was concerned, but affirmed that* she reluctantly yielded to the urging of Booth in aiding the plot of assassination. He insisted that her oath of fidelity bound her to see the fatal end of the conspiracy."

Here is shown the policy of the Jesuits. Booth, while he was the instrument to commit the deed, after it was done, is made to be the scapegoat to bear the sins of the real conspirators, to direct suspicion from themselves, while the two priests, Wigert and Walter, keep close watch and attention over the condemned woman, for fear she might, at last, let something out, and they steered her to the close of the drama. Mother-like, she had prepared for the escape of her son after he had performed his part in making every preparation for the crime and the retreat of the assassins, so that he might not incur any risk of danger when the deed was done; so under the watchful care of two Jesuit fathers in disguise, he is out of harm's way over the border to Canada.

Says Chiniquy: "Surratt was harbored and protected by the Jesuit Bishop Bourgette, of Montreal, until he could safely send him to a Jesuit priest Bouché, at the mouth of the Loup River, where he was hidden a short time, and taken thence to the Jesuit Bishop of Quebec, who sheltered him until he could send him to Paris, where he would be forwarded to Rome and be safely sheltered and concealed by Pope Pius IX."

The information which Father Chiniquy received seems to be the most correct one, and it was revealed to him by those who knew, and when they afterwards left the Roman Catholic Church and became Protestants.

"An Englishman in Montreal," says Gen, L. C. Baker, "who previous to the murder of Mr. Lincoln, had sympathized strongly with the South, and associated with their agents in Canada, and has been fully posted in their movements, said that the assassination was too much for him, and stated that he knew that during the 20th of April the Southern agents heard from the party that murdered the

President, *and they expected him to arrive in Montreal within forty-eight hours—not sure that it was Booth, but one closely connected with the assassination, if not the principal,"* etc.

This information was given to Alderman Lyman of Montreal, who gave it to a brother of Cheney, of the Express Company; he gave it to Gov. Smith of Vermont. It seems, however, that in making his escape into Canada, that Surratt dropped or left his handkerchief in the Burlington Depot of the Vermont Central Railroad, which was picked up, bearing the name of "John H. Surratt" in the corner. Reports in regard to the matter duly reached the headquarters of the army. But during all this time he was safely covered under the black wings of the Jesuit vampire bats of Rome, where, at last, he is enlisted as a soldier in the Papal service, and protected by the Pope himself. But the Vatican itself could not effectually secrete him, and the Pope had to surrender him on the peremptory demand of the Government of the United States, in connection with which the following extract will not be uninteresting:

"HOW SURRATT ESCAPED.

"One of the most familliar figures in the neighborhood of West Broadway, near Hudson street, is a strongly-built, low-sized truckman, with a smooth-shaven face and sharp features. He passes among his comrades and friends under the name of 'the dominie,' not because of any excessive piety on his part, but because in the course of his highly checkered career he has managed to pick up a very fair knowledge of history, geography, physics, etc., and to learn several European languages, which he speaks with wonderful fluency. He is, moreover, a pleasant little man, and when his day's work is done nothing pleases him better than to gather his friends together in a quaint, old-fashioned beer-saloon on Hudson street, and to relate experiences of his past. One story he repeats to satiety, *and that is the part he took in the escape from imprisonment in Italy of John H. Surratt, one of the conspirators against Abraham Lincoln.* The other day a reporter for the *Mail and Express* chanced to meet this peculiar little man, and, of course, the latter was willing to go over the old ground. 'I was born and brought up in Deventer, Holland, near the German frontier,' said he. 'I was always of a roving, I might almost say romantic disposition, and in 1867, after reaching my twenty-first year, I began to look around for an opportunity to distinguish myself. Just about this time *Pope Pius IX was greatly in want of soldiers to defend himself against the Garibaldians, and several Papal recruiting bureaus had been started in Switzerland, Belgium and other countries.* Here was a brilliant opportunity, I thought, and—how well I remember the day—on February 14, 1867, I left home, received a bounty of sixty francs and journeyed to Rome. *In the Holy City I was drafted into the Sixth Company of the First Battalion of Pontifical Zouaves,* whose headquarters had just been transferred to Velletri, a small fortified village forty miles north of Rome. Of course, I felt very proud on first donning the pretty gray Pontifical uniform, striped with red, a tasseled *fur kepi* and white gaiters—not to mention my shouldering an improved Minnie rifle.

"'I think it must have been about three weeks after my enlistment that I took advantage of a first leave of absence to visit Rome, where the Easter ceremonies were in full progress. While sitting in the cars on the return journey to Velletri, my attention was directed to a Zouave, *wearing a uniform similar to mine.* He was young and handsome, and wore a curly black moustache and goatee. Becoming interested in his person, I finally summoned courage enough to address him in French—this was the language mostly spoken by the Zouaves. But he did not understand me. Then I tried Italian, German and Dutch, but with equally poor result. At last, I scraped a few English words together, and to my great satisfaction the stranger was able to understand. *He told me he was an Irish-American, and had crossed the Atlantic out of enthusiasm for the cause of the Pope.* He also said his name was Watson, and that he was serving the Third Company of the First Battalion of Zouaves, stationed at Veroli. He was not very talkative, however, and soon after we parted company, he having to get out at a station on the road. I think it must have been two months later, in consequence of the movements of certain Garibaldian bands, that my company was transferred to Veroli. Here I met Watson again, and we became very intimate together, and shared the same room in the barracks. However, the man always remained an enigma to me, and do my best, I was unable to learn anything of his past. After some weeks' stay at Veroli the Sixth and Third Companies were detailed for duty to Coll Pardo, where a band of brigands had been committing depredations. Just at this time another American, who called himself St. Mery, enlisted in my company, and soon attracted attention by his strange questions and the persistency with which he inquired whether any of his countrymen were serving with the Zouaves. As the First Battalion was some fourteen hundred strong, you will readily understand that it was no easy task for him to obtain the desired information. In the meantime, I noticed a marked change in Watson's manner. He seemed more worried and nervous than usual, and if anything, spoke less. *We had not remained many days at Coll when he asked me whether I thought he could obtain leave of absence for a few days.* I referred him to our sergeant, a Frenchman named Halgand; but he had no authority to grant the request, *and advised Watson to go to Veroli and seek permission of the Battalion commander. This advice Watson followed,* bidding me good-bye most affectionately. Hardly had he started on his trip, however, than a detachment of fifty men, under Lieut. DeMousty, arrived and asked for him. Then for the first time it became known that our reserved and melancholy comrade was none *other than John H. Surratt, one of the accomplices in the assassination of President Abraham Lincoln, of the United States of America.* St. Mery proved to have been a detective in search of the fugitive,

"'*Immediately upon hearing of Watson's departure, DeMousty concluded that he had not gone to Veroli, but was on his way to the frontier.* The detachment therefore started in pursuit of him, *and by the merest chance in the world caught up with him at a village near the Tuscan border.* He was seized and brought in irons to Veroli, where he was thrown into the barracks dungeon. Now you must know that the barracks are built on an elevation overlooking Veroli, and that while the entry to the dungeon staircase is on the crest of the hill, the dungeon window is almost at its base, thirty feet below. *Orders had been received from Rome to secure and keep the prisoner at any cost,* and so DeMousty detailed twelve of us, among whom was a Maltese named Catania, a Scotchman named McCrossen and myself—*all three of us tried friends of Surratt,* to *guard the dungeon and its inmate.* Ten of us were posted on the narrow staircase, and two (Cantania and McCrossen) were outside. Next to the dungeon was a small compartment containing the entrance to the barrack sewer. When night came, *in accordance with an arrangement made between Surratt and ourselves, the prisoner was allowed to enter this compartment,* as prisoners were in the habit of doing. *Apparently we totally forgot his presence, but at ten minutes of two we all made a rush for the dungeon, and, as three among us expected, Surratt had disappeared.* He had lowered himself into the sewer and had made his way out by an opening into the neighboring rivulet. This *supposed* discovery led to a furious fusillade on our part, its object being naturally *to create suspicion from us by creating the impression that we were trying to stop the fugitive.* As soon as the Lieutenant heard of the escape he ordered the entire party on watch under arrest, *but I recollect clearly that a smile of satisfaction played around his lips at the time, and I sincerely believe he was in secret sympathy with Surratt.*

"'The same cannot be said of the Battalion commander. When news of the occurrence was broken to him he exclaimed, "*Je suis ruiné!*" [I am ruined] and sent an entire cavalry regiment in pursuit of Surratt; but they never got him. He was afterwards arrested in Egypt, I think.'"

But it will be seen that with all the schemes and connivances for his escape, that he had to be returned to his own country, and when for his personal safety it could be done. All the active conspirators and accomplices were out of the way, either by having been hung, imprisoned or otherwise. Martial law had given way to the civil, and the protection that had been thrown around him by the "Militia of the Pope," and the witnesses hung, and others which could not be found, he therefore could not be convicted of the crime in which he was an aider and abettor, so was released, as God released Cain, with a mark upon him to follow him to the grave.

Of letters of sympathy, resolutions of condolence and condemnation received at the office of the Secretary of State, numbering nearly a thousand, which are to be found in the bound volume of "TRIBUTES OF THE NATIONS TO ABRAHAM LINCOLN," ordered to be printed by Congress, embracing diplomatic correspondence, the actions of parliaments, provincial and municipal governments, the entire Masonic Fraternity and other similar associations throughout the world, and the entire foreign Protestant organizations of pastors and laity everywhere, and all other organizations and societies, benevolent, political, educational, scientific and otherwise, with the exception of one only, and that of a diplomatic necessity and form of courtesy at Rome. Not a single Roman Catholic society of either cardinals, archbishops, priests, monks, nuns or of the laity of that Church in any form or manner of expression of any kind or character was received at the office of the Secretary of State at Washington, or to be found in this bound volume, which contains the "TRIBUTES OF THE NATIONS TO ABRAHAM LINCOLN." Even policy should have dictated some expression of sorrow and regret at his assassination and death; but Rome had no tears to shed over the victim whom the Jesuits, the "Militia of the Pope," "The Engineer Corps of Hell," who had slaughtered him in the hour of his triumph of civil and religious liberty and the maintenance of the Union.

In contrast to this silence of the Papal hierarchy and laity, we present the following extracts from various Masonic and other bodies in Italy to the memory of Abraham Lincoln:

"BROTHERS OF AMERICA: Our soul is grieved because our first utterance to you must consist of words of sorrow and consolation. His martyrdom will be a baptism more powerful than that required by the Roman Church. It is a baptism of blood—the other is of water. Brothers, your President was one of those wonderful men, like our Mazzini or Garibaldi, who tower above the meanness of common humanity and show how great a true man may become."

"We Italians see in the misfortunes of America repetitions of our own misfortunes. Italy mingles her tears with America."

"Americans of the Union: Despotism, priestly and political, diplomatic hypocrisy and a tradition of blood have fettered the Italian emancipation with so many snares that we, overwhelmed with grief and disgusted with this depraved Old World, turn with confiding looks to the New one, and our souls rejoice at the grand spectacle you show us. Oh, Americans! you who have conquered your own independence by your virtue only in the sacredness of the laws, constitutes only one, a free family, without kings or myrmidons, *without priests* or deceitful idols."

"Americans of the Union: Every one in Europe does not hold for its divinity the cotton or the sword; permit that our crowns of laurel and of myrtle go to garnish the tomb of Lincoln. Let our flowers be mixed with yours, our tears with yours, and with yours our oaths; to gratify the spirit of Lincoln for the complete destruction of slavery, we will encourage and imitate you in the battle for the redemption of humanity."

"And remember, also, that besides the poor blacks, there are many political slaves not less afflicted and oppressed, crying out for their lost liberty robbed from them by a foreign power. They expect fraternal aid from you in shaking off the yoke imposed upon their necks by brutal force. Help them, and proclaim to the world that America belongs to the Americans."

"Now Liberty in stigmatizing the cause of her enemies, * * and the people looking upon them cannot do otherwise than recollect that despots have had a share in this, and that in some courts of Europe they found protection, encouragement and applause, *and finally, the wicked instigator of the civil war, Jefferson Davis, obtained consolation, praises and hopes even in the paternal benediction of the Pope.*"

"Accept our sympathy and friendship as brothers; for we are hoping the day is not far distant when we will be free, and can call you really brothers of one family—a smiling, free and happy people."

"May the malediction of God descend upon those who conceived and consummated the most abominable deed. Brothers, we feel the blow that struck you. But now that your country is free, swear upon the tomb of your deliverer to rescue your brethren from the bonds of slavery. His memory will be the terrible leader in your battles—the compact of alliance that binds you together. His love shall be the example to guide you against those who seek to disunite you."

"Long may America flourish! Glory to the memory of the immortal LINCOLN, whose name will be recorded in the eternal pages of history as the greatest ever honored by humanity."

"Hail in eternity, O spirit of LINCOLN! Thou hast gone to the embrace of WASHINGTON. Look down from the supernal spheres with the smile of pardon and faith in the human beings that are contending for the triumph of the eternal laws of moral progress. O, great spirits, welcome the greeting and love of those who remain to struggle, and may your thoughts of great things and of the constant virtue of sacrifice inspire us all, men and nations, to continue in the right."

And so the heart and hand and voice of suffering Italy were lifted up in sympathy with America in its great affliction. Cities and towns in Italy gave the name of Lincoln to public squares and streets, that his name and memory might be honored among them. But the despotism and tyranny of the Papacy crushing that noble and generous people, called for Roman Catholic volunteers even from America, to aid in riveting their fetters more closely, which call was responded to by native-born as well as naturalized citizens who were subject to Rome; still, embracing even John H. Surratt, the conspirator and accomplice of the assassin Booth (whom Rome had to deliver up upon the demand of America), and in spite of the efforts of the hordes of hirelings, assassins and the despots of the earth who were the slaves and tools of the Papal hierarchy, Italy became united, redeemed and disenthralled, the temporal power of the Pope was overthrown by the armies of freedom under Garibaldi, Mazzini, Cavour, Victor Emanuel and Gavazzi, the foreign mercenaries were driven in shame and dishonor from her no longer polluted and invaded soil. Mexico arose in like manner and avenged her wrongs upon the usurper and invader, and the corpse of a monarchy and Jesuit treason was forever borne away and not allotted even a tomb from which it might have in the future any reasonable resurrection, to again submerge that republic in blood by a foreign foe, and erect the bastile of tyranny again upon the ruins of the temple of freedom.

Our own beloved land, watered with the blood and tears of a people forced into a fratricidal war by the schemes and plottings of superstition and slavery, directed by the Pope at Rome and engineered by the Jesuits from the beginning (and who are still in our midst), was destined to arise from the crimson flood which had engulfed it, but not until it was reddened deeper with the life-blood of its Saviour, the "Martyr President, ABRAHAM LINCOLN," proving the *Secret Monitor of the Jesuits*, when they declare *"that those who do not love them shall fear them;"* and in the declaration made, " *In whatever place of the Catholic world a Jesuit is insulted or* RESISTED, *no matter how insignificant he may be, he is sure to be* AVENGED."

The struggle commenced by Abraham Lincoln as a lawyer in defense of Father Chiniquy, at Urbana, Illinois, in May, 1856, against that terrible power, which combined with treason, slavery and rebellion to destroy the American Union, and in the event of its failure or success to make the South unjustly bear the stigma of the crime, was ended in his assassination at Washington on the night of the 14th of April, 1865; and in attempting to rob the tomb of his body at Springfield, Illinois, on the night of November 6, 1876, that it might no longer be a shrine for the pilgrims of the world to visit who revere his memory.

For eighteen years we have devoted our time and our means in following up this hellish plot from the beginning, and we thus have made our statement, presented the evidence and made our argument before our readers, and leave them as a fair-minded jury to say whether or not our conclusions and premises are correct, and that the enemies of the American Union, and those who conspired against the life and liberty and the Republic, and who were the instigators, aiders, abettors, accomplices and authors of the murder of the "*Martyr President*, ABRAHAM LINCOLN, were not the members of the "ENGINEER CORPS OF HELL, OR ROME'S SAPPERS AND MINERS," as named in the title of this book.

EDWIN A. SHERMAN, Compiler.

PART THIRD.

PART THIRD.

SYLLABUS ERRORUM.

THE PAPAL SYLLABUS OF ERRORS, A. D. 1864.

[This document, though issued by the sole authority of Pope Pius IX, Dec. 8, 1864, must be regarded now infallible and irreformable, having been approved by the Vatican Ecumenical Council July 18, 1870. It is purely negative, but indirectly it teaches and enjoins the very opposite of what it condemns as error. We omit the Latin, and give the full translation.]

" *The Syllabus of the principal errors of our time, which are stigmatized in the Consistorial Allocutions, Encyclicals and other Apostolical Letters of our Most Holy Father, Pope Pius IX.*

§ I. PANTHEISM, NATURALISM AND ABSOLUTE RATIONALISM.

1. There exists no supreme, most wise and most provident Divine Being distinct from the universe, and God is none other than nature, and is therefore subject to change. In effect, God is produced in man and in the world, and all things are God, and have the very substance of God. God is therefore one and the same thing with the word, and hence spirit is the same thing with matter, necessity with liberty, true with false, good with evil, justice with injustice.

2. All action of God upon man is to be denied.

3. Human reason, without any regard to God, is the sole arbiter of truth and falsehood, of good and evil; it is its own law to itself, and suffices by its natural forces to secure the welfare of men and nations.

[Allocution, *Maxima quidem*, 9th June, 1862.]

4. All the truths of religion are derived from the native strength of human reason; whence reason is the master rule by which man can and ought to arrive at the knowledge of all truths of every kind.

5. Divine revelation is imperfect, and, therefore, subject to a continual and definite progress, which corresponds with the progress of human reason.

6. Christian faith contradicts human reason, and divine revelation not only does not benefit but even injures the perfection of man.

7. The prophecies and miracles set forth and narrated in the Sacred Scriptures are the fictions of poets; and the mysteries of the Christian faith are the result of philosophical investigations. In the books of both Testaments there are contained mythical inventions and Christ is himself a mythical fiction.

[Encyclical Letters, *Qui pluribus*, 9th November, 1846. Allocution, *Maxima quidem*, 9th June, 1862.]

§ II. MODERN RATIONALISM.

8. As human reason is placed on a level with religion, so theological matters must be treated in the same manner as philosophical ones.

[Allocution, *Singulari quâdum perfusi*, 9th December, 1854.]

9. All the dogmas of the Christian religion are, without exception, the object of scientific knowledge or philosophy; and human reason, instructed solely by history, is able, by its own natural strength and principles, to arrive at the true knowledge of even the most abstruse dogmas, provided such dogmas be proposed as subject-matter for human reason.

10. As the philosopher is one thing and philosophy is another, so it is the right and the duty of the philosopher to submit to the authority which he shall have recognized as true; but philosophy neither can nor ought to submit to any authority.

11. The Church not only ought never to animadvert upon

philosophy, but ought to tolerate the errors of philosophy, leaving to philosophy the care of their correction.

12. The decrees of the Apostolic See and of the Roman congregations fetter the free progress of science.

[Letter, *ad Archiep. Frising. Tuas libenter*, 21st December, 1863.]

13. The method and principles by which the old scholastic doctors cultivated theology are no longer suitable to the demands of the age and progress of science.

[Letter, *ad Archiep. Frising, Tuas libenter*, 21st December, 1863.]

14. Philosophy must be treated of without any account being taken of supernatural revelation.

[Epist., *ad Achiep. Frising. Tuas libenter*, 21st December, 1863.]

[N. B.—To the rationalistic system belong in great part the errors of Anthony Günther, condemned in the letter to the Cardinal Archbishop of Cologne, *Eximam tuam*, June 15, 1857, and in that to the Bishop of Breslau. *Dolore haud mediocri*, April 30, 1860.]

§ III. INDIFFRENTISM, LATITUDINARIANISM.

15. Every man is free to embrace and profess the religion he shall believe true, guided by the light of reason.

[Apostolic Letter, *Multiplices inter*, 10th June, 1851. Allocution, *Maxima quidem*, 9th June, 1862.]

16. Men may in any religion find the way of eternal salvation and obtain eternal salvation.

[Encyclical Letters, *Qui pluribus*, 9th November, 1846. Allocution, *Ubi primum*, 17th December, 1845. Encyclical Letters, *Singulari quidem*, 17th March, 1856.]

17. We may entertain a well-founded hope for the eternal salvation of all those who are in no manner in the true Church of Christ.

[Allocution, *Singulari quâdum*, 9th December, 1854. Encyclical Letters, *Quanto conficiamur*, 17th August, 1863.]

18. Protestantism is nothing more than another form of

the same true Christian religion, in which it is possible to be equally pleasing to God as in the Catholic Church.

[Encyclical Letters, *Noscitis et Nobiscum*, 8th December, 1849.]

§ IV. SOCIALISM, COMMUNISM, SECRET SOCIETIES, BIBLICAL SOCIETIES, CLERICO-LIBERAL SOCIETIES.

Pests of this description are frequently rebuked in the severest terms in the Encyc., *Qui pluribus*, Nov., 1846; Alloc., *Quibus quantisque*, April 20, 1840; Encyc., *Noscitis et Nobiscum*, Dec. 8, 1849; Alloc., *Singulari quâdum*, Dec. 9, 1854; *Encyc. Quanto conficiamur mœrore*, Aug. 10, 1863.

§ V. ERRORS CONCERNING THE CHURCH AND HER RIGHTS.

19. The Church is not a true and perfect and entirely free society, nor does she enjoy peculiar and perpetual rights conferred upon her by her Divine Founder, but it appertains to the civil power to define what are the rights and limits with which the Church may exercise authority.

[Allocution, *Singulari quâdum*, 9th December, 1854. Allocution, *Gravibusque*, 17th December, 1880. Allocution, *Maxima quidem*, 9te June, 1862.]

20. The ecclesiastical power must not exercise its authority without the permission and assent of the civil government.

[Allocution, *Meminit unusquisque*, 30th September, 1861.]

21. The Church has not the power of defining dogmatically that the religion of the Catholic Church is the only true religion.

[Apostolic Letter, *Multiplices inter*, 10th June, 1851]

22. The obligation which binds Catholic teachers and authors apply only to those things which are proposed for universal belief as dogmas of the faith by the infallible judgment of the Church.

[Letter, *ad Archiep. Frising. Tuas libenter*, 21st December, 1863.]

23. The Roman Pontiffs and Ecumenical Councils have

exceeded the limits of their power, have usurped the rights of princes, and have even committed errors in defining matters of faith and morals.

[Apostolic Letter, *Multiplices inter*, 10th June, 1851.]

24. The Church has not the power of availing herself of force, or any direct or indirect temporal power.

25. In addition to the authority inherent in the Episcopate, a further and temporal power is granted to it by the civil authority, either expressly or tacitly, which power is on that account also revocable by the civil authority whenever it pleases.

[Apostolic Letter, *ad apostolicæ*, 29th June, 1851.]

26. The Church has not the innate and legitimate right of acquisition and possession.

[Allocution, *Nunquam fore*, 15th December, 1856. Encyclical Letters, *Incredibili*, 18th September, 1863.]

27. The ministers of the Church and the Roman Pontiff ought to be absolutely excluded from all charge and dominion over temporal affairs.

[Allocution, *Maxima quidem*, 9th June, 1862.]

28. Bishops have not the right of promulgating even their apostolical letters without the permission of the government.

29. Dispensations granted by the Roman Pontiff must be considered null, unless they have been asked for by the civil government.

[Allocution, *Nunquam fore*, 15th December, 1856.]

30. The immunity of the Church and of ecclesiastical persons derives its origin from civil law.

[Apostolic Letter, *Multiplices inter*, 10th June, 1851.]

31. Ecclesiastical courts for temporal causes of the clergy, whether civil or criminal, ought by all means to be abolished, either without the concurrence and against the protest of the Holy See.

[Allocution, *Ascerbissimum*, 27th September, 1862. Allocution, *Nunquam fore*, 15th December, 1856.]

32. The personal immunity exonerating the clergy from

military service may be abolished, without violation either of natural right or of equity. Its abolition is called for by civil progress, especially in a community constituted upon principles of civil government.

[Letter to the Archbishop of Montreal, *Singularis nobisque*, 29th September, 1864.]

33. It does not appertain exclusively to ecclesiastical jurisdiction by any right, proper and inherent, to direct the teaching of theological subjects.

[Letter, *ad Archiep. Frising. Tuas libenter*, 21st December, 1863.]

34. The teaching of those who compose the Sovereign Pontiff to a free sovereign acting in the universal Church, is a doctrine which prevailed in the Middle Ages.

35. There would be no obstacle to the sentence of a General Council, or the act of all the universal peoples, transferring the Pontifical sovereignty from the Bishop and City of Rome to some other bishopric and some other city.

36. The definition of a National Council does not admit of any subsequent discussion, and the civil power can regard as settled an affair decided by such National Council.

[Apostolic Letter, *ad apostolicæ*, 22d August, 1851.]

37. National Churches can be established, after being withdrawn and plainly separated from the authority of the Roman Pontiff.

[Allocution, *Multis gravibusque*, 17th December, 1861.]

38. Roman Pontiffs have, by their too arbitrary conduct, contributed to the division of the Church into Eastern and Western.

[Apostolic Letter, *ad apostolicæ*, 12d August, 1851.]

§ VI. ERRORS ABOUT CIVIL SOCIETY, CONSIDERED BOTH IN ITSELF AND IN ITS RELATION TO THE CHURCH.

39. The commonwealth is the origin and source of all rights, and possess rights which are not circumscribed by any limits.

[Allocution, *Maxima quidem*, 9th June, 1862.]

40. The teaching of the Catholic Church is opposed to the well-being and interests of society.

[Encyclical Letters, *Qui pluribus*, 9th November, 1846. Allocution, *Quibus quantisque*, 20th April, 1849.]

41. The civil power, even when exercised by an unbelieving sovereign, possess an indirect and negative power over religious affairs. It therefore possesses not only the right called that of *exequatori*, but that of the (so-called) *appelatis ab abusu*.

42. In the case of conflicting laws between the two powers, the civil law ought to prevail.

[Apostolic Letter, *ad apostolica*, 22d August, 1851.]

43. The civil power has a right to break, and to declare and render null, the conventions (commonly called *Concordats*), concluded with the Apostolic See, relative to the use of rights appertaining to the ecclesiastical immunity, without the consent of the Holy See, and even contrary to its protest.

[Allocution, *In Consistoriali*, 1st November, 1850. Allocution, *Multis gravibusque*, 17th December, 1860.]

44. The civil authority may interfere in matters relating to religion, morality and spiritual government. Hence it has control over the instructions for the guidance of consciences issued, conformably with their mission by the pastors of the Church. Further, it possesses power to decree in the matter of administering the divine sacraments, as to the dispositions necessary for their reception.

[Allocution, *In Consistoriali*, 1st November, 1850. Allocution, *Maxima quidem*, 9th June, 1862]

45. The entire direction of public schools in which the youth of Christian States are educated, except (to a certain extent) in the case of episcopal seminaries, may and must appertain to the civil power, and belong to it, so far that no other authority whatsoever shall be recognized as having any right to interfere in the discipline of the schools, the arrangement of the studies, the taking of degrees, or the choice and approval of the teachers.

[Allocution, *In Consistoriali*, 1st November, 1850. Allocution, *Quibus luctuosissimis*, 5th September, 1851.]

46. Much more even in clerical seminaries, the method of study to be adopted is subject to the civil authority.

[Allocution, *Nunquam fore*, 15th December, 1856.]

47. The best theory of civil society requires that popular schools open to the children of all classes, and generally all public institutes intended for instruction in letters and philosophy and for conducting the education of the young, should be freed from all ecclesiastical authority, government and interference, and should be fully subject to the civil and political power, in conformity with the will of rulers and the prevalent opinion of the age.

48. This system of instructing youth, which consists in separating it from the Catholic faith and from the power of the Church, and in teaching exclusively, or at least primarily, the knowledge of natural things and the earthly ends of social life alone, may be approved by Catholics.

[Letter to the Archbishop of Fribourg, *Quam non sine*, 14th July, 1854.]

49. The civil power has the right to prevent ministers of religion and the faithful from communicating freely and mutually with each other and with the Roman Pontiff.

[Allocution, *Maxima quidem*, 9th June, 1862.]

50. The secular authority possesses, as inherent in itself, the right of presenting bishops, and may require of them that they take possession of their dioceses before having received canonical institution and the apostolic letters from the Holy See.

[Allocution, *Nunquam fore*, 15th December, 1856.]

51. And, further, the secular government has the right of deposing bishops from their pastoral functions, and it is not bound to obey the Roman Pontiff in those things which relate to episcopal sees and the institution of bishops.

[Apostolic Letter, *Multiplicis inter*, 10th June, 1851. Allocution, *Acerbissimum*, 27th September, 1852.]

52. The government has of itself the right to alter the

age prescribed by the Church for the religious profession, both of men and women; and it may enjoin upon all religious establishments to admit no person to take solemn vows without its permission.

[Allocution, *Nunquam fore*, 15th December, 1856.]

53. The laws for the protection of religious establishments, and securing their rights and duties, ought to be abolished; nay, more, the civil government may lend its assistance to all who desire to quit the religious life they have undertaken and break their vows. The government may also suppress religious orders, collegiate churches and simple benefices, even those belonging to private patronage, and submit their goods and revenues to the administration and disposal of the civil power.

[Allocution, *Acerbissimum*, 27th September, 1852. Allocution, *Probe memineritis*, 22d July, 1855.]

54. Kings and princes are only exempt from the jurisdiction of the Church, but are superior to the Church in litigated questions of jurisdiction.

[Apostolic Letter, *Multiplices inter*, 10th June, 1851.]

55. The Church ought to be separate from the State, and the State from the Church.

[Allocution, *Acerbissimum*, 27th September, 1852.]

§ VII. ERRORS CONCERNING NATURAL AND CHRISTIAN ETHICS.

56. Moral laws do not stand in need of the divine sanction, and there is no necessity that human laws should be conformable to the law of nature and receive their sanction from God.

57. Knowledge of philosophical things and morals, and also civil laws, may and must depart from divine and ecclesiastical authority.

58. No other forces are to be recognized than those which reside in matter; and all moral teaching and moral excellence ought to be made to consist in the accumulation and increase of riches by every possible means and in the enjoyment of pleasure.

59. Right consists in the material fact, and all human duties are but vain words, and all human acts have the force of right.

60. Authority is nothing else but the result of numerical superiority and material force.

[Allocution, *Maxima quidem*, 9th June, 1862.]

61. An unjust act, being successful, inflicts no injury upon the sanctity of right.

[Allocution, *Jumdudum cernimus*, 18th March, 1861.]

62. The principle of *non intervention*, as it is called, ought to be proclaimed and adhered to.

[Allocution, *Novos et ante*, 28th September, 1860.]

63. It is allowable to refuse obedience to legitimate princes; nay, more, to rise in insurrection against them.

[Encyclical Letters, *Qui pluribus*, 9th November, 1846. Allocution, *Quisque vestrum*, 4th October, 1847. Encylical Letters, *Nosci tis et Nobiscum*, 8th December, 1849. Apostolic Letter, *Cum Catholica*, 26th March, 1860.]

64. The violation of a solemn oath, even every wicked and flagitious action is repugnant to the eternal law, is not only not blamable, but quite lawful, and worthy of the highest praise, when done for the love of country.

[Allocution, *Quibus quantisque*, 20th April, 1848.]

§ VIII. THE ERRORS CONCERNING MARRIAGE.

65. It cannot be by any means tolerated that Christ has raised marriage to the dignity of a sacrament.

66. The sacrament of marriage is only an adjunct of the contract, and separable from it, and the sacrament itself consists in the nuptial benediction alone.

67. By the law of nature the marriage tie is not indissoluble, and in many cases divorce, properly so-called, may be pronounced by the civil authority.

[Apostolical Letter, *ad apostolicæ*, 22d August, 1851. Allocution, *Acerbissimum*, 27th September, 1852.]

68. The Church has not the power of laying down what are diriment impediments to marriage. The civil authority

does possess such a power, and can do away with existing impediments to marriage.

[Apostolical Letter, *Multiplices inter*, 10th June, 1851.]

69. The Church only commenced in later ages to bring in diriment impediments, and then availing herself of a right not her own, but borrowed from the civil power.

70. The canons of the Council of Trent which pronounce censure of anathema against those who deny to the Church the right of laying down what are diriment impediments, either are not dogmatic, or must be understood as referring to such borrowed power.

71. The form of solemnizing marriage prescribed by the said Council, under penalty of nullity, does not bind in cases where the civil law has appointed another form, and where it decrees that this new form shall effectuate a valid marriage,

72. Boniface VIII is the first who declared that the vow of chastity pronounced at ordination annuls nuptials.

73. The merely civil contract may, among Christians, constitute a true marriage; and it is false, either that the marriage contract between Christians is always a sacrament, or that the contract is null if the sacrament be excluded.

74. Matrimonial causes and espousals belong by their very nature to civil jurisdiction.

[Apostolic Letter, *ad apostolicæ*, 26th August, 1851. Letter to the King of Sardinia, 9th September, 1852. Allocution, *Acerbissimum*, 27th September, 1852. Allocution, *Multis gravibusque*, 17th December, 1860.]

N. B.—Two other errors may tend in this direction—those upon the abolition of the celibacy of priests, and the preference due to the state of matrimony over that of virginity. These have proscribed: the first, in the Encyclical *Qui pluribus*, November 9, 1846; the second, in the Apostolical Letter, *Multiplicis inter*, June 10, 1851.

§ IX. ERRORS REGARDING THE CIVIL POWER OF THE SOVEREIGN PONTIFF.

75. The children of the Christian and Catholic Church

are not agreed upon the compatibility of the temporal with the spiritual power.

[Apostolic Letter, *ad apostolicœ*, 22d August, 1851.]

76. The abolition of the temporal power, of which the Apostolic See is possessed, would contribute in the greatest degree to the liberty and prosperity of the Church.

[Allocution, *Quibus quantisque*, 20th April, 1849]

N. B —Besides these errors, explicitly noted, many others are impliedly rebuked by the proposed and asserted doctrine which all Catholics are bound most firmly to hold, touching the temporal sovereignty of the Roman Pontiff. These doctrines are clearly stated in the Allocutions, *Quibus quantisque*, 20th April, 1849, and *Si semper antea*, 20th May, 1850, Apostolical Letter *Quam Catholica Ecclesia* 26th March, 1860; Allocutions, *Novos*, 28th September, 1860; *Jumdudum*, 18th March, 1861; and *Maxima quidem*, 9th June, 1862.]

§ X. ERRORS HAVING REFERENCE TO MODERN LIBERALISM.

77. In the present day it is no longer expedient that the Catholic religion shall be held as the only religion of the State, to the exclusion of all other modes of worship.

[Allocution, *Nemo vestrum*, 26th July, 1855.]

78. Whence it has been wisely provided by law, in some countries called Catholic, that persons coming to reside therein shall enjoy the public exercise of their own worship.

[Allocution, *Acerbissimum*, 27th September 1852.]

79. Moreover, it is false that the civil liberty of every mode of worship, and the full power given to all of overtly and publicly manifesting their opinions and ideas, of all kinds whatsoever, conduce more easily to corrupt the morals and minds of the people and to the propagation of the pest of indifferentism.

[Allocution, *Nunquam fore*, 15th December, 1856.]

80. The Roman Pontiff can and ought to reconcile himself to, agree with progress, liberalism and civilization as lately introduced.

[Allocution, *Jumdudum cernimus*, 18th March, 1861.]

EXTRACT FROM THE FINAL DOGMATIC DECREE OF THE VATICAN ECUMENICAL COUNCIL OF THE INFALLIBILITY OF THE POPE.

"Knowing most fully that this See of Holy Peter remains ever free from all blemish of error, * * * * that the occasion of schism being removed, * * the Sacred Council approving, we teach and define that it is a dogma divinely revealed; that the Roman Pontiff, when he speaks *ex cathedra*, that is, when in discharge of the office of pastor and doctor of all Christians, by virtue of his supreme Apostolic authority, he defines a doctrine regarding faith or morals to be held by the universal Church, by the Divine assistance promised to him in blessed Peter, is possessed of that infallibility with which the Divine Redeemer willed that his Church should be endowed for defining doctrine regarding faith or morals; and that therefore such definitions of the Roman Pontiff are irreformable of themselves, and not from the consent of the Church. But if any one—which may God avert—presume to contradict this one definition; let him be *anathema*.

"Given at Rome, in public session solemnly held in the Vatican Basilica, in the year of our Lord one thousand eight hundred and seventy, on the eighteenth of July, in the twenty-fifth year of our Pontificate."

THE BULL OF POPE SEXTUS V AGAINST QUEEN ELIZABETH.

"We, Sixtus the Fifth, the universal Shepherd of the flock of Christ, the Supreme Chief, to whom the government of the whole world appertains, considering that the people of England and Ireland, after having been so long celebrated for their virtues, their religion and their submission to our See, have become putrid members, infected, and capable of corrupting the whole Christian body, and that on account of their subjection to the impious, tyrannical government of Elizabeth, *the bastard queen,* and by the influence of her adherents, who equal her in wickdeness, and who refuse, like her, to recognize the authority of the Roman Church; regarding that Henry the Eighth, formerly, for motives of debauchery, commenced all these disorders by revolting against the submission which he owed to *the Pope, the sole and true sovereign of England;* considering that the usurper Elizabeth has followed the path of this infamous king, we declare that there exists but one mode of remedying these evils, of restoring peace, tranquility and union to Christendom, of re-establishing religion, and of leading back the people to obedience to us, which is, *to depose from the throne that execrable* ELIZABETH, who falsely arrogates to herself the title of Queen of the British Isles. Being then inspired by the Holy Spirit for the general good of the Church, we renew by virtue of our apostolic power, the sentence pronounced by our predecessors, Pius the Fifth and Gregory the Thirteenth, *against this modern Jezebel;* we proclaim her deprived of royal authority, of the rights, titles or pretentions to which she may claim over the kingdoms of Ireland and England, affirming that she possesses them unlawfully and by usurpation. We relieve all her subjects from the oaths that they have taken to her, and we prohibit them from rendering any kind of service to *this execrable woman. It is our will that she be driven from door to door like one possessed of a devil, and that all human aid should be refused her;* we declare moreover that FOREIGNERS OR ENGLISHMEN are *permitted as a* MERITORIOUS WORK TO SEIZE THE PERSON OF ELIZABETH AND SURRENDER HER, LIVING OR DEAD, TO THE TRIBUNALS OF THE INQUISITION. *We promise to those* WHO SHALL ACCOMPLISH THIS GLORIOUS MISSION, *infinite recompenses, not only in the life eternal but in this world!* Finally, we grant plenary indulgences to the faithful, who shall willingly unite with the Catholic army, which is going to combat the impious Elizabeth, under the orders of our dear son, Philip the Second, to whom we give the British Isles in full sovereignty, as a recompense for the zeal he has always shown for our See, and for the particular affection he has shown for the Catholics of the low countries."

This terrible bull was published in the ecclesiastical States, with tolling of bells and by the light of candles. At Madrid they dressed the chapel of the Palace of the Escurial in black, and Philip dressed in black, and followed by all the grandees of his court, caused the anathema pronounced against the Queen of England to be read by the Nuncio.

Fortunately for England and the Protestant world, the fleet of the Invincible Armada was almost destroyed by a frightful tempest which assailed it at the mouth of the Thames. The vessels which escaped the violence of the sea were routed by Francis Drake, the Vice-Admiral of England, and obliged to return in disgrace to Spain.

THE ROMAN CATHOLIC BISHOP'S OATH.

"I, N., elect of the Church of N., from henceforward will be faithful and obedient to St. Peter the Apostle, and to the Holy Roman Church, and to our lord, the Lord N., Pope N., and to his successors canonically coming in. I will neither advise, consent, or do anything that may lose life or member, or that their persons may be seized or hands anywise laid upon them, or any injuries offered to them under any pretence whatsoever. The counsel which they shall intrust me withal, by themselves, their messages or letters, I will not knowingly reveal to any to their prejudice. I will help them to defend and keep the Roman Papacy and the royalties of St. Peter, saving my order against all men. The legate of the Apostolic See, going and coming, I will honorably treat and help in his necessities. The rights, honors, privileges and authority of the Holy Roman Church, of our lord, the Pope, and his foresaid successors, I will endeavor to preserve, defend, increase and advance. I will not be in any council, action or treaty in which shall be plotted against our said lord and the said Roman Church anything to the hurt or prejudice of their persons, right, honor, *State or power;* and, if I shall know any such thing to be treated or agitated by any whatsoever, *I will hinder it to my power*, and as soon as I can, will signify it to our said lord, or to some other, by whom it may come to his knowledge. The rules of the Holy Fathers, the apostolic decrees, ordinances or disposals, reservations, provisions and mandates, I will observe with all my might and cause to be observed by others. *Heretics, schismatics and rebels to our said lord or his foresaid successors*, I WILL TO MY UTMOST POWER PERSECUTE AND WAGE WAR WITH. I will come to a council when I am called, unless I be hindered by a canonical impediment. I will by myself, in person, visit the threshold of the apostles every three years, and give an account to our lord and his foresaid successors of all my pastoral office, and of all things anywise belonging to the state of my Church, to the discipline of my clergy and people, and lastly to the salvation of souls committed to my trust, and will in like manner humbly receive and diligently execute the apostolic commands. And, if I be detained by a lawful impediment, I will perform all the things aforesaid by a certain messenger hereto specially empowered, a member of my chapter, or some other in ecclesiastical dignity or else having a parsonage; or in default of these by a priest of the diocese; or in default of one of the clergy (of the diocese), by some other secular or regular priest of approved integrity and religion, fully instructed in all things above mentioned. And such impediment I will make out by lawful proofs to be transmitted by the foresaid messenger to the cardinal proponement of the Holy Roman Church in the congregation of the Sacred Council. The possessions belonging to my table I will neither sell, nor give away, nor mortgage, nor grant anew in fee, nor anywise alienate—no, not even with the consent of the chapter of my Church—without consulting the Roman Pontiff. And, if I shall make any alienation, *I will thereby incur the penalties contained in a* CERTAIN CONSTITUTION *put forth about this matter.* So help me, God, and those Holy Gospels of God."

EXTRACT FROM THE ROMAN CATHOLIC PRIEST'S OATH.

(See "Profession of Faith.")

"I acknowledge the Holy Catholic Apostolic Roman Church to be the Mother and Mistress of all Churches: *and I promise true obedience to the Bishop of Rome*, the successor of St. Peter, Prince of the Apostles, and Vicar of Jesus Christ on earth. I also undoubtedly receive and profess all other things delivered, defined and declared by the Sacred Canons and General Councils, and particularly by the Holy Council of Trent; *and I also condemn, reject and anathematize all things contrary thereto, and all heresies whatsoever* condemned, *rejected and anathematized by the Church.*

"This true Catholic faith, *without which none can be saved,* and which I now freely profess and truly hold, *I promise, vow and* SWEAR most constantly to hold, and to profess the same, whole and entire, with God's assistance to the end of my life; and to take care to the best of my power that it shall be held, taught, and preached by those over whom I shall have authority, or with the care of whom I shall be charged, by virtue of my office. *Amen.*

THE RIBAND CONSPIRACY IN IRELAND, OR THE SO-CALLED LAND LEAGUE MOVEMENT.

The *Dublin Evening Mail* gives the following picture of the state of Ireland, on account of this secret conspiracy against the Government of Great Brtiain and Protestants in general:

"A Riband Lodge is an affiliated branch of the Land League, which has for its object the two-fold purpose of extirpating heresy and regulating the occupation and possession of land. Each separate Lodge is composed of forty members. It has a Master, Secretary and thirty-four members. These are admitted with a solemn oath to yield unlimited obedience to the authorities of the institution, and to maintain the utmost secresy. They swear to wade knee-deep in Protestant blood, and spare none of the heretic race from cradle to crutch, and that they will not serve the Queen unless compelled, and that, when the day comes, to fight, and that neither the groans of men nor the moans of women shall daunt him, etc.

"The members are known to each other by secret signs and passwords, changed every three months by a central authority unknown even to conspirators themselves. They meet by conceit at fires and on market days at some public house known to be friendly, and drop in one by one till the room is full, and then proceed to business. They avoid night meetings as much as possible, lest they attract attention; and when they do meet at night, it is generally at dances got up for the purpose, when the junior members are dressed in women's clothes; all that appears to the observer is rustic hilarity and merriment, but the work of death is going on within.

" When an offence is committed against the barbarous code of laws this society has established, either by an agent ejecting non-paying tenants from land for which they are unwilling or unable to pay any rent, or by a farmer in becoming tenant for such ejected land, or by a landlord preferring a Protestant to a Roman Catholic tenant, or by information given for the purpose of bringing to justice members of the association, then, on the next meeting, of the Lodge, a complaint is brought forward against the offending individual; a jury is forthwith empanneled and sworn, consisting generally of seven members; the Master of the Lodge acts as Judge; the complaint is sworn to and examined by counsel; members volunteer evidence on one side or the other, and the Judge charges the jury, the verdict is brought in by the majority, and the sentence of death pronounced in hideous mockery of justice by the presiding conspirator. The appointment of the executioner next follows. Lots are drawn, and they on whom the fatal billet falls must, on the pain of death, carry out the merciless sentence. Frequently, however, the trial and sentences are reported to a distant Lodge, which furnishes the executioners, on the understanding of the services being returned in kind when demanded. There is no hurry about the matter—all is conducted in the most sedate and business-like manner. The victim is watched, his habits examined and reported; accurate information of all his movements obtained; a time is fixed for his execution. If unfavorable, it is deferred with perfect coolness; if favorable, he is executed without remorse and without mercy."

A POPISH BULL OR CURSE.

PRONOUNCED ON REV. WM. HOGAN, FORMERLY A PAPAL PRIEST IN PHILADELPHIA.

"By the authority of God Almighty, the Father, Son and Holy Ghost, and the undefiled Virgin Mary, Mother and Patroness of our Saviour, and of all Celestial Virtues, Angels, Archangels, Thrones, Dominions, Powers, Cherubim and Seraphim, and of all the Holy Patriarchs, Prophets, and of all the Apostles and Evangelists, of the Holy Innocents, who in the sight of the Holy Lamb are found worthy to sing the new song of the Holy Martyrs and Holy Confessors, and of all the Holy Virgins, and of all Saints, together with the Holy Elect of God—may he, William Hogan, be damned. We excommunicate and anathematize him from the threshold of the Holy Church of God Almighty. We sequester him, that he may be tormented, disposed and be delivered over with Dathan and Abiram, and with those who say unto the Lord, 'Depart from us, we desire none of thy ways.' As a fire quenched with water, so let the light of him be put out for evermore, unless it shall repent him and make satisfaction. Amen.

"May the Father, who creates man, curse him! May the Son, who suffered for us, curse him! May the Holy Ghost, who is poured out in baptism, curse him! May the Holy Cross, which Christ for our salvation, triumphing over his enemies, ascended, curse him!

"May the Holy Mary, ever Virgin and Mother of God, curse him! May St. Michael, the advocate of the Holy Souls, curse him! May all the Angels, Principalities and Powers, and all Heavenly Armies, curse him! May the glorious band of the Patriarchs and Prophets, curse him!

"May St. John the Precurser, and St. John the Baptist, and St. Peter and St. Paul and St. Andrew, and all other of Christ's Apostles together, curse him! And may the rest of the Disciples and Evangelists, who by their preaching converted the universe, and the holy and wonderful company of Martyrs and Confessors, who by their works are found pleasing to God Almighty; may the Holy Choir of the Holy Virgins, who for the honor of Christ have despised the things of the world, damn him! May all Saints, from the beginning of the world to everlasting ages, who are found to be beloved of God, damn him!

"May he be damned wherever he be, whether in the house or in the alley, in the world or in the water, or in the Church! May he be cursed in living and dying!

"May he be cursed in eating, in being hungry, in being thirsty, in fasting and sleeping, in slumbering and in sitting, in living, in working, in resting and * * * * and in blood-letting!

"May he be cursed in all the faculties of his body!

"May he be cursed inwardly and outwardly! May he be cursed in his hair! Cursed be he in his brains and his vertex; in his temples, in his eyebrows, in his cheeks, in his jawbones, in his nostrils, in his teeth and grinders, in his lips, in his shoulders, in his arms, in his fingers!

"May he be damned in his mouth, in his breast, in his heart and purtenances, down to the very stomach!

"May he be cursed in his * * * * and his * * *, in his thighs, in his * * * * * * and his * * * and in his knees, his legs and his feet and toe-nails!

"May he be cursed in all his joints and articulation of the members, from the crown of his head to the soles of his feet may there be no soundness!

"May the Son of the Living God, with all the glory of His Majesty, curse him! And may Heaven, with all the powers that move therein, rise up against him, and curse and damn him, unless he repent and make satisfaction! Amen! So be it, be it so. Amen!"

EXTRACTS FROM BISHOP DUPANLOUP'S BOOK AGAINST FREEMASONRY.

Bishop Dupanloup of Orleans, France, was deputed by Pope Pius IX, in 187–, to prepare a work against Freemasonry, and to echo the anathemas and thunders of the Vatican against this noble Order:

"I have often been asked the following questions on the subject of Freemasonry:

"'Is it an institution hostile to religion?'

"'May a Christian become a Freemason?'

"'Can one be at the same time a Freemason and a Christian?'"

Some years ago Mgr. de Ketteler, Bishop of Mayence, one of the most learned bishops and large-minded men in Germany, was also obliged to give his attention to this subject, and he has published a pamphlet with this title, "*Can a Catholic become a Freemason?*"

His answer was the same as mine, and after a careful study of the question, I must reply as he does: "*No!* a Catholic, a Christian, cannot be a Freemason."

Why? Because Freemasonry is the enemy of Christianity, and in the depth of its heart an irreconcilable enemy. I will go still further, and ask, "Can a serious-minded man, a man of sound, common sense, become a Freemason?" And I must answer equally clearly, "*No!* Because Freemasonry, in its true spirit, in its very essence and in its last acts is the declared enemy of Christianity, and by its fundamental principles an irreconcilable enemy."

"Was it not with a deeply-seated, hostile intention that, in 1869, at Brussels, Naples and Paris, those new Councils (in Masonic language, *Conventions*), were convened *in the face of the Œcumenical Council?* And quite lately, has not a similar Convention tried to meet in Rome itself? We may remember that this Paris Convention was announced by a circular of the Grand Master of the Order as follows:

"The undersigned, considering that, under present circumstances, *in the face of the Œcumenical Council,* which is about to open, *it is important* that Freemasonry *should solemnly affirm its great principles,"* * * * etc.

I only wish to make one remark upon this circular. It is upon the motive of this projected Convention. It is to elaborate and vote *a solemn manifesto*—for what purpose? To affirm *certain principles* which it was *important* to lay down *in face of the* Œcumenical Council. Would it be possible to declare in a more explicit manner the flagrant antagonism between Freemasonry and the Catholic Church? And if it were possible to have any doubt left on the subject, would it not be enough to remove it, to remember a letter published at that time by M. Michelet, and in which the "*manifestation*" which it was incumbent on the Freemasons to make, "in face of the Œcumenical Council," would be "THE TRUE COUNCIL WHICH WOULD JUDGE THE FALSE ONE?"

Freemasonry is, then, a serious war declared against all religion. But the odious object of the Freemasons appears specially in the zeal they show in preaching morality without God, and, in consequence, in separating the instruction of youth from all religious belief.

"Christianity" (Catholicism), it is said incessantly in the

Lodges, "is a *lying, bastard* religion, *repudiated by common sense, brutalizing*, and which must be *annihilated*. It is *a heap of fables, a worm-eaten fabric. Catholicism is a used-up formula*, repudiated by every sensible man. *It is not the lying religion of the false priests of a Christ* which will guide our steps." Thus spoke, at the installation of the Lodge of "*Hope*," the *great orator* of the Lodge, the Brother Lacombie. According to this *orator*, the ministers of the Gospel (priests) are a party "which has undertaken to *enchain all progress, stifle all light and destroy all liberty*, in order to reign quietly over a *brutalized population of ignorant slaves.*"

Further on he continues: "To-day, that the light is beginning to shine through the clouds, we must have the courage to make short work of all this *rubbish of fables*, even should the torch of reason *reduce to cinders* all that still remains standing of these *vestiges of ignorance and superstition.*"

This is the way Freemasonry speaks; this is what it calls "not troubling its head about Christianity." What in fact is the principle—free-thinking. "Free-thinking is the FUNDAMENTAL PRINCIPLE. Not RESTRAINED, but COMPLETE and universal liberty. A liberty which shall be ABSOLUTE, without limit, *in its fullest extent*. Absolute liberty of conscience is the ONLY BASIS of Freemasonry. Freemasonry is, in fact, ABOVE all dogmas. It is above all religions. Liberty of conscience is SUPERIOR TO ALL FORMS of religious belief. And this unlimited, complete and universal liberty is a RIGHT. Thus liberty, right not in regard to the civil law, but to the interior conscience—liberty, the absolute, universal right to believe what one wills, as he wills, or not to believe anything at all. This *right*, which is proclaimed to be anterior and superior to all religious convictions or forms of belief—this is the fundamental principle and the sole basis of Freemasonry. The Masonic principal is, therefore, exclusive of Christianity, and hence a Christian cannot be a Freemason."

"But besides, has not Garibaldi, the accomplice, and perhaps the agent at this moment in Rome, of the great persecutor of the Church in Germany—has not Garibaldi been Grand Master of the Italian Freemasons? And when the great conspirator, Joseph Mazzini, died, what happened? All the Italian Lodges went into mourning; many of them sent deputations to his funeral, and the Grand Orient of Italy invited all Freemasons, of whatever nationality, who found themselves at that moment in the valley of the Tiber, to assemble themselves in the Piazza del Popolo. At the hour appointed a host of brothers surrounded the Masonic banner, which for the first time had been displayed in Rome, and followed it to the capitol, bearing the bust of Mazzini."

Can we wonder, after all this, that popes and bishops should have condemned Freemasonry? And is it not a great duty that they have thus fulfilled, and a great service rendered to humanity? For the two centuries during which Freemasonry has been, I will not say founded, but developed in Europe, the Popes have never ceased their anxious watch over its movements; and in the eighteenth century two Sovereign Pontiffs, Clement XII and the learned Benedict XIV, and, lastly, Pius IX, pronounced against this association the most explicit and the most solemn condemnations.

Let it suffice to quote here some passages of the celebrated Bull *Quo graviore* of Leo XII, and a recent allocution of Pius IX.

The Pope Leo XII, in this Bull, first calls to mind the condemnations pronounced against Freemasonry since the reign of Clement XII, declares this institution to be the *open enemy of the Catholic Church*, and finally recalls the Bull of Pius VII, his immediate predecessor; then he himself renews all these condemnations:

"Beware of the seductive and flattering speeches which are employed to induce you to enter into these societies. Be convinced that no one can enter them without being guilty of grave sin."

Further on, in accents of the *warmest charity*, he conjures those who have allowed themselves to be seduced to give up the Lodges as soon as possible and forbids, under pain of all the penalties pronounced by his predecessors [including confiscation of property and death], any Catholic to be received into the Society of Freemasons.

Lastly, Pius IX, recalling in his allocution of the 25th September, 1865, the warnings given to Freemasonry by his predecessors, he continues thus:

"Unfortunately, these warnings have not had the hoped for result; and we look upon it, therefore, as a duty to condemn this Society anew. We condemn this Masonic Society, and all other societies of the same nature, and which, though differing in form, tend to the same object, under the same pains and penalties as those specified in the constitutions of our predecessors, and this concerns all Christians of every condition, rank or dignity all over the world."

It is for this reason that all the Belgian Bishops, in a collective circular on Freemasonry, made the following declaration:

"It is positively foridden to take any part in this Society, and those who persist in so doing are unworthy of receiving absolution as long as they shall not have sincerely renounced their error."

It is for this reason, again, that the Irish Bishops, assembled together in Dublin, in April, 1861, in a pastoral letter addressed to the clergy and faithful of these dioceses, pointed out Freemasonry among other contemporary perils, saying:

"It is for us a sacred duty to warn you to avoid these secret societies, and especially that of the *Freemasons*."

Finally, not to multiply quotations any further, it is for this reason that the Bishops of free Northern America, assembled in Council at Baltimore, pointed out and unanimously condemned the Society of Freemasons in a pastoral letter addressed to their diocesans.

[NOTE BY THE COMPILER.—At Cincinnati, Ohio, on the 19th of March, 1882, the Provincial Council of Roman Catholic Bishops re-condemned Freemasonry and all other similar societies, and repealed and annulled the Declaration of American Independence].

"In France, how often has not the Episcopate lifted up her voice to repeat the Pontifical condemnations, and demonstrated the incompatibility of Freemasonry with Christianity (Roman Catholicism). What the Bishops think of Freemasonry in France, Belgium, England and America, they equally think in Germany."

I have before me at this moment a pamphlet published by Mgr. de Ketteler. The conclusion of this calm and exhaustive treatise is this:

"There is, then, on the one hand, the *Catholic Church*, and on the other, *modern Freemasonry*. A Catholic who becomes a Freemason *deserts the temple of the living God to work at the temple of an idol.*"

Says Mgr. the Bishop of Autun: "If one wishes honestly to remain a Christian (Catholic), one cannot be at the same time a Freemason."

Yes, in reply to Bishop Dupanloup's tirades and false assertions, excepting one, and in that we most heartily concur, "*a Roman Catholic cannot be a Freemason, nor a Freemason be a Roman Catholic.*"

Adopting the language of the Rev. Bro. E. H. Ward, at the laying of the corner-stone of the new Masonic Temple in Stockton, California, he uttered the following truths:

"You will seek in vain for a higher morality than Masonry inculcates. I bear this testimony gladly, for it has rejoiced my heart to learn that Masonry grounds its morality not upon utilitarianism, or any philosophical theories of the past or present, but (where alone a true system of morals can be based) upon God's existence and man's accountability to him. It does not profess to have discovered its system, but to have derived it from the Bible, 'The Great Light of Masonry.' For every intelligent Mason that book is essentially different from any other book. * * * This book, 'every line bedewed with drops of love divine, and with the eternal heraldry and signature of the Almighty stamped,' we (Masons) accept as the revelation of God's will to man, and from it derive our moral precepts. * * * Purity, brotherly love, relief, truth, temperance, fortitude and justice, are only a few of them, and flowers more beautiful than these grow not in the garden of God."

Contrast the above beautiful and eloquent eulogium with the following from the *Roman Catholic Monitor* of San Francisco, the mouth-piece of Rome, in speaking of the Knights Templars of America, at their Twenty-second Triennial Conclave in San Francisco, August 20, 1883. It says:

"They are simply a band of men belonging to the Masonic Order, and all their Latin devices, crosses, religious ceremonies and sham knightly armor, are merely so many gaudy, glittering feathers plucked from the peacock to ornament the buzzard. The ceremonies on Sunday at the Pavilion were a hollow mockery, and the Knight Templar Order merely an association of oath-bound grippers, who believe in having a 'good time' under borrowed plumes and under knightly names, that are only soiled by being used by such unworthy imitators of the invincible Knights of the ages of chivalry.

"There is no more connection between the real Knights of the past and the dressed-up dudes of the present, than there is between the architecture of St. Peter's in Rome and the brick-pile abortion called the City Hall. These men are merely Freemasons, who are void of the first principles of the dignity, honor and religious zeal which animated the Knights of the past, when the Church blessed their banners.

"Every man in the sham Knights' Society is under the ban of the Catholic Church, and this of itself is sufficient to prove that there must be something dangerous to Christianity, to morality and to society in such an oath-bound secret organization. Individually, the men who intend to parade themselves in public—like so many circus-riders, dressed up in the tawdry trappings of the ring—may be very decent dish-washers, counter-jumpers, cocktail manipulators, or members of any of the various crafts by which money is made rapidly, if not honestly; but it would take considerable magic to transform one of these dressed-up dudes into the genuine Knight who flourished in an age when courage passed current for character, and when men were valued for their faith and valor, and not because they could put on borrowed clothes and ride a borrowed horse, and call themselves by the doubly-ridiculous title of Sir Knights."

In response to which we offer the following brief poem, by the gifted authoress, Mrs. Eliza A. Pittsinger of San Francisco:

THE TEMPLARS' CROSS AND MARTYR'S CROWN.

BY ELIZA A. PIITSINGER,

(Author of "The Bugle Peals.")

[Respectfully dedicated to the Knights Templar of America, at their Triennial Conclave, and the laying of the corner-stone of the GARFIELD Monument at San Francisco, California, on the 24th day of August, 1883, the 311th Anniversary of St. Bartholomew.]

> What means this pageant of display,
> These symbols of an Ancient Day,
> That o'er our city float and play?
>
> What means these men? this mighty host,
> Of which the Nation well may boast,
> That bears its banners to our coast?
>
> The banquet, dance, procession grand,
> With valiant type and model manned?
> O, answer, heroes of the land?
>
> While thus I question, fleet and fast
> Like peals from some far bugle-blast,
> Comes up an answer from the past.

All that I hear I cannot tell;
Suffice it, brothers, that we dwell
In bonds of peace, and all is well!

Some fragments of your Order grand,
So ancient and so wisely planned,
I do most clearly understand!

I pluck a blossom from the tree
Of olden records, that shall be
With us a bond of unity!

And to this great, momentous time,
'Mid scenes of grandeur most sublime,
I sing the song of death and crime!

A valiant Knight was DeMolay,
Who, on a dark, intriguing day,
Was murdered by his foes, they say.

Burned at the stake, by those who sought,
(Who with infernal weapons wrought),
To crush the golden germs of thought.

Who were these foes? what was their creed?
What demon crouched behind the deed,
Did those rebellious spirits lead?

Full fifteen thousand men were slain,
And in a crimson pool were lain,
O, why this slaughter, sons of Cain?

Knights of to-day, sheep of the fold,
Who still preserve those symbols old,
What mystery do these deeds unfold?

Five hundred and seventy years have sped,
Since those brave Knights of Freedom bled,
With DeMolay at the front and head.

What force was hid behind the scene?
By what nefarious machine
Burst forth that flood of hate and spleen?

By whose command or edict came
Those thunderbolts of wrath and shame,
That wrapt this olden Knight in flame?

Go back to Rome! to bomb and shell
Of Pope Clement, who now doth dwell
Deep in the fiery pit of Hell!

Behold in this lost soul the foe!
Behold the seas of blood and woe,
From Popish Bulls of long ago!

Ye wardens of the mystic rite,
O, deadly is the wrath and spite
Of bigotry against the light!

Go back to Rome! Behold to-day
The same old craft that once did slay
The Prince of Orange and DeMolay!

The Harlot sits upon her throne!
Her hands are crimson, and her zone
Is flecked with colors not her own!

The demon lurks within his lair,
The foe behind his pledges fair,
O, soldiers of the land, beware!

O, brothers, keep your armor bright!
Our LINCOLN fell beneath the blight
Of Romish hate and Papal spite!

With problems solved and battles past,
The mourning Goddess stands aghast,
And bares her visage to the blast.

In fifteen hundred and seventy-two,
This day of August we review
The bloody St. Bartholomew!

That time when brave Coligny fell,
When Catharine, Patron Saint of Hell,
Shuffled her Romish cards so well!

But love outspeeds the shafts of hate;
It twines its laurels with the great
Immortal names we consecrate.

O, GARFIELD, LINCOLN! to the line
Of Martyrdom ye bear the sign
Of all that's deathless and divine!

As Master Builders ye were known,
And as we lay this corner-stone,
A fragment of our craft is shown!

With sword in hand, and burnished shield,
To no intriguing power we yield,
Our rights in Temple, State or Field!

Beneath the sacred folds that glow
Above our Nation's ebb and flow
We throw our gauntlet to the foe!

We bear our colors to the light,
And with the enemy's camp in sight,
Hew to the line, strike to the right!

Our Temple rises, block by block,
With granite borne from Plymouth Rock,
It braves the fiery lightning's shock!

And standing by the Golden Gate,
This sword and shield we consecrate
To LIBERTY OF SCHOOL AND STATE!

[NOTE.—In reply to the attack made by the Roman Catholic *Monitor* upon the Knights Templar, and the Masonic Fraternity generally.—E. A. P.]

INTERESTING INFORMATION FROM PERU AND CHILI.

[Extract from a letter from a distinguished officer of the U. S. Navy, and an eminent Freemason, to the Compiler of this work, dated at Payta, Peru, August 6th, 1883]:

"There is but little in the news line to write about. The war still lingers in Peru, with no great amount of fighting. The people are too ignorant (from their Church education) to know how to form a government, and their teachers are too much frightened to tell them how to do so. In Chili there is a strong party opposed to the Church and State. It will come finally. In Peru the clergy are afraid to oppose a peace or to favor one, as either action may cause a loss of power for them. The degradation of these countries is sublime in its thoroughness. Treachery is a characteristic of the men and lechery of the women, though the women are far superior to the men. Virtue in office is unknown in Peru. Fidelity to the marriage laws, *or even to the laws of nature, is rare among the men!* Among a lot of fifteen hundred prisoners taken in the early part of the war, it was found that after two months' confinement, OVER TWO HUNDRED HAD THE SYPHILIS IN THE ANUS! But such is to be expected in a country wholly controlled by a celibate priesthood who have unlimited license.

"I only wrote the above to show the utter degradation which seems to follow an absolute monkish rule. There is said to be an old priest in Lima who is now living in open and undenied intercourse WITH HIS OWN GRAND-DAUGHTER! What makes the matter worse, HE IS THE FATHER OF HIS GRAND-DAUGHTER! I suppose he will look after a young baby girl recently born to him, if he does not lose his virility through old age. The priest at this little town (Payta, Peru), *has four children,* AND IS STILL RESPECTED! He supports the children. You can have no idea of how low this man has gotten, and I believe all through the celibacy of the Pope's priesthood.

"I could write a most disgusting letter on this topic, but to send it would be to violate the chastity of the United States mails.

"There was quite a little skirmish the other day in the mountains, and, as usual, the Peruvians were defeated. *Their conquerors killed all the wounded and prisoners, first making the prisoners* DIG THEIR OWN GRAVES! It is said that before killing the men *they were mutilated in the most disgusting and barbarous way!* I can see really but little to admire in either the Peruvians or Chilenos. The lower classes in each country are very low indeed, and scarcely deserve to be called human. The Peruvians are more degraded, but the cruelty of the Chilenos is unequalled."

CRITICISM BY ONE OF THE LITERATI OF CALIFORNIA.

"Home, Sweet Home," made its author, Howard Payne, immortal. "The Battle Hymn of the Republic" has given Julia Ward Howe a place in the pantheon of lyric verse. There are tributes to pathetic destiny, to lofty inspiration and to the holiest memories of the human heart; hence their everlasting enshrinement. Others have become immortal through their works because of adverse and relentless criticisms. The Scottish reviewers undoubtedly gave the prime and main impulse to the grand creations of Byron. "The Wandering Jew," because of the anathemas of Rome, has made Eugene Sue the conspicuous figure he is in fictitious narrative. And there exists no doubt but that the author of "The Jesuit," this spirited and talented poet of the Golden State, is to have placed upon her temple the wreath of the undying. Surely, if the brilliant efforts of an earnest worker against the designing and Anti-Republican Jesuit can give conspicuity of immortality, then our poet is verily to become a living memory.

"The Jesuit" is an embodiment of an inspiration that is scarcely surpassed, unless by other efforts of the same writer. It is an incision as of a blade of fire, CLEAVING THE HARLOT OF THE TIBER. The whole nature of the *personnel* of the military arm of the Roman Catholic hierarchy is laid open to inspection by the masterly effort of Mrs Pittsinger. "The Jesuit," however, is only one of many creations of a similar character from the pen of this really meritorious poet of the "Far West." The fact that Rome writhes beneath the strokes of her subtle and penetrating lance proves that she has power, and is finally to become a conspicuous figure in the annals of Roman hate.

The poem is as follows:

> In Rome a tyrant, and in Spain a thing
> That wears a mask and bears a poisonous sting;
> In India a strangler, in France a knave,
> In Ireland a bigot and a slave;
> In our Republic a designing tool
> And traitor warring with the Public School—
> And whether in Greece, in Hindoostan or Spain,
> His record bears the progeny of Cain.
>
> In the black arts a chieftain and a king,
> Moving *en rapport* with a sudden spring.
> And in the game of infamy and sin
> He steals a march long ere his foes begin;
> His dupes he marks, and with a ruthless greed,
> Wherein his conscience glorifies the deed,
> No means are left untried by which to take
> The last lone Peter's pence, for Jesus sake!
>
> In a most marvellous and crafty way
> He flatters, fawns and pounces on his prey;
> If at his hands a kindly deed is done,
> O, then beware of some dark plot begun!
> The robes of light he dons, and serves his creed
> In garments filched and suited to his need!
>
> Hid from the light in some dark, musty aisle,
> He learns to feign, to meddle and beguile;
> And in his skill avoids no toil nor care,
> As link on link he weaves his wily snare,
> Spins his dark web, and most adroitly plies
> On poor confiding bats and helpless flies
> The vilest of all arts and blackest of all lies.

His breath is like some dire and dread simoon,
Forever blasting with a curse and doom;
Whate'er he touches droops beneath the spell
Of some dark, haunting shade, cruel and fell—
Where'er he journeys, wheresoever toils,
There virtue weeps and innocence recoils,
And the fair cup of life doth overflow
With desolation, infamy and woe.

And thus he stands, a stigma and a blot,
With deeds confined to no especial spot—
Where carnage, superstition, death and crime
Despoil an age or devastate a clime
There hath he wandered, there upon the sand
Hath left the print of his unrighteous hand.

MIKE'S CONFESSION.

Now Mike was an 'ostler of very good parts,
   Yet only a church-mouse was he;
And he came to confess to the new parish priest,
   Like a pious and true devotee.

When his sins were reeled off till no more could be found,
   Said the priest: "Are you sure you've told all?
Have the mouths of the horses never been greased,
   So they couldn't eat oats in the stall?"

"With respict to yer riv'rence," said Mike, with a grin,
   "Sure for that ye may lave me alone;
I've scraped till there's niver a sin lift bahoind—
   Me conscience is clane to the bone!"

So absolved, happy Mike went away for more sins,
   Till the day came round to tell all;
And the very first thing he confessed, he had greased
   The mouth of each horse in the stall.

"How is this?" said the priest, "when here but last week,
   You never had done this, you swore."
"Faith, thanks to yer riv'rence," said Mike,
   "*Till you mintioned it, I niver had heard it before.*"

DEVOTION TO THE BLESSED VIRGIN.

MARY THE MASTERPIECE OF OMNIPOTENCE.

She is the Most Perfect Likeness of Her Son.

"How can we, who are so insignificant and impotent, praise Mary? *For even if all the members of all men were changed into tongues*, they would not altogether be able to praise her as she deserves." Mary is, indeed, after the incarnation of the Divine Word, her Son, the masterpiece of Omnipotence, for, after God, she is truly the aggregation of all good. St. Bernardine of Sienna beautifully expresses the idea in the mind of the Church with respect to Mary's greatness and majesty, when he says that "He alone who has created her can comprehend the height of His work, and *He has reserved to Himself the perfect knowledge of her*—'tanta fuit perfectio ejus, ut soli Deo cognoscenda reservetur.'" "The love of Jesus Christ for His Mother," says Mgr. Malou, Bishop of Bruges (tom. ii, ch. 11, art. 3 and 4), "is the true measure of the graces with which He adorns her. In creating her His Mother, He constituted her the heiress of all His treasures. * * * * *

"If, before being born, we could chose our own mother, with what qualities would we not wish to have her endowed? And had we the power to create her, with what perfection would we not adorn her? What was not in our power the Son of God could do. *He has chosen and created His own Mother. He has made her as He wished.*"

Hear the magnificent expressions of the learned Dominican Contenson (lib. 10, diss. vi, cap. 2): "Between the Mother of God and her Son there is a remote, substantial union, and certain identity, because the substance of the Son and Mother is one and the same, for the flesh of Christ is the flesh of Mary, and, certainly, if man and wife are two in one flesh, how much more so are not the Mother and the Son? Mary has supreme sanctity, and the highest possible resemblance to her Son (Summa cum Filio similitudo). The maternity of Mary enters into the hypostatic order, and as St. Thomas says, it closely touches the boundaries of the divinity (fines diuinitatis proxime attingit)."

Never can the Mother be separated from her Son, she is ever with Him, and He is ever with her. They rule together. Hence that grand expression of Arnod of Carnot: "The Mother cannot be separated from her Son in His government or power. The flesh of Christ and that of Mary is one and the same, and I consider the glory of the Son and Mother not so much as being common to them, as being the same in both—Nec e dominatione vel potentia Filii Mater potest esse sejuncta. Una est Christi et Mariæ Caro; et Filii gloriam cum Matre non tam communem judico quam eamdem."

St. Thomas, following St. Bernard, says (Opuscul. de charitate), that "God made Mary the infinite image of His own goodness—Fecit hanc Deus bonitatis suae infinitam imaginem."

Hear the devout Bernard addressing Mary (Serm. in Signum Magnum): "How familiar you have deserved to become with Him (God); in you He remains, and you in Him; you clothe Him with the substance of your flesh, and He clothes you with the glory of His Majesty; you cover the sun with a cloud, and you yourself are covered with the sun—Quam familiaris ei fieri meruisti; in te manet, et tu in eo, vestis eum et vestiris ab eo; vestis eum substantia carnis, et vestit ille te gloria majestatis; vestis Solem nube et Sole ipsa vestriis."

Compare the words of St. Bernard with what the "Divine Life of the Blessed Virgin" records the Divine Infant to have said to His Mother, and you will discover a very close and striking similarity of expression and idea. "God," says St. Peter Damian (Serm. 14 in Nativ. B. V. Mariæ), "is in the Virgin Mary by identity, because He is what she is—Inest (Deus) Mariæ Virgini identitate, quia idem est quod ille." "Let then every creature be silent and tremble," continues the same Saint, "and let him hardly dare to lift his eyes to the immensity of so great a dignity, and of such great merit—Hic taceat et contremiscat."

On these words of the Canticles, "My beloved to me and I to Him," Philip of Harvenge (Comment. in Cantic., lib. 3 c. 16), represents the Immaculate Mary as saying: "*My beloved gives me what He has, and I give Him what I have, so that what He has is mine, and what I have is His. We live in community by love and union.*"

Father LePoire says (12 e Etoile, chap. 12 e): "Jesus and Mary are so closely united together that there is no means of separating them, or as conceiving them as separated from each other. Jesus was conceived by Mary, and Mary was conceived for Jesus. Jesus wishes to come to us only through Mary, and Mary exists only on account of Jesus."

Peter DeBlois (in Nativ. B. M. M. Serm., 38), says: "Mary was born in order that Jesus might be born from her."

Salazar (DePraedestin. Virg. ad existent., cap. 19), says: "All the virtues which shine out so grandly in Jesus Christ, are also conspicuous in Mary, and Jesus has in turn appropriated to Himself all the virtues of His Mother." Truly, then, can Mary be styled the form and the idea of God. "The most holy Virgin," says St. Augustin, "is the idea and the form of God, not only under the relation of the humanity of Christ taken from her, but also under the relation of the divinity—Est virgo sanctissima idea it forma Dei, non solum ratione humanitatis assumptæ, sed etiam ratione divinitatis. "Mary is not only the idea and image of the essence and perfections of God," says Barbier, "*but also what is given to no other creature, she represents in herself in a certain manner, the Divine Persons and the Divine processions.*"

To the Holy Virgin are applied by the Church these words of wisdom (vii, 26): "For she is the brightness of eternal light, and the unspotted mirror of God's majesty, and the image of His goodness." Well has Amadeus of Lusanne in the 12th century said (Homil. 7, de laud., B. M. V.): "*Never has anything like to Mary been seen among the sons or daughters of Adam, nothing like her among the prophets, apostles or evangelists, nothing in Heaven or on earth; for I ask who amongst the children of God can be compared or equalled to the Mother of God?*" "I DARE TO SAY," WRITES BARBIER, "THAT IT SEEMS TO ME THAT GOD IMITATED NARCISSUS, WHO ON SEEING HIS OWN IMAGE IN THE WATER, BECAME SO ENAMORED OF IT, THAT TO ENJOY IT, HE PLUNGED INTO THE WATER AFTER IT. IT WAS SO WITH GOD, WHO GAZING ON MARY AS A MOST LIMPID FOUNTAIN, AND SEEING IN HER HIS OWN IMAGE MOST PERFECTLY REPRESENTED, AND BECOMING CAPTIVATED WITH HER, HE DESCENDED INTO HER CHASTE WOMB."

Hear how our Lord Himself addresses His august Mother, as we read in the Revelations of St. Bridget (1st Book, chap. 46): "You are to me the most sweet and dear of all creatures. Many figures are seen in a mirror, but the image of oneself is always considered with the most pleasure. Hence, though I love all my saints, I love you in a manner altogether special, because I have been engendered from your flesh. You are the chosen myrrh whose perfume has ascended to the Divinity, *and has caused Him to descend into your body. This same heavenly odor has lifted your body and your soul up to the Divinity, with whom you now are both as to your body and your soul.*"

St. John Damascene (Orat. DeDormit. Deip), assures us that Mary has ascended beyond the choirs of the angels, in order to be at the side of her Son, in the highest Heavens, *so that there is nothing between the Son and Mother. Yes, her place is next to God, her throne is close to that of her*

Son, *on the mountain of the Trinity.* Long since has the Church of God ranked her after her adorable Son.

St. Ephrem, that eloquent interpreter and defender of the ancient faith, says that *Mary is our Sovereign after the most adorable Trinity, our Comfortress after the Holy Ghost, and after Mediator, the Mediatrix of the Universe,* and that she is more exalted and infinitely more glorious than the Cherubim and the Seraphim, that she is an unfathomable abyss of Divine goodness, the plenitude of the graces of the Trinity, and that she occupies the next place to God.—*Roman Catholic Monitor of San Francisco, of Wednesday, November 8, 1882.*

[The *italics* are our own.]

FREDERICK THE GREAT AND THE FREEMASONS.

In the year 1778 the defunct Lodge at Aix-la-Chapelle was reinstated through the mother Lodge at Wetzlar.

The rector of the Dominican Convent at Aix-la-Chapelle, Father Greineman, and a Capuchin monk, Father Schiff, were trying in the cathedral to excite the lower classes against the Lodge. When Frederick heard of this he wrote the following letter, dated February 7, 1778, to the instigators:

"MOST REVEREND FATHERS: Various reports, confirmed through the papers, have brought to my knowledge with how much zeal you are endeavoring to sharpen the sword of fanaticism against quiet, virtuous and estimable people called Freemasons. As a former dignitary of this honorable body, I am compelled, as much as it is in my power, to repel this dishonoring slander and remove the dark veil that causes the temple which we have erected to all virtues to appear to your vision as a gathering point for all vices.

"Why, my Most Reverend Fathers, will you bring back upon us those centuries of ignorance and barbarism that have so long been the degradation of human reason? Those times of fanaticism upon which the eye of understanding cannot look back but with a shudder! Those times in which hypocrisy, seated on the throne of despotism, with superstition on one side and humility on the other, tried to put the world in chains, and commanded a regardless burning of all those who were able to read!

"You are not only applying the nickname of masters of of witchcraft to the Freemasons, but you accuse them to be thieves, profligates, forerunners of anti-Christ, and admonish a whole nation to annihilate such a cursed generation.

"Thieves, my Most Reverend Fathers, do not act as we do, and make it their duty to assist the poor and the orphans. On the contrary, thieves are those who rob them sometimes of their inheritance and fatten on their prey in the lap of idleness and hypocrisy. Thieves cheat, Freemasons enlighten humanity.

"A Freemason returning from his Lodge, where he has only listened to instructions benefited to his fellow beings, will be a better husband in his home. Forerunners of anti-Christ would, in all probability, direct their efforts towards an extinction of Divine law. But it is impossible for Freemasons to sin against it without demolishing their own structure. And can those be a cursed generation who try to find their glory in the indefatigable efforts to spread those virtues which constitute the honest man? FREDERIC."

THE CATHOLIC CHURCH AND THE SCHOOLS.

BOSTON, November 25th.—The announcement is made of the policy of the Roman Catholic Church in New England toward the public schools. The Archbishop, following the advice of the Pope to a European Bishop, has directed all priests in the Archdiocese of New England to at once establish parochial schools, and threatens parents who refuse to patronize them with the terror of the Church. In locations where the influence of the public schools is thought to be particularly injurious to the Catholic youth, priests are instructed to withdraw children at once, even if there be no parochial schools in the vicinity.

SCHOOL WAR IN BELGIUM.

The contest being between the clerical or parish schools and the communal or secular schools. Every effort was made on the part of the ecclesiastical authorities to induce the teachers of the public schools to desert them for the other. As the majority of the female teachers were *religieuses*, they naturally sided with the clerical party; and in one place, after giving a written promise to remain, they left the communal schools in a body, marching in solemn procession, with sacred banners flying, to take possession of the new Catholic school building. The teachers who persisted in the public schools, which, like the American, are neutral in matters of religion, complained of great persecution from the zealous religionists, being called all manner of hard names, "whited sepulchers," "apostles of Satan," etc., and their schools are characterized as "places where children would learn, beside the three R's, to practice gymnastics, to live like brutes and to die like dogs." "Send your children to a neutral school? Better cut their throats at once!" cries one preacher. The public secular schools are "filthy holes," said another priest. But the most effective weapon against the public schools is the refusal on the part of the priests to allow children who attend them to take their first communion, which is a very important event in the life of a Catholic child.

SECRETARY LINCOLN CENSURED.

The *Monitor* protests strongly against the justice of the decision recently rendered by Secretary of War Lincoln denying the petition of Catholic officers and others residing at the Presidio Reservation near this city, to be allowed the use of sufficient ground to erect a Catholic church. The petition, it says, was first presented to General Schofield, Commander of the Post, who referred to Secretary Lincoln, with "a personal and official recommendation" that it be granted. "A few days ago the answer came back from Robert T. Lincoln, Secretary of War for the Republic which *Catholic blood created, fostered and protected*, that no Catholic church would be permitted on that or no other military reservation. Catholics can imagine the indignation roused in the breasts of the Catholic soldiers as they heard of this mandate from *a mushroom military martinet*, who owes his present place and power entirely to the prestige which the name Lincoln received through the exalted worth of his eminent father.

The *Monitor* adds that *such narrow and bigoted views could only emanate "from a degenerate son of a great father, over whose head were poured the baptismal waters of Catholic."* [Which *statement* is an infernal lie.—COMPILER.]

BOSTON, August 10.—The *Herald* this morning has a Washington special detailing the circumstances of the case referred to by Secretary Lincoln to justify his refusal to allow a Catholic church to be built on the Presidio Reservation at San Francisco. There has been a strong feeling in the matter among prominent Catholics, as it was understood it was one of the old western missions that the Secretary referred to. It is now ascertained that reference was made to the St. James Mission in Washington Territory, established in 1838, which claimed 640 acres under the law of 1848, confirming certain religious societies in possession of lands occupied for Indian missions in Oregon. A bill was introduced in Congress in 1873 for the issuance of a patent. The committee to whom it was referred found questions of jurisdiction involved, some of the land claimed being comprised in a Government Reservation, the committee declined to determine as to the value of the adverse claim, the bill having been amended so as to permit the claimants to assert their rights in the courts to any part or the whole of the 640 acres. Chief Clerk Tweedle of the War Department says that in the Mission of St. James the only title ever held by the claimant was under the Hudson Bay Company, and this reverted to the United States on the possession of the Territory of Oregon. It cannot be ascertained whether the War Department was ever asked for permission by the mission to locate its church on the reservation, but from the fact that all the buildings were erected while the land belonged to the Hudson Bay Company, the inference is plain that no permission would be required.

UNITED STATES PROPERTY.

WHY THE SECRETARY OF WAR DECLINED THE REQUEST FOR THE ERECTION OF A CHURCH ON THE PRESIDIO RESERVATION.

[The annexed letter from Robert Lincoln, Secretary of War, to a resident in this city, explains why the recent request to erect a church on the Presidio Military Reservation was denied]:

"WAR DEPARTMENT,
"Washington, D. C., July 7, 1883.

"DEAR SIR: I have your letter of the 29th June, and am much obliged for your kind expressions. My action in the matter of the proposed Catholic chapel in the Presidio Reservation has, I understand, occasioned some abuses of me in the newspapers, but I have not been disturbed by it.

"The circumstances were merely that application was made for the grant of a suitable piece of ground on the Military Reservation, for the erection of a building to be used exclusively as a place of worship for the Catholic portion of the garrison, it being stated that the men, with their friends, were willing to pay for the building. When the paper was first seen by me it bore the indorsement of General Sherman, stated that he doubted the wisdom of permitting anybody to build on a Military Reservation any building whatever, not wholly the property of the United States. My action was a concurrence in the views of the General of the Army, and was based on business views alone. I am entirely opposed to giving anybody the use of Government land without the authority of an act of Congress, and I refuse requests of this kind whether they are from railroad corpoiations or religious societies of any denomination. If it was at all necessary I could furnish a number of examples where very great trouble has been caused by different action. In one case, what appears to have been originally a harmless license has now been expanded into a claim for a whole Military Reservation and all the buildings that the Government has put on it, at an expense of more than $300,000. I am, very truly yours, ROBERT LINCOLN."

[NOTE.—The whole Military Reservation of Fort Vancouver, Washington Territory, is the one referred to, which the Hudson Bay Company surrendered to the United States Government when the boundary question between the United States and Great Britain was settled. A simple permission granted by the Hudson Bay Company for a chapel to be erected close by its Fort, which was surrendered to the United States Government. The Fort, garrison buildings and all which have since been erected by the United States Government under this original permit of the Hudson Bay Company are now claimed under this preposterous and ridiculous pretension, when no deed, lease or contract recognizing any such claim is to be found.]

ABRAHAM LINCOLN'S ASSASSINATION AND DEATH AN EVENT TO COMMEMORATE THE FOUNDING OF THE ORDER OF THE JESUITS.

JESUIT CELEBBRATION.

NEW YORK, April 15, 1883.—The 250th anniversary of the founding of the Society of Jesus, and the 50th anniversary of the establishment of the Joint Province of Maryland, which embraces Massachusetts, New York, Pennsylvania, New Jersey, Maryland and the District of Columbia, was celebrated with great pomp in the new and beautiful Church of St. Francis Xavier. Many dignitaries of the Catholic Church were within the sanctuary rails. The congregation was very large. At Baltimore Archbishop Gibbons celebrated the anniversary mass in the Jesuit Church. In Boston Bishop Orr of Springfield, preached a sermon in the Church of the Immaculate Conception. In Philadelphia, in St. Joseph's Church, in addition to the above anniversaries, there were also commemorated the 200th anniversary of the establishment of the Jesuit Mission in America, the 150th anniversary of the building of St. Joseph's Church, and the 50th anniversary of its restoration to the Sons of Loyola.—*S. F. Post.*

WHAT THE AMERICAN PEOPLE WERE DOING.

Honoring Lincoln's Memory.

SPRINGFIELD, Illinois, April 16, 1883.—Memorial services on the eigthteenth anniversary of the death of Abraham Lincoln was held at the catacomb of the National Lincoln Monument, yesterday, under the auspices of the Lincoln Guard of Honor. The programme embraced religious exercises, music, reading of President Lincoln's Sunday Order to the Army and Navy, and an oration. At the conclusion of the stated exercises, the catacomb was opened, and the large concourse passed in and placed flowers and evergreens on the sarcophagus.—*S. F. Post.*

TELEGRAMS.

The election of a successor to Pere Beckx, General of the Order of Jesuits, has terminated. The successor, whose name is kept secret, was presented to the Pope on Saturday, September 22, 1883. The selection was made after a warm contest.

The Pope has ratified the election of the German Father Auderilitz, who has just been chosen the successor to Pere Beckx, the General of the Order of Jesuits.—*Sept.* 28, 1883.

FREEMASONRY AMONG THE CATHOLICS.

MONTREAL, Sept. 27th.—The Papal Ambassador is now on his way from Rome to Montreal, to inquire into the rapid spread of Freemasonry among the adherents of the Catholic faith.

EXTRACTS

FROM
PETER DEN'S AND FRANCIS P. KENRICK'S

ROMAN CATHOLIC MORAL THEOLOGY,

WHICH MAY BE RIGHTLY CALLED

"THE SEWAGE OF THE CONFESSIONAL,"

OR THE

"CESSPOOL OF HELL."

INTRODUCTORY.

On the 14th of September, 1808, in a Provincial Council of Roman Catholic Bishops and Priests, it was "unanimously agreed that *Den's Complete Body of Theology* was the best book on the subject that could be published." This resolution was subsequently confirmed by another Council, on the 25th of February, 1870, which was unanimous as follows:

"*Resolved*, That we do hereby confirm and declare our unalterable adherence to the resolutions unanimously entered into at our last general meeting, on the 14th September, 1808." *Wyse's History of Catholic Associations, Vol. II, page* 20.

The "Moral Theology" of Peter Den's was most heartily approved and commended by the Archbishop of St. Louis, Missouri, in February, 1850, as will be seen by reference to the journals of that date.

Bishop Kenrick's "Theology" is of the same characteristic if not worse, and he frequently cites St. Thomas Aquinas and St. Alphonsus Liguori as authorities, which Bishop Foley admitted in Court to be true, when he was forced to translate and read publicly, or be sent to jail for contempt of Court, as already stated in Part II of this book. Peter Den's "Theology" has been in use among the priests of Rome for nearly a century and a half, both in Europe and America, with the approval of Popes Gregory XVI and Pius IX. It is used as a text-book in the Royal College of Maynooth. The Mechlinæ edition, from which we have taken the extracts, bears date of 1864, and is published by "*De Propaganda Fide*" (Society for the Propagation of the Faith), with the title "*Theologia ad usum Seminarium, et Sacræ Theologicæ Alumnorium*"—(" Theology in use in the Theological Seminary, and Sacred Theology for Students." KENRICK's "THEOLOGY" was first published in Philadelphia in 1841-2-3, and "entered according to Act of Congress, by FRANCIS PATRICK KENRICK, in the Clerk's Office of the District Court in the Eastern District of Pennsylvania." It is in three volumes, and the extracts are from the first edition. The "Society for the Propagation of the Faith," published a later edition from Mechlinæ, in two volumes, in 1861. It is catalogued in Latin, and is for sale in nearly all the large Catholic bookstores everywhere.

In presenting these extracts to our readers, we do so solely for the purpose that every true, independent, free-souled man, whether married or single, may see for himself what a damnable, infernal and foul institution the Confessional of the Roman Catholic Church is. It must have been a Romish priest in the disguise of the serpent who tempted Eve to sin in Paradise, and Adam had to father the devil's offspring, and live in doubtful paternity of the first-born, who proved to be a murderer, and slew his only brother. The same temptation, the same breaking down of the moral and modest nature of a pure girl or woman, by the slimy, devilish priest, who as a third party comes between the husband

and wife, father and daughter, and claims the paramount and superior right of the priest in the state of matrimony, thrusl., the parent and the husband aside (for to the priest they are not one flesh, nor one soul or being), and questions are propounded that would make an honest, free man recoil with horror, shame and indignation if he knew them, and avenge the insult to the honor and purity of his wife, sister or daughter, offered by the adulterous, lecherous reptile who befouls and pollutes both soul and body, and destroys the home of happiness, the heaven on earth to man. Is not the Romish priesthood truly the "Engineer Corps of Hell, and Rome's Sappers and Miners," indeed, and whose constant aim and occupation is to destroy all morality, all purity, all true religion, all family ties and all governments but that of hell incarnate?

Read the whole without any false sensitiveness or false notions of delicacy, but, rather, as if you were one of a grand jury, solemnly sworn to inquire into and examine every foul spot and every condition of secret crime and practice that is poisoning the very atmosphere you breathe, sapping the foundations of society, of the family and of the State, and as if you were appointed one of a Board of Health with power to abate a nuisance, and without any squeamishness on your own part whatever, give it your undivided attention, and see what a cancer, what a putrid sore, what a foul, malaria-breeding curse, destroying both soul and body, this cursed system is, which falsely calls itself the only true religion, and aims to control every avenue to happiness on earth and to eternal bliss in heaven, and maintains a toll-gate on every road and pathway that leads to hell, while it drives its legions of victims with whip and spur through the portals of the gateway of death, where souls already smitten with its leprosy are utterly damned and lost.

"Be ye not unequally yoked," says Paul. If you are a single man, let the Roman Catholic girl alone, and do not marry where the slimy priest has the key to the soul and the body of your wife, and your children (if they were yours) would be mortgaged before they were begotten to that damnable institution, for after they were born, you would not be certain that they were your own, and all your after life be a miserable slavery, and all you have on earth be the chattels of Rome.

Protestant fathers and mothers, do not give your children up to this Papal Moloch, keep them away from their schools, colleges and convents. They will be educated away from you; the fountains of natural affection will be poisoned and polluted, and the sweet, innocent babe that was given to you by a kind and Heavenly Father to be the pride and comfort of your old age, will be converted into a deadly asp upon your breast, that will sting you to death, or abandon you for a life that will be lost in a Dead Sea worse than that that was fed by the streams that flowed through Sodom and Gomorrah.

To the private citizen, to the statesmen, to him who is entrusted the government of the town, the city, the State and the Nation, we commend a careful perusal of this system which is a nursery of every sort of pollution, of lust and of crime, which compounds felony of the darkest dye, under the seal of Confession, which is covering the whole land with gloom as with the pall of death, and which has plunged nations in blood and tears, mourning the loss of the noblest and best of earth. And while the sorrow of a lamented Lincoln is yet fresh in our hearts, and swear by the Eternal God who rules the universe that this vile tape-worm that is consuming the vitals of our nation shall be expelled from the body politic and utterly destroyed.

EDWIN A. SHERMAN, Compiler.

EXTRACTS.

[Taken from "*The Garden of the Soul,*" touching Extreme Unction, or Anointing with Oil, with the approbation of the late Archbishop Hughes of New York]:

Page 263 (James v and xiv): "And as the eyes, the ears and other organs of sense are the instruments by which men are led to offend Almighty God, and they will, on that account, be anointed with holy oil; whilst the priest applies this holy oil to your eyes, your ears and the REST," etc., etc.; "do you with a contrite and humble heart implore the mercy of God for the forgiveness of all the sins which through these avenues have made their way into your soul." Those who have defloured a virgin must pay six gios (seven French sous). "Whoever has carnally known mother, sister, cousin germain or his godmother, is taxed one ducat and five corlins" (or five sous). [*Pope, John xxii.*]

[The Rev. W. Hogan says, in his book on Auricular Confession, page 49: "That he was acquainted with three priests in Albany who in less than three years were the fathers of between sixty and one hundred children, besides having debauched many who had left the place previous to their confinement. Many of these children were by married women."]

Pages 213 and 214: "VI. Have you been guilty of fornication, or adultery, or incest, or any sin against nature, either with a person of the same sex, or with any other creature? How often? Or have you designed or attempted any such sin, or sought to induce others to do it? How often?"

"Have you been guilty of self-pollution? or of immodest touches of yourself? How often?"

"Have you touched others, or permitted yourself to be touched by others, immodestly? or given or taken wanton kisses or embraces, or any such liberties? How often?"

"Have you looked at immodest objects with pleasure or

danger? read immodest books or songs to yourselves or others? kept indecent pictures? willingly given ear to, and taken pleasure in hearing loose discourse, etc.? or sought to see or hear anything that was immodest? How often?"

"Have you exposed yourself to wanton company? or played at any indecent play? or frequented masquerades, balls, comedies, etc., with danger to your chastity? How often?"

"Have you been guilty of any immodest discourses, wanton stories, jests, or songs, or words of double meaning? How often? and before how many? and were the persons to whom you spoke or sung, married or single? For all this you are obliged to confess, by reason of the evil thoughts these things are apt to create in the hearers."

"Have you abused the marriage bed by any actions contrary to the laws of nature? or by any pollutions? or been guilty of any irregularity, in order to hinder you having children? How often?,'

"Have you, without a just cause, refused the marriage debt? and what sin followed it? How often?"

"Have you debauched any person that was innocent before? havej you forced any person, or deluded any one by deceitful promises, etc.? or designed or desired to do so? How often? You are obliged to make satisfaction for the injury you have done."

"Have you taught anyone evil that he knew not of before? or carried any one to lewd houses, etc.? How often?"

Page 216: "IX. Have you willingly taken pleasure in unchaste thoughts or imaginations? or entertained unchaste desires? Were the objects of your desires maids or married persons, or kinsfolks, or persons consecrated to God? How often?

"Have you taken pleasure in the irregular motions of the flesh? or not endeavored to resist them? How often?"

"Have you entertained with pleasure the thoughts of saying or doing anything which it would be a sin to say or do? How often?"

"Have you had the desire or design of committing any sin? Of what sin? How often?"

EXTRACTS FROM PETER DEN'S THEOLOGY.

DE SIGILLO CONFESSIONIS.

Quid est sigillum confessionis sacramentalis?

R. Est obligatis seu debitum celandi eu quæ ex sacramentalis confessione cognoscuntor. Dens, tom vi, p. 227.

ON THE SEAL OF CONFESSION.

What is the seal of sacramental confession?

Ans. It is the obligation or duty of concealing those things which are learned from sacramental confession. Dens, Vol. VI, p. 227.

An potest dari casus, in quo licet frangere sigillum sacramentale?

R. Non potest dari; quamvis ab es penderet vita aut salus hominis, aut etiam interitus Reipublicæ; neque summus Pontifex in es dispensare potest; ut provinde hoc sigili arcanum magis liget, quam obligatis juramenti, voti secreti naturalis, etc., idque ex voluntati Dei positiva.

Can a case be given in which it is lawful to break the sacramental seal?

Ans. It cannot; although the life or safety of a man depended thereon, or even the destruction of the commonwealth; nor can the Supreme Pontiff give dispensation in this; so that on that account this secret of the seal is more binding than the obligation of an oath, a vow, a natural secret, etc., and that by the positive will of God.

Quid igitur respondere debet Confessarius interrogatus super veritate, quam per solam confessionem sacramentalem novit?

R. Debet respondere se nescire lam, et si opus est, idem juramento confirmare.

What answer, ought a confessor to give when questioned concerning a truth which he knows from sacramental confession only?

Ans. He ought to answer that he does not know it, and if it be necessary to confirm the same with an oath.

Obj. Nullo casu licet mentiri; atqui Confessarius ille mentiretur quia scit veritatem, ergo, etc.

R. Neg. min., quia talis Confessarus interrogatur ut homo, et respondet ut homo; jam aritem non scit ut homo illam veritatem, quamvis scint ut Dens, ait S. Th. q. II, Art. 1 ad 3, et iste senous sponte in est responsioni; nam quando extra confessionem interrogatur, vel respondet, consideratur ut homo.

Obj. It is in no case lawful to tell a lie, but that confessor is questioned as a man, and answers as a man; but now he does not know that truth as a man, *though he knows it as God*, says St. Thomas (q. II, Art. 1, 3), and that is the free and natural meaning of the answer, for when he is asked, or when he answers outside of confession, he is considered a man.

Quid si directe a Confessario quæratur, utrum illud scint per confessionem sacramentalim?

R. Hoc casu nihil oportet respondere; ita Steyart cum Sylvis; sed interrogatis rejicienda est tanquam impia rel etiam posset absolute, non relative ad petititionem dicere; ego nihil scio; quia vox *ego* restringet ad scientiam humanam. *Dens, tom, vi, p.* 228.

What if a Confessor were directly asked whether he knows it through sacramental confession?

Ans. In this case he ought to give no answer (so Steyart and Sylvius), but reject the question as impious; or he could even say absolutely, not relatively to the question, I know nothing. because the word I restricts to his human knowledge. *Dens, v.* 6, *p.* 228.

DE ABSOLUTIONE COMPLICIS.

"Advertendum quod nullus Confessarius, extra mortis periculum, licet alius harbent potestatem absolvendi a reservatis absolvere possit ant valeat a peccato quolibet mortali externo contra castitatem, complicem in eodem secum peccato."

Hic casus complicis non collocatur inter casus reservatos, quin Episcopus non reservat sibi absolutionem, sed quilibet alius Confessarius potest ab eo absolvere, præterquam sacerdos complex. *Ib.* 6, 297.

ON THE ABSOLUTION OF AN ACCOMPLICE.

"Let it be observed that, except in case of danger of death, no Confessor, though he may otherwise have the power of absolving from reserved cases, may or can absolve his accomplice in any external mortal sin against chastity committed by the accomplice with the Confessor himself."

This case of an accomplice is NOT *placed among the reserved cases, because the Bishop does* NOT *reserve the absolution to himself, but any other confessor can absolve from it, except the priest, who is himself the partner in the act.*

An comprehenditur masculus complex in peccato venereo v. g. per tactus?

R. Affirmative, quia Pontifex extendit ad qualemcumque personam.

Non requiritur ut hec peccatum complicis patratum sit in confessione, vel occasione confessionis; quocumque enim loco vel tempore factum est, etiam antequam esset Confessarius, facit lasum complicis. *Ib.* 6, 298.

Is a male accomplice in venereal sin, to-wit, by touches, comprehended in this degree?

Ans. Yes; because the Pope extends it to whatsoever person. It is not required that this sin of an accomplice be committed in confession or by occasional confession; for in whatever place or time it has been done, even before he was her confessor, it makes a case of an accomplice.

Nota ultimo, cum restrictis fiut ad peccata carnis poterit Confessarius complicem in aliis peccatis, v. g. in furto, homocidis, etc., valide absolvere. *Dens, tom, vi* 293.

Las'ly, take note, that since the restriction is made to

carnal sins, the Confessor will be able to give valid absolution to his accomplice in other sins, namely, in theft, in homocide, etc. *Dens, v.* 6, *pp.* 297-8.

After telling us, that in obedience to a Bull of Gregory the Fifteenth, and a constitution founded thereon by Benedict the Fourteenth, any priest is to be denounced who endeavors to seduce his penitents in the Confessional, he asks the following question:

Confessarius sollicitavit pœnitentem ad turpiu, non in confessionis, sed ex alia occasione extraordinaria, un est denuntiandus?

R. Negative. Aliud foret, si ex scientia confessionis sollicitaret; quia v. g. ex confessione novit, illam personam deditam tali peccato venero. *P. Antoine, t. lv, p.* 480.

A Confessor has seduced his penitent to the commission of carnal sin, not in confession, nor by occasion of confession, but from some other extraordinary occasion, is he to be denounced?

Ans. No; if he tampered with her from his knowledge of confession it would be a different thing, because, for instance, he knows that person, from her confession, to be given to such carnal sins. *P. Antoine, t. iv, p.* 430.

Propterea monet Steyærtius, quod Confessarius pœnitentem, que confitetur se peccasse cum sacerdote, vel sollicitatum ab eo ad tupiu, interrogare possit utrum ille sacerdos sit ejus Confessarius. an in Confessione sollicitaveret, etc.

For which reason Steyart reminds us that a Confessor can ask a penitent, who confesses that she has sinned with a priest, or has been seduced by him to the commission of carnal sin, whether that priest was her Confessor or had seduced her in the Confessional.

A denuntratio fieri debet, quando dubium est, utrum fuerit vera sufficiens sollicitatio ad turpiu?

R. Ruidam negant, sed Card. Cozza cum aliis quos citat, dub. 15, affirmat, si dubium non sit leve, dicens examen illud relinquendum Episco sive Ordinario. *Dens. t. vi. p.* 301.

Ought the denunciation be made when there exists a

doubt whether the solicitation to carnal sin was real and sufficient?

Ans. Some say, No; but Card. Cozza, with others whom he cites, doubt 25, says, Yes, if the doubt be not light, adding that the examination of the matter is to be left to the Bishop or the Ordinary. *Dens, v. vi,* p. 301.

DE MODO DENUNTIANDI SOLLICITANTEM PRÆFATUM.

Primus modus conveniens est, si ipsa persona sollicitata immediate, nulli, alteri revelando, accedat Episcopum sive Ordinarium. 20. Potest Episcopo scribere epistolam clausam et signatam sub hac forma: "Ego Catharina N., habitans Mechlinæ in plateâ N., sub signo N.. hisce declaro me 6 Martii, anno 1758, occasione confessionis fuisse sollicitatum ad inhonesta a Confessario N. N., excipiente confessiones Mechlinæ, in Ecclesia N. quod juramento confirmare parata sum." *Dens, tom. vi,* 302.

ON THE MODE OF DENOUNCING THE AFORESAID SEDUCER.

The first and most convenient mode is this. If the person upon whose chastity the attempt had been made, would proceed herself to the Bishop or to the Ordinary, without revealing the circumstance to any one else. 2. She can write a letter closed and sealed to the Bishop in the following form: "I, Catherine N., dwelling at Mechlin, in the street N., under the sign N., by these declare that I, on the 6th day of March, 1758, on the occasion of confession, have been seduced to improper acts by the Confessor N. hearing confessions at Mechlin, in the Church N., which I am ready to confirm on oath.

3. Si autem scribere noqueat, similis epistola scribatur ab alio v. g. à secundo Confessario cum licentia pœnitentis, et nomen pœnitentis seu personæ sollicitantis, experimatur ut supra; sed nomen Confessarii sollicitantis ut occultum maneat scribenti, no exprimatur, verim à tertio aliquo, rei ignaro, in chartula aliqua nomen ejus scribatur sub alio prætexta; quæ chartula epistolæ præfatæ includatur.

3. But if she cannot write let a similar letter be written by another, namely, by a second Confessor, with the license of the penitent, and let the name of the penitent or person seduced be expressed as above, but let the name of the seducing confessor, in order that it may remain a secret to the writer, be not expressed, but let his name be written under a different pretext, by some third person ignorant of the circumstances, on some scrap of paper, which may be inclosed in the aforesaid letter.

In hoc casu (denunciationis) tamen quidam putant moderandum, et considerandas esse circumstantias frequentiæ, periculi, etc. *Dens, tom vi, y.* 301.

In this case (of denouncing), however, some are of opinion that moderation must be observed, and that the circumstances of frequency of danger, etc., must be considered. *Dens, vol. vi, p.* 301.

Momentur interea Confessarii, ut mulierculis quibuscumque accusantibus priorem Confessarium, fidem leviter non adhibeant; sed prius scrutentur accusationis finem et causam, examinent earum mores, conversationem, etc. *Ib. vi,* 302.

In the meantime, Confessors are advised not lightly to give to any woman whatsoever accusing their former Confessor, but first to search diligently into the end and cause of the occasion, to examine their morals, conversation, etc.

Quocirca observa, quod quæcumque persona, quæ per se vel per alium, falso denuntia sacerdotem tanquam solicitatorem, incurrat casum reservatum summo Pontifici. Ita Benedictus XIV, Constit. Sacramentum Pœnitent, apud Antoine, p. 418.

For which reason observe, that whatever person, either by herself or another, falsely denounces a priest as a seducer, incurs a case reserved for the Supreme Pontiff. Thus Benedict XIV, in the Constitution, called "Sacramentum Pœnitentiæ," in Antoine, p. 418.

Benedictus XIV, in Constit. citata numero 216, reservavit sibi et successoribus peccatum falsæ denuntiationis Confessarii sollicitantis ad turpia. *Dens, tom. vi p* 303.

Benedict XIV, in the Constitution, cited in No. 216, reserves to himself and his successors the sin of falsely denouncing a Confessor for seducing his penitent to commit carnal sin. *Dens, vol. 6, p. 303.*

Alloquium pullæ est occasio proximo illi qui ex decem vicibus bis vel ter solet cadere in peccatum carnis vel in delectationem carnis deliberatam. *Ib. vi. 185.*

Speaking to a girl is a proximate occasion (of sin) to him, who, out of every ten times, is wont to fall twice or thrice into carnal sin, or into deliberate carnal delight. *Ib. vi 185.*

Frequentatio quotidiana tabernæ aut puellæ censetur esse occasio proxima respectu ejus, qui ex ea bis vel ter inmense prolabitur in simile peccatum mortale. *Vol. vi, p. 175.*

Daily frequenting a tavern or a girl is considered a proximate occasion (of sin) in respect of him, who, on that account, falls twice or thrice a month into like mortal sin. *Vol. vi, p. 185.*

Idem resolvit P. DuJardin, p. 51, de administratione quotidiana alicujus officii licet honesti, v. g. Medicii, Confessari, Mercatoris, si inde quis bis terve per mensem deliberate cadere solent, pag. 53, concludit Confessarium obligari ad deserendum illud ministerium. *Ib. vi, 185.*

P. DuJardin is of the same opinion (p. 51) respecting the administration of any office, however honest; for instance, of a physician, a confessor, a lawyer, a merchant, if any should on that account be accustomed to fall deliberately two or three times a month; and in page 53 he concludes that the Confessor is bound to desert that ministry. *Vol. vi, p. 185.*

Obj. Confessarius ille occupatus in ministerio audiendi confessiones raisissimo cadit comparative ad vices, quibus non cadit; ergo ministerium audiendi confessiones respectu illius non est occasis proxima.

Nego cons. quia ille, licet non comparative, absolute frequentur cadit; qui enim per singulos menses committeret duo vel tria injustæ, diceretur absolute frequentur committere homiocidium, ille Confessarius toties accidit animam suam ergo. *Dens, tom. vi, p. 185.*

Obj. That Confessors every day occupied in the ministry of hearing confessions falls very seldom in comparison with the times he does not fall; therefore, the ministry of hearing confessions is not with respect to him a proximate occasion (of sin).

Ans. I deny the consequence, because he, though not comparatively, does, however, absolutely fall frequently, for he who would commit two or three unjust homicides every month should be said absolutely to commit homicide frequently, so often does that Confessor slay his own soul. *Dens, v, vi, p.* 185.

DE JUSTIS CAUSIS PERMITTENDI MOTUS SENSUALITATIS.

JUSTU CAUSA EST AUDITUS CONFESSIONUM.

Quanta debet esse causu, ob quam quis se possit habere permissive ad motus inordinatus, sic ut illi motus non censeantur voluntarii nec calpabiles?

R. Debet esse tanta ut cum sus effectu bono in his circumstantiis præalent istis motibus seu effectui malo, juxta regulam. N. 15 explicatum. *Vol. i, p.* 315.

ON JUST CAUSES FOR PERMITTING MOTIONS OF SENSUALITY.

HEARING OF CONFESSION IS JUST CAUSE.

How great ought to be the cause for which one can hold himself permissively with regard to inordinate motions, so as that they may be considered neither voluntary nor culpable?

Ans. It ought to be so great as to prevail with its good effect in its circumstances, over those motions or the bad effect, according to the rule explained in No. 15, vol. i p. 315.

Hujusmodi justæ causæ sunt auditis confessionum, lectio casuum conscientæ pro Confessario, servitum necessarium rel utile Præstitum infirmo. *Vol. i, p.* 315.

Just causes of this sort are the hearing of confessions, the reading of cases of conscience drawn up for a Confessor, necessary or useful attendance on an invalid. *Vol. i, p* 315.

Justa causa facere potest, ut opus aliquod, ex quo motus oriuntur, non tantum licite incœtur, sed etiam licite continuetur; et ita Confessarius ex auditione Confessionis eos percipiens, non ideo ab auditione abstinere, debet, sed justacœ habet perseverandi rationem, modo tamen ipsi motus illi semper displiceant, nec inde oriatur proximum periculum consensus. *Dens, tom. i, p.* 315.

The effect of a just cause is such that anything from which motions arise, may be not only lawfully begun, but also lawfully continued, and so the Confessor receiving those motions from the hearing of confessions ought not on that account to abstain from hearing them, but has a just cause for persevering, providing, however, that they always displease him, and there arise not therefrom the proximate danger of consent. *Dens, v. i, p.* 315.

In omni peccato carnali circumstantia conjugii sit experimenda in confessione. *Vol. vii, p.* 167.

In every carnal sin, let the circumstance of marriage be expressed in confession.

An aliquando interrogandi sunt conjugati in confessione circa negotionem debiti?

R. Affirmative drœsertim muliefes, quæ ex ignorantia rel præ pudore peccatum istud quandoque reticent; verum non ex abrupto, sed prudenter est interrogatio instituenda v. g. an cum marito rixatœ sint, quœ hujusmodi rixarum causa; num protu talem occasionem maritis debitum negarint; quod si se deliquisse fateantur, caste interrogari debent, an nil secutum fuerit continentiœ conjugali contrarium, v. g. pollutio, etc. *Vol. vii, p.* 167.

Are the married to be at any time asked in confession about denying the marriage duty?

Ans. YES! particularly the WOMEN,* who through ig-

---

* WOMEN.—The following passage is taken from the Moral Theology in which the young priests are lectured in Maynooth; the reader will perceive that it is almost word for word the same as selected from Peter Den's:

Quæres 1. An teneantur conjuges reddere debitum?

norance or modesty are sometimes silent on that sin; but the question is not to be put abruptly, but to be framed prudently; for instance, whether they have quarreled with their husbands; what was the cause of the quarrels; whether they did upon these occasions deny their husbands the mar-

---

R. Tenere utramque conjugem sub mortali injustitæ peccato comparti reddere debitum, dum rel expresse rel tacite exigitur, nisi legitima catsa de negandi intervenerit. Id constat. ex S. Pauls. 1 Corinth. vii.

Dixi autem 1. UTRAMQUE CONNEUGEM TERJI, in eo enim pares sunt ambo conjuges, ut palet ex verbis Apostoli.

Dixi eos teneri SUB PECCATO MORTALI, quin res est per se gravis, cum inde nascantur'rixæ odia dissensiones parsaque debito fraudata incontinentiæ periculo exponatur, quod lethale est Hine Parochus aut per se in Tribunali Pœnitentiæ aut saltem, et quidem, aliquando prudentius priæ matris ministerio, adocere debet sponsas, quid in hac parte observandum sit. Cum verro mulieres ejusmodi peccata in confessione sacramentali præ pudore ant ignorantia non raro reticeant expedit aliquando de iis illas interrogare, sed cante et prudentur, non ex abrupto; v. g. inquiri potest an disidia fuerint inter eam et conjugem, quæ eorum causæ qui effectus, an proptere marito denegaverit quod ex conjugii legibus ei debetur.—[Maynooth Class Book, Tract de Matrimo, p. 482.]

Are man and wife bound to render each other matrimonial duty?

Ans. Each is bound under a mortal sin of injustice to render matrimonial duty to his or her partner, whilst it is expressly or tacitly required, unless there should occur a legitimate reason for refusing. That is manifest from St. Paul, 1 Corinth., chap. vii.

But I have said that each is bound, for in this affair both man and wife are equal, as is clear from the words of the Apostle.

I have said, in the second place, that they are bound under MORTAL SIN, because it is a weighty affair in itself, since it the active cause of quarrels, hates, dissensions, and since the party defrauded of duty is exposed to the danger of incontinence, which is a deadly sin; hence the parish priest, either himself personally in the Tribunal of Penance (the Confessional), or least (and sometimes more prudently) by the agency of a pious matron, ought to inform married persons, and PARTICULARLY MARRIED WOMEN, of what they should observe with repect to this matter. But since women through modesty or ignorance, not unfrequently conceal sins of that sort in sacramental confession, it is expedient sometimes to interrogate them regarding those sins, but cautiously, prudently, not abruptly; for instance, it may be asked

riage duty; but if they acknowledge they did upon these occasions deny their husbands the marriage duty; but if they acknowledge they have transgressed, they ought to be asked chastely, WHETHER ANYTHING FOLLOWED CONTRARY TO CONJUGAL CONTINENCE, viz: POLLUTION,* etc.

Hine uxor se accusans in confessione quod negaverit adbitum interrogatur, un maritus ex pleno rigore juris sui id petiverit; idque colligetur, ex eo, quod petiverit intanter, quod graviter fuerit offensus, quod, quod aversiones rel alia mala sint secuta, de quibus etiam se accusare debet, nuia fuit eorem causa; contia si confiteatur rixas rel aversiones adversus maritum interrogari potest; an debitum negaverit? *Dens, vii, p.* 168.

Hence let the wife, accusing herself in confession of having denied the marriage duty, be asked whether the husband demanded it with the full rigor of his right; and that shall be inferred from his having demanded it instantly, from his having been grievously offended, or from aversions or any other evils having followed of which she ought also to accuse herself, because she was the cause of them; on the other hand, if she confess that there exist quarrels and aversions between her and her husband, she can be asked whether she has denied the marriage duty. *Dens, vii, p.* 168.

---

whether there have been any dissension between her and her husband; what was the cause and what the effect of them—whether she has on that account denied to her husband what is due to him by the laws of marriage.—[Maynooth Class Book, p. 482.]

Notatur, quod pollutio in mulieribus quando que pessit perfici ita ut semen non effluat extra membrum genitale; indicium istius allegat Billuart, si scilliclt mulier sentiat seminis resolutionem cum magno voluptudis sensu qua completa passio satiatur. *Dens, tom. iv, p.* 363;

*It is remarked that women may be guilty of perfect pollution even without a flow of their semen to the outside of the genital member (the passage). of which Billuart alleges a proof, if, for instence, the woman feel a resolution (loosening) of the semen with a great sense of pleasure, which being completed, HER PASSION IS SATIATED.

Variis modis peccari potest contra bonum prolis, scilicet.*

Io pecant viri, qui committat peccatum. Her et Onan quos, quia rem hanc detestatem fecerunt interfecit Dominus Genesis 38.

Sin can in various modes be committed against the good of the offspring. 1st, the men sin who commit the sin of Her and Onan, whom because they did this detestable thing the Lord slew. Genesis xxxviii.

2. Pecant uxores, quæ potionibus fœtus conceptionem impediunt, ant susceptum visi semen ejciunt, rel ejicere conantur. *Dens, tom.* 7, *p.* 165.

2. The wives sin who prevent the conception of the fœtus with potions or eject, or endeavor to eject, the seed received from the man. *Dens, v. vii, p.* 165.

Notent hic Confessarii, quod conjugati, ne proles nimium multiplicentur, aliquando committant detestabilem turpitudinem Her et Onan, circa quod peccatum examinandi sunt. *Dens, tom.* 7, *p.* 172.

Here let the Confessors take note, that the married, lest their children multiply too fast, sometimes commit a detestable turpitude like that of Her and Onan, about which sin THEY ARE TO BE EXAMINED. *Dens, v. vii, p.* 172.

Ne Confessarius hæreat iners in circumstantiis alicujus peccati indagandis, in promptu habeat hunc circumstantiurum:

Quis, quid, ubi, quibus, auxiliis, cur, quomodo, quando? *Dens, tom.* 5, *p.* 123.

Lest the Confessor should indolently hesitate in tracing out the circumstances of any sin, let him have the following versicle of circumstances in readiness:

---

*Quid est bonum prolis?

R. Legitima prolis generatio et ejusdem inveri Dei culta educatio. Dens, t. 7, p. 164.

What does the good of the offspring mean?

Ans. It means the legitimate generation of the offspring, and the education of the same in the worship of the true God. Dens, v, vii, p. 146.

Who, which, where, with, why, how, when? *Dens, v.* 6, *p.* 123.

An Confessarius protest absolvere sponsam dug cognoscit ex solo confessione sponsi, quon sponsa in confessione reticeat fornicationem habitam cum sponso?

R. Varsas reperio opiniones; La Croix, lib. G. p. n. 1969, existimat sponsam non esse absolvendam, sed dissimalanter dicendum; Miseriatur tui, etc., ita ut ipsa ignoret sibi abslutisnem negari.

Can a Confessor absolve a young woman going to be married, whilst he knows solely from the confession of the betrothed husband that she does not disclose in her confession the fornication she has been guilty of with her betrothed?

Ans. I find various opinions: LaCroix thinks that she ought not to be absolved; but that the Confessor should dissemble, and Miseriatur, tui, etc., so that she may not know that absolution has been denied her.

Prudentes Confessarii solent et statuunt regulariter inquirere ab omnibus sponsis, utrum occasione futuri matrimonii occurrint cogitationes quædam inhonesta? Utrum permisciunt oscula, et alias majores libertates, ad, invicem exeo, quad forte putaverint jum sibi plura licere?

Prudent Confessors are wont and lay it down regularly to ask from all young women going to be married, whether from occasion of their approaching marriage there occurred to them any improper thoughts? Whether they permitted kisses and other greater alternate liberties, because perhaps they thought greater freedoms would soon be allowed them?

Cum verecundia solent magis corripere sponsum, ut sponsa postea confidentius exponat, quod novit jam esse notum Confessario.

And since the young woman is more under the influence of modesty, we are wont for that reason to hear the betrothed husband's confession first, that she may afterwards more confidently reveal to the Confessor what she knows to be known to him.

Addunt aliqui, sponsam qui prius confitetur, posse, induci; ut dicat sponsæ, se peccatum illud aperte esse confessum. Post confessionem sponsæ id non licet ampliue. *Dens, tom. 6 pp.* 239-40.

Some divines add that the betrothed husband who makes his confession first, can be induced to tell her that has openly confessed that sin. After the young woman's confession that would be no longer in the Confessor's power. *Dens, v. 6, pp.* 289-40.

An licita est delectatio morosa de opere jure naturæ prohibitio, sed sine culpe formuli hic et nuc posito, v. g. delectatio de pollutione nocturno involuntaria?

R. Neg. quia objectum delectationis est intrinsecus malum, adeoque deliberate delectatio de ea est mala. *Vol. I, p.* 326.

Is morose delight allowed on a thing prohibited by the law of nature, but here and now having taken place without a formal fault, for instance, delight on nocturnal involuntary pollution?

Ans. No; because the object of the delight is intrinsically bad, and therefore deliberate delight respecting it is also bad.

Multi tamen, ut Salmanticenses, Vasquez, Billuart, Antoine, etc., putant quod licet illicitum sit delectari de homicidio, ebrietate, etc., involuntarie commissis, illicitum tamen non sit, obfinem conum de pollutione mere naturali et involuntaria delectari; rel affectu simplici et inefficaci eam desideare.

Hujus sententiæ etiam est S. Antonius, parte 2, tit. 6, cap, 5.

Many, however, as Salmanticenses, Vasquez, Billuart, Antoine, etc., think that, although it is unlawful to delight on homicide, drunkenness, etc., involuntarily committed, it is not unlawful, however, on account of the good end, to delight on merely natural and involuntary pollution or to desire it with a simple and inefficacious affection.

Of this opinion also is Saint Anthony, part 2, tit. 6, chap. 5.

Decitur "affectu simplici et inefficaci;" quia si desideretur efficacita, ita ut ex desiderio pollutis causetur, rel media ut eveniat, adhibeantur, certum est juxta omnes quod pollutis mere naturalis et involuntaria nullo jure prohibeatur; cum sit effectus mere naturalis seu mera naturæ evacuatio, ut sudor, saliva, etc., ac proindene quidem materialter seu objective, mala, unde illam ut talem inefficaciter velle non est peccatum. *Dens, i, pp.* 826-7.

They say "with a simple and efficacious affection," because if it be desired efficaciously so as that pollution be caused by the desire or means employed that it may happen, it is certain according to all a mortal sin. The reason of these authors is, that pollution merely natural and involuntary is prohibited by no law; since it is merely a natural effect, or a mere evacuation of nature, like sweat, saliva, etc., and, therefore, it is by no means materially or objectively bad; whence it is not a sin to wish for it inefficaciously as such. *Dens, v. i, pp.* 326-7.

Quid est morosa delectatis?

R. Est voluntaria complacentia circa objectum illicitum absue voluntate implendo seu exequendo opus. *Vol. I, pp.* 318-19.

What is morose delight?

Ans. It is a voluntary complacence about an illicit object without a wish of performing or executing the work.

Vocatur "morosa" non a mora temporis, quo durat; nam unico instanti perfici potest; sed a mora rationis, quæ delectationem hanc postquam eam advertit, repellere negligit; et sic ratio est in mora fungendi suo officio. Potest etiam dici morosa quia ratio ei immoderatua ab que voluntate procendi ad ipsum opus. *I,* 318-19.

It is called "morose," not from the delay (mora) of time during which it lasts, for it may be complete in an instant, but from the delay of reason, which neglects to repel this delight after it has perceived it; and thus reason delays in discharging its own office. It can also be called "morose," because reason dwells on it without a wish of proceeding to the work itself.

In qua materia hace delectatio locum habet?

R. Quamvis delectatio morosa frequentius contingat circa venera, locum famen habere potest in quacumque materia, ut cica furtum, pugnam, vindictam, etc. *Dens, t. i, p.* 319.

In what manner does this delight take place?

Ans. Although morose delight more frequently happens about venereous matters, however it can take place in any matter whatsoever, as about theft, about fighting, about revenge, etc. *Dens, vol. i, p.* 319.

An persona conjugata peccat delectando veneree de copula vel tactibus cum comparte habitis ant habendis, si compars sit absens tempore delectationis infirma, etc., adeo ut copula hic et nunc sit impossibillis?

R. Si delectando se exponat periculo pollutionis, certo peccat mortaliter, contra castitatem et etiam contra justitiam. Si vero absit periculum pollutionis, Sanchez, Sylvius, Steyært, et Daelman, eam a mortali liberant, quia honestas status matrimonialis videtur talem delectationem a mortali excusare. Alli tamen probabilius similem delectationem consent mortalem ut Navarrus, Billuart, Collet, Antoine, etc. *Dens, tom. i, p.* 331.

Does a married person sin in delighting venereously on copulation or on touches, which she has had or is to have, if at the time of the delight her partner be absent or infirm, etc., so as that copulation be here and now impossible?

Ans. If in delighting she expose herself to the danger of pollution, she certainly sins mortally against chastity, and also against justice. But if there be no danger of pollution, Sanchez, Sylvius, Steyart and Daelman free her from mortal sin, because the honesty of the matrimonial state seems to excuse such delight from mortal sin. Others, however, as Navarrus, Billuart, Collet and Antoine, etc., think with more probability, that such delight is a mortal sin. *Dens, v· i, p.* 331.

An quis piam voto castitatis obstrictus facit contra suum votum, si aliis personis liberis sit causa libidinis, v. g. si consulat ut illi inter se fornicentur?

R. Peccat peccato scandali, et fit reus fornicationis, aliorum; verumtamen non videtur violare votum proprium mere ob fornicationem aliorum, si absit complaceutur propria, quia non vovit servare castitatem alienam, sed propriam, sicuti conjugatus id consulens non peccat contra fidem matrimonii sui. *Vol. iv, p.* 360.

Does any one bound by a vow of chastity act against his vow if he be the cause of lechery to others, who are free from such vows; for instance, if he advise others to commit fornication with one another?

Ans. He is guilty of the sin of scandal, and stands arraigned of their fornication; however, he does not seem to violate his own vow merely on account of the fornication of others, if he feels no complacency himself; because he has made no vow to preserve the chastity of others but his own, just as a married man advising it does not sin against the faith of his matrimony. *Vol. iv, p.* 360.

Obj. Vovens castitatem vovet non co-operari aut consentire alli peccato contra castitatem.

R. Id negatur. *Dens, tom.* 4, *p.* 360.

Obj. He that makes a vow of chastity vows not to co-operate with or consent to any sin against chastity.

Ans. That is denied. *Dens, v. iv, p.* 360.

Quantum est peccatum exercere actum conjugalem ob solam voluptatem?

R. Cum S. Aug. et S. Thom. Supp. p. 49 a. 6, in corp esse solummodo ex natura sua veniale; quia haeretur, ut supponitur, in tra limites legitimi matrimoni; potest tamen esse mortale ratione finis, vel aliarium circumstantiarum; puta v. g. vir ita voluptate captus sit, ut accedens ad uxorum, paratus sit ad eam accedere, licet, uxor non foret, vel si tempore actus conjugalis affectum et delectationem habeat erga aliam, cujus etiam qualitates tunc erunt in confessione exprimenda, puta quod sit conjugata, consanquinla, etc., idque præcipue est cavendum in bigamis, no dum copulatar conjugi secundæ, affectum ponat in priori. *Vol. vii, p.* 182.

How great is the sin to exercise the conjugal act solely for pleasure?

I answer with St. Augustine and St. Thomas (Supp. 40, etc.), that it is only venial in its own nature, because it is fixed, as is supposed, within the limits of legitimate matrimony, however it may be a mortal sin by reason of the end, or other circumstances; suppose, for instance, if the man were so seized with pleasure, that going to his wife, he were ready to go to her, though she were not his wife, or if, at the time of the conjugal act, he have his affection and delight towards another, whose qualities also (*i. e.*, as well as the foregoing circumstances) shall then (in that case) be expressed in confession, suppose that she is married, that she is his blood relation, etc., and this is particularly to be guarded against in those who are married a second time, lest, while he is copulating with his second wife, he may fix his affection on the first. *Vol. vii, p.* 132.

An licet actum conjugalem exercere partim ob debitum finem puta generationem prolis et partim ob delectationem?

R. Negative, quia tunc finis equidem partialiter est inordinatus, cum ex parte obediatur libidini, sicque partialiter invertitur ordo a Deo et natura constitutus. *Dens, t. vii, p.* 182.

Is it lawful to exercise the conjugal act partly for the due end, namely, the generation of offspring, and partly for delight?

Ans. No; because then, indeed, the end is partially inordinate, since in part obedience is given to lust, and thus the order appointed by God and by nature is partially inverted. *Dens, v. vii, p.* 182.

An licitum est petere debitum conjugale ex solo fine vitandi propriam incontinentiam, non concurrente fine generationis prolis, vel redditionis dsbili?

R. Pontius cum multis aliis affirmat, sed melius cum SS. Augustino et Thomas videtur negatum. *Vol. vii, p.* 183.

Is it lawful to ask conjugal duty solely with the end or view of avoiding incontinence in one's self, and without the concurring end of generating offspring or of rendering duty?

Ans. Pontius and many others say Yes; but it seems better to say No, with St. Augustine and St. Thomas. *Vol. vii, p.* 183.

Conjugatis proponi potest: an pacifice vivient? An honesto modo utantur matrimonia? An periculo pollutionis sese exposerint? An proles Christiane educent?

To the married it can be proposed: Whether they live peaceably? Whether they enjoy matrimony in an honest way? Whether they have exposed themselves to the danger of pollution? Whether they bring up their children like Christians?

Circa quæ specialiter examinari possunt adolescentes ætatis circiter viginiti annorum, sati vegeti et mundani, vel potui dediti?

R. Circa peccata luxuriæ primo per generales interrogationes et a longinqus: v. g. an pœnitens frequentet personas alterius sexus? Si concedat; an sint dicta quædam verba inhonesta? Quid secutum? etc. Si negat, potest inquiri: an aliquando vexetur inhonestis cogitationibus vel somniis? Si affirmet, ad interrogationes u'terioris progedi apostet. *Vol. vii, p.* 134.

About what can young men be specially examined at the age of about twenty years, sufficiently vigorous and like many men of the world, or given to drink?

Ans. About the sins of luxury, first by general questions and from afar; for example, whether the penitent frequents persons of the other sex? If he allows that he does, whether any improper words were said? What followed? etc. If he answer in the negative, it can be asked, whether he is at any time tormented with improper thoughts or dreams? If he says Yes, it is fit to proceed to other questions.

Eadem prudentiæ forma observabitur circa adolescentulam vel mulierem comptam. *Dens. t.* 6, *p.* 134.

The same form of prudence shall be observed about a *young girl* or a *woman* vainly decked. *Dens. v.* 6, *p.* 131.

DE PECCATIS CARNALIBUS CONJUGUM INTER SE.

Certum est, conjuges inter se peccari posse, etiam graviter virtutem castitatis, sive continentiæ, ratione quarundam circumstantiarum; in particulari antem definire, quæ sint mortales, quæ solum veniales, per obscurum est, nec eadem omnium sententia; ut vel ideo sollicite persuadendum sit conjugatis, ut recordentur se esse fillios sanctorum quos decet in sanctitate conjugali filius procreare. Quidum auctores circumstantius circa actum conjugalem præcipue observandas, exprimunt his versibus. *Vol. vii, p.* 186.

OF THE CARNAL SINS WHICH MAN AND WIFE COMMIT WITH EACH OTHER.

It is certain that man and wife can sin grievously against the virtue of chastity or continence, with regard to certain circumstances relating to the use of their bodies; but to define particularly what are mortal, what only venial, is a matter of very great difficulty, nor are all writers of one opinion on the subject; so that, even on that account, the married ought to be anxiously advised to recollect that they are the children of the saints, and should therefore beget children in conjugal sanctity. The circumstances which are chiefly to be observed in the performance of the conjugal act, some authors express in the following verses (*Vol. vii, p.* 186):

'Sit modus, et finis, sine damno solve, cohære.

Sit locus et tempus, tactus, nec spernito votum.''

[These lines are so extremely obscene that we think it best not to give them in English.]

Ergo debet servari modus, sive situs, quia dupliciter invertitur. Io si non servetur defitum vas, sed copula, habeatur in vase, sed copula, habeatur in vase præpostero, vel quocumque ali non naturali; quod semper mortale est spectans ad sodomiam minorem, seu imperfectam, idque tenendum contra, qnosdam laxitas, sive copula ibi consummetur tive tantum in chœtur consummanda in vase naturali. *Vol. vii, p.* 186.

Modus sive invertitur ut servetor debitum vas ad copulam natura ordinatum, v. g., si fiat accendo præpostero, a latere, stando, vel si vor sit succumbus. Modus is mortalis est si inde suboriatur periculum pollutionis respectu alterutrius quando periculum, ne semen perdatur, prout sæpe accidit, dum actus exercetur stando sedendo, aut viro succumbente; si absit et sufficienter præcaveatur istud periculum, ex communi sententia id non est mortale; est que generatim modus ille sine causa taliles corundi graviter a Confessaris reprehendendus si tamen ob justam rationem situm naturalem conjuges immutent, secludaturque dictum periculum nullam est peccatum, ut dictum est in numero 48. *Vol. vii, p.* 186.

An uxor possit se tactibus exituare ad seminationem, si a copula conjugali se retraxerit, maritus, postquam ipse seminavit sed antequam seminaverit uxor.

R. Plurimi negant; eo quod, cum vir se retraxerit, actus sit completus, adeoque illa seminatis mulieris foret peccatum pollutionis; alii vero affirmant; quia ista excitatio spectat ad actiis conjugalis complimentum et perfectionem; excipeunt tamen cosum, ubi periculem et perfectionem; excipeunt tamen casum, ubi periculum est ne semen ad extra profudatur. *Vol. vii, p.* 188.

Hanc posteriorem sententiam ad exorbitantes opiniones laxiorum refert Henricus a S. Ignatio. *Tom vii, p.* 188.

Henricus, from St. Ignatius, refers this last opinion to the exhorbitant opinions of the more lax divines. *Vol. vii, p.* 188.

EXTRACTS FROM BISHOP KENRICK'S THEOLOGY.

152. Fellatores vocat Martialis "lingua maritos et ore mœchos." (L., XI, epigr, 61.] Pessimam hoc libidinis genus mortale esse et naturæ repugnare liquet. Rui linguam mulieris os imittunt, in proximo pollutionis discrimine versantur, et contra naturam voluptatem quærere connicuntur: quapropter nequeunt a lethali eximi culpæ, nisi obiter fiav absque venerea delectatione. *T. I., p.* 1130.

VOLUME III, PAGE 308.

§ II. DE USU CONJUGII.

67. Conjugii usus, modo rationi convenienti, licitus est, nam ex ipso Conditoris instituto fit ut maris et femnæ conjunctione genus propagetur humanum. "Situs naturalis est, et mulier sit succuba, ut vir incubus; hic enim modus aptior est effusione seminis virilis, et receptioni in vas femineum ad prolem procreandam. Situs autem innaturalis est si coitus aliter fiat, nempe sedendo, stando, de latere, vel præpostere more pecudem, vel si vir sit succubus, et mulier, incubus." *L. vi, n.* 917.

68. Si conjuges incœpta copula, ex mutus consensa cohibeant seminationem absque effusionis periculo, per se non est peccatum mortale. * * * * * * * *

69. "Si vero fœmina jam seminaverit, vel sit in probabili periculo seminandi, non poteni quidem vir data opera a seminatione se retrahere. sine gravi culpa, quia tunc ipse est causa, ut sement uxoris prodigatur." *L. vi, n.* 918.

70. Si vir jam seminaverit, femina retrahendo se a seminando plerisvue videtur peccare lethaliter, quia juxta plures utrumque semen ad generationem requiritur.

73. Peccat mortaliter vir copulam inchoando in vase

debito eam consummet. Ita communias et verius sentiunt theologi. "Ratio quia ipse hujusmodi coitus (etsi absque seminatione) est vera sodomia, quamvis non consummata, sicut ipsa copula in vase naturali mulieris alienæ est ver fornicata licet non adsit seminatio." Virilia perfricare circa vas præposterum uxoris est etiam mortale; "ratio est quia saltem talis tactus non potest moraliter fieri sine afftu sodomitico." *L. vi, n* 616,

79. In loco sacro copula habenda non est, extra necessitatem, quæ contigit exercitu in ecclesia diversante.

81. Coire tamen cum prægnante S. Alphonso videtur culpa venialis, "nisi adsit periculum incontinentiæ vel alia honesta casa." *S. Alph. i, vi, n.* 924.

92. Non debet vir jejuniis nimiis se reddere impotentem, nec mulier jejunando fieri nimis deformis, ades ut eam vir aversetur.

95. Si actus sit venialiter malus S. Alphonsus sic distinguit: "actus est illicitus ex parte petentis, puta si petat ob voluptatem, vel alium finem leviter malum, vel die quo vult Eucharistian accipere, tunc tenetur reddere; quia cum actus sit per se honestus, tenetur ex justitia ad reddendum, etiamsi exigens peccet graviter in petendo, ut diximus. *N.* 944, *Dub.* 1. Si vero actus est venialiter illicitus ex parte ipsius actus, copulæ, ut si petatur situ innaturali, vel tempore menstrui, aut puerperii tunc quando adest justa potest quidem reddere, cum quælibet justa causa excuset a veniali. Justa autem causa erit, v, g., ne incurrat indignationem alterius, sive rancorem illius quodammodo notabilem, et non possit cum commode avertere. * * * * * * *
Dixi *potest reddere*, sed non tenetur, quia licet vinculum justitiæ fortius sit vinculo charitatis, attamen cum actus, sit tali modo per se illicitus, alter non habet jus ad illum." *L. vi, n.* 946.

96. Si homo extra vas seminaturus noscatur, utrum uxor possit eum excipere inquiritur. Equidem constat eam non

posse id consilii, quam detestandum, sit, probare; sed excusant eam pluses, eum excipientum; quia copula inchoata per Cæterum quoties cumque possit precibus et monitis eum inducere ut coitum integrum habeat, videtur teneri; nec facile excusatur si ipsa absque gravi causa petat debitum, quando novit eum ita rem habiturum, nam ex caritate tenetur impedire peccatum viri: "Justam autem causam habet petendi, si ipsa esset in periculo, incontineniæ, vel si deberet alias privari suo jure petendi plusquam semel, vel bis, cum perpetus scrupulo an ei sit satis grave incommodum, vel ne, nunc se continere." *L. vi, n.* 947.

97. Non tenetur reddere debitum conjuji gui remisit jus suam, v. g., castitatem vovendo ex consensu mutuo. Quod so ita eo senserit, ut non cesserit suo juro, tunc instanter petenti videtur reddendum, quam per se debeatur, et alter suo jure non ceciderit bono voluntodis proposito. Amenti reddendum non est debitum, quam dominii usus ratione indigeat. Altamen si non sit omnino mente captus, licet ei petento obtemperare præsestim ne prodigatur semen, quando ex cita nullum incommodum grave timendum sit. Cum muliere amente non licet corie, nisi sterili, noscatur, proli enim inferretur damnum. Peccaret qui conjuges amentes conjungeret ad copulam, quam proles carreret necessaria educatione.

98. Non tenetur conjux debitum reddere alteri adulterii reo, fides enim semel fructa alterum obligatione solvit, manente tamen conjugii vinculo. Igitur si de delicto constet vel vehementia sint ejus indicia culpanda non est uxor quæ renuit subesse murito.

99. Erbio non tenetur conjux morem quere, caret enem usu rationis, qui ad exercendum dominium requiritur. Quod si non adeo ebrires sit ut nequreat rem habere, licet utique obtemperan, quamvis vix teneatur. Ad impiendum dissidia rixas, et blasphemias plerumque oportet pretenti acquiescere: quod si contigat effundi extra vas semen, id ebrio imputandum erit.

100. Qui ob incestum privatus est jure petendi debiti, tenetur nihilominus ad reddendum; nec enim alter ob ejus culpam puniendas est. Qui castitatem vovit, absque conjugis consensu, paniter tenetur reddere, quamvis nequeat petere, nam eon potuit conjugis jus afficere suæ volentatis proposito.

101. Conjuges tenentur ad reddendum debitum cum levi suo incommodo et damno, nam conjugio ineundo, se obligarunt ad ea quæ huic insunt. Si contingat alterutrum morbo aliquo laborare, qui contagiosus non sit, non debet alter ejus effugere consortium, nam et leproso debitum reddendum est. Quod si infectio timenda sit, ex medicorum judicio, vel si conjux sanus vehementur abhoreat ab alterius consortio, execusandus videtur, impossibilium enim nulla est obligatio.

103. Uxor quæ experta est se non posse parere absque vitæ periculo, non tenetur reddere debitum, nam cum tanto sui detrimento nequit obligari: attamen potest reddere, nam licet illi se objicere periculo quod ex sui conditione oritur, præsertim si id ad vitandam sui, vel conjugis incontinentiam necessariam sit. Si semper pariat filios mortuos, plures dicunt eam posse reddere, quamvis non teneatur, nam præstet infasites esse, etram cum peccato originis, quam non esse, et per accidens eorum mors contigit, quam conjugii usus per se licitus sit. Ego distinquendum preto. Si fœtus mors in utero contigat, vel alias, absque actu chirurgi vitam tollentis, uti que videtur licere uti matrimonio, etsi prævideatur eventura: sed si fœtam forcipibus tollendum constet, dubitari posset utrum liceat conjugis uti, cum tanto prolis detrimento. Equidem optandum ut abstinerent conjuges; sec quam incontinentiæ sit periculum, excusari forsan poterunt, chirurgorum permitttentes arbitrio, quomodo cum uxore parturiente agendum sit. *T. iii, p.* 317.

104. Uxor quæ in usu matrimonii se vertit, ut non recipriet semen, vel statim post illud exceptum surgit, ut expellatur, lethaliter, peccat; sed opus non est ut diu resupina jaceat; quam matrix brevi semen attrahat, et mox arctissime

clandatur. Puellæ vim patenti licet se vertere, et conari ut non accipiral semen, quod injuria ei immittitur; sed exceptum non licet expellere, quia jam possessionem pacificam habet, et haud absque injuria ejiceretur. *T. iii. p.* 317.

105. Conjuges senes plerumque cocunt absque culpa, licet contingat semen extra vas effundi, id enim per accidens fit ex infirmitate naturæ. Quod si vires adeo sint fractæ ut nulla sit seminandi intra vas speo, jam nequeunt conjugii uti. *T. iii, p.* 317.

106. Tactus, aspectus, et verba turpia inter conjuges, directa ad copulam, permittuntur, quia veluti media sunt ad finem licitum adhibita. Hinc licet illis se invicem ita excitare ut copulam facilius perficiant. Quæ antem ad copulam non referuntur, et solius voluptatis causa fiunt, non excedunt culpam venialem, si tactus per se non sit valde fœdus, et si non adsit periculum pollutionis. Equidem status conjugalis jure censetur hæc pleraque quaodummado cohonestare, et gravem anferre turpitudinem; secus plurimis scrupulisque foret obnoxisus. "Et hoc" inquit S. Alphonsus, "etiamsi copula tunc ipsis esset vetita ob morbum, vel esset impossibilis ob impotentiam quæ supervenisset," *L. vii,* 933. Quod si quis voto castitatis se ligasset, tunc plane forent illa omnia mortalia. Si impedimentum copulæ proveniat ex affinitate vel cogatione spirituali, etiam tunc tactus hujusmodi excusari possunt a mortali, quam pœna legis sit strictæ interpretationis. *T.iii, pp.* 317-18.

107. Quand periculum pollutionis in se, vel in altero prævidetnr, difficilisis excusantur tactas husmodi a gravi peccato, præsertim si videantur inchoata quædam pollutio ("prout esset digitum morose admovere intra vas femineum.") S. Alphonsi judicum damus. "Puto probabilus decendum, quod actus turpes inter conjuges cum periculo pollutionis, tam in pretente quam in reddente, sunt mortalia, nisi habeantur, ut conjnges se excitent ad copulam proxime secuturam, quia cum ipsi ad copulam jus habeant, habent etiam jus ad tales actus, tametro pollutio per acci-

dens copulam præveniat. Actus vero pudicos etiam censeo esse mortalia, is fiant cum periculo pollutionis in se, vel in altero, casu quo habeantur absolam votuptatem, vel etiam ob levem causam: secus si ob causam gravem, puta si aliquando adsit urgeno causa ostendendi indicia affectus ad fovendum muturem amorem, vel ut conjux avertat suspionem ab altero, quod ipse sit erga aliam personam propensus. Probabiliter dicunt Sanchez, Bosius et Escobar: "in reddente, tactus etiam impudicos, nisi sint tales ut videantur inchoata pollutio, esse licitos, quamvis adsit periculum pollutionis in alterutro, quia tunc reddens dat operam rei licitæ, ad quam obligatur propter jus pretentis, qui tamelsi peccat, non tamen jus amittit, cum culpa se teneat ex parte peronæ." *L. vi, n.* 933. Immittur prudenda in os uxoris etiam obiter, videtur peccatum mortale "tum quia in hoc actu ob calorem oris adest proximum periculum pollutionis, tum quia hæc per se videtur nova species luxunæ contra naturam (dicta ab aliquibus *irrumnatio*)." (*L. vi, n.* 935.) *Vol. iii, p.* 318.

108. Tactus turpes sui ipsius, conjuge absente, vix possunt carere periculo proximo pollutionis, ideque plerumque damnatur peccati mortalis. "Ratio, tum quia conjux non habet jus per se in proprium corpus, sed tantum per accidens nempe tantum, ut possit se disponere ad copulam; unde cum copula tunc non sit possibilis; tactus cum seipso omnino ei sunt illiciti; tum quia tactus predendorum, quando fiunt morose, et cum commotione spirituum, per se tendunt ad pollutionem, suntque proxime connexi cum ejus periculo." (*L. vi, n.* 936.) *T. iii. pp.* 318-19.

109. Conjuge absente, delectatio de copula cogitata non caret gravi periculo. "Si delectatio habeatur non solum cum commotione spirituum, sed etiam cum titilatione seu voluptate venere, sentio cum Concina. * * * contra Sporer, eam non posse excusari a mortali, quia talis delectatio est proxime conjuncta cum periculo pollutionis. Secus vero puto dicendum, si absit illa voluptuosa titillatio quia

tunc non est delectationi proxime adnexum periculum pollutionis, etiamis adsit commotio spirituum, et sic revera sentit Sanchez, eum ibi non excuset delectationem cum voluptate venera sed tantum (ut ait) cum commotione et alteratione partium absque pollutionis periculo. At quia talis commotio propinqua est illa titillationi voluptuosæ, ideo maxime hortandi sunt conjuges, ut abstineant ab hujusmodi delectatione morasa." *L. v, n.* 937. Venia sit dictis.*

VOLUME I, PAGE 318.

§ VII. — DE LUXURIA.

92. Ex causa autem necessaria, vel utili, rel convenienti animæ aut corpori, si pollutio preventura præ videatur, quam quis tamen animo aversatur, nulla est culpa, nisi adsit consensus periculum. "Hinc etiam aliis confessariis mulierum, ac legere tractatus de rebus turpibus; chirengis aspicere ac tangere partes feminæ ægrotantis, ac studere rebus medicis: licet quoque aliis alloqui, osculari, aut amplexari mulieris juxta morem patriæ servire in balneis, et similia. (Hæc pessime detorsit infelix redux ad hæreticos.) II. Licet alicui, qui magnum pruritum patitur in verendis, illum tactu abigere, etiamsi pollutio sequatur. Caute tamen abtinendum est, si puritus non sit valde molestus. III. Sic etiam licet, etiam prœvisa pollutione, equitare causa utilitatis. IV. Licet decumbere alixuo situ ad commodius quiescendum. V. Cibos calidos aut potus moderate sumere, et honestus choreas ducre." *St. Alphonsus,* 1, *iii, n.* 483.

---

*Inclytos scriptor DeMaistre ce conjugii abusu hæc notavii quæ ponderent operet qui affectantes morum puri'ate mia scrutandis rebus matrimonii abhorrent: "Si nous pouvions aparcevoir clairement tout les maux qui resultent des generations desordonees, et des innombrables profanations de la premiere loi du monde, nous reculerious d'horreur. Voila pourqui la seule religion vraie est aussi la scule qui sans pouvoir tout dire a l'homme, se soit nanmoins emparee du marriage et l'ai t soumit a de sainte ordonnances." *Le Compte DeMaistre, Soirees de Saint Petersburg:* 1 *Entretien, p.* 55.

VOLUME III, PAGE 172.

DE SIGILLO COFESSIONIS.

87. Interrogatus confessarius utrum quis apud eum confessus fuerit, potent plorumque respondere, prout res se habet. Quod si clam accessrit, ipsam confessionem celatam voluns, putant plures, et quidem recte, judice St. Alphonso, frangi sigillum si accessus ejus a confessario dclaretur, nam gravioris, peccati suspicionem facile injicil. *L. vi, n.* 638. De iis autem quæ confitendo declarantur, nihil prorsus dicendum est; ea enim ignorare causetur, quam nonisi Dei vices gerenti innotescant. "Homo non adducitur in testimonium, nisi ut homo. Et ideo sine læsione conscientæ potest jurare se nescire, quod scit tantum ut Deus. *St. Thom. Suppl. iii, p. qu., XI Art. i ad iii.* Igitur simpliciter denegare debet se eo nosse; quod si aliunde noverit, cavendum ne quid ceitius ex confessione proferatur.

www.ingramcontent.com/pod-product-compliance
Lightning Source LLC
Chambersburg PA
CBHW030755230426
43667CB00007B/975